THE FLYER VAULT

DANIEL TATE & ROB BOWMAN

THE FLYER VAULT

150 Years of Toronto Concert History

Foreword by Geddy Lee

DUNDURN
TORONTO

Publisher: Scott Fraser | Editor: Allison Hirst | Designer: Laura Boyle
Toronto music venue word map illustration: © Dave Murray
Printer: Marquis

Library and Archives Canada Cataloguing in Publication

Title: The flyer vault : 150 years of Toronto concert history / Daniel Tate & Rob Bowman ; foreword by Geddy Lee.
Names: Tate, Daniel, 1980- author. | Bowman, Rob (Robert Maxwell James), author. | Lee, Geddy, writer of foreword.
Identifiers: Canadiana (print) 20190152982 | Canadiana (ebook) 20190152990 |
ISBN 9781459745421 (softcover) | ISBN 9781459745438 (PDF) | ISBN 9781459745445 (EPUB)
Subjects: LCSH: Concerts—Ontario—Toronto—History. | LCSH: Concerts—Ontario—Toronto—
Posters. | LCSH: Music—Ontario—Toronto—History. | LCSH: Music—Posters—Ontario—Toronto. |
LCSH: Advertising—Music—Ontario—Toronto—History. | LCSH: Music-halls—Ontario—Toronto—History.
| LCSH: Nightclubs—Ontario—Toronto—History.
Classification: LCC ML205.8.T6 T216 2019 | DDC 780.78/713541—dc23

We acknowledge the support of the Canada Council for the Arts and the Ontario Arts Council for our publishing program. We also acknowledge the financial support of the Government of Ontario, through the Ontario Book Publishing Tax Credit and Ontario Creates, and the Government of Canada.

VISIT US AT

dundurn.com | @dundurnpress | dundurnpress | dundurnpress

Dundurn
3 Church Street, Suite 500
Toronto, Ontario, Canada
M5E 1M2

For Gary Tate, who evidently passed the music history gene to his son, and all the loyal followers of The Flyer Vault Instagram account who've made this project all the more worthwhile.
— Daniel Tate

For Maureen, Rylan, and Miranda as well as all the great promoters who made Toronto such an amazing city by bringing to town such an incredible array of artists year in and year out.
— Rob Bowman

A NOTE TO THE READER

The Flyer Vault project started in April 2015 when I rediscovered a trove of old hip hop concert and rave flyers that I collected over the years. I started posting them to Instagram, and slowly but surely, the audience grew. Soon, my account became a meeting place for people to reflect and reminisce on shows that profoundly impacted them. This book is the culmination of what was originally a digital project. It's a testament to the thousands of people who both presented and experienced live music in our city over the years.

Each chapter in *The Flyer Vault* is accompanied by an Apple Music playlist (@theflyervault), custom curated by Rob and me. These playlists cover the hundreds, if not thousands, of artists and songs that are noted in the book. For those who want the true time machine experience, we recommend giving them a listen during or after each chapter.

We commissioned renowned Toronto-based illustrator Dave Murray to put together the first Toronto music venue word map (see pages x–xi). The map depicts over 200 club and concert venues that span a century. It's a breathtaking illustration and will surely take many of you down memory lane.

— Daniel Tate

 Follow The Flyer Vault on Apple Music to listen to playlists that include the artists and songs featured in each chapter.

#theflyervault 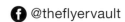 theflyervault.com 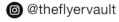 @theflyervault ◉ @theflyervault

CONTENTS

FOREWORD by Geddy Lee

Over a year ago I was drifting through my Instagram "explore" page (what a modern dude, eh?), when I came across a photo of a program from a Rush show at Massey Hall back in 1976. Being curious, and a little vain, I clicked on it and found myself on a visual journey across my fair city's popular musical history. I became a follower. A few of the clippings and poster images were from concerts I attended back in the day, but more importantly, when viewed as a whole, the posts came together as an evocative mosaic, a powerful reminder of how lucky I was to have grown up in such a culturally diverse and open-minded place as was, and still is, the city of Toronto.

Now, what was simply a digital idea has grown into a fine and proper print publication — *The Flyer Vault: 150 Years of Toronto Concert History* — a historical document which expands upon that mosaic and brings to life the music and the performances that charged our community for over 150 years, from vaudeville to jazz to rock to electronica; blasts from the past such as Buffalo Bill's Wild West Show, Ella Fitzgerald, Josephine Baker, and Bill Haley & His Comets, at venues like the Club Top Hat, Shea's, the Colonial Tavern, the Riverboat, (my beloved) Rock Pile and, still going strong, Massey Hall. The festivals, arenas, and stadiums that featured all the gods of rock, from Elvis to Zeppelin, the raves and the punk shows in small clubs like the Rivoli, the BamBoo, and Lee's Palace, plus the small theatres like the New Yorker and the Victory Burlesque — all these and beyond are well represented here.

The time span is impressive, the breadth of talent expansive, and more than anything else, it's a truly fun ride for any time-traveller to take. It's a record of the musical life of a city that, thanks to The Flyer Vault, is gone but no longer forgotten.

— **Geddy Lee**
Musician, songwriter, and author; lead vocalist, bassist, and keyboardist for Rush
July 2019

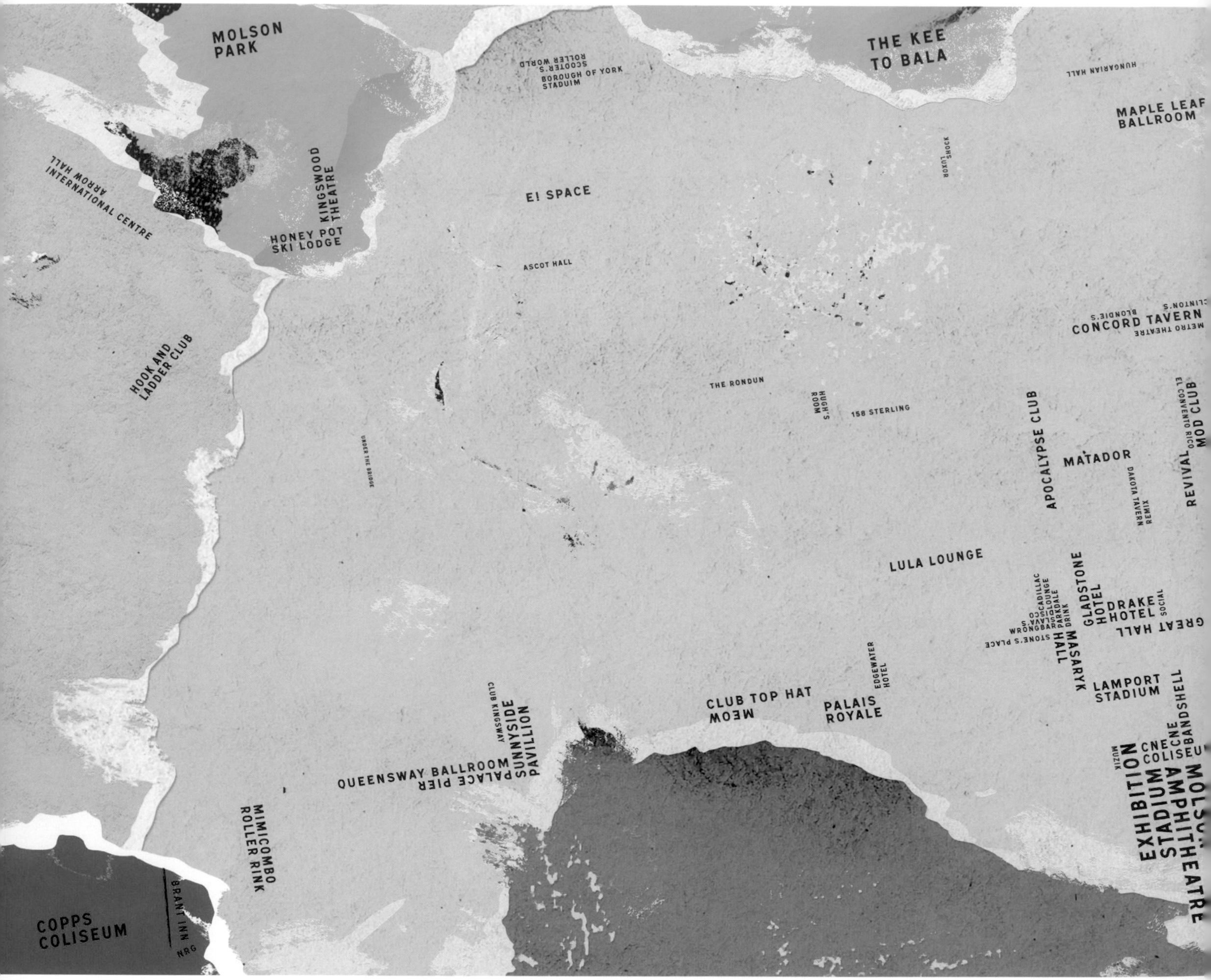

MOLSON PARK

THE KEE TO BALA

SCOOTER'S ROLLER WORLD

BOROUGH OF YORK STADIUM

HUNGARIAN HALL

MAPLE LEAF BALLROOM

ARROW HALL
INTERNATIONAL CENTRE

KINGSWOOD THEATRE

HONEY POT SKI LODGE

E! SPACE

HUGH'S ROOM

ASCOT HALL

CLINTON'S

BLONDIE'S

CONCORD TAVERN

METRO THEATRE

HOOK AND LADDER CLUB

THE RONDUN

HUGH'S ROOM

158 STERLING

EL MOCAMBO RICO

MOD CLUB

REVIVAL

APOCALYPSE CLUB

MATADOR

DAKOTA TAVERN
REMIX

UNDER THE BRIDGE

LULA LOUNGE

GLADSTONE HOTEL

DRAKE HOTEL

CADILLAC LOUNGE

WRONGBAR

BOVINE SEX CLUB

STONE'S PLACE

BRANT AVA.'S

SOCIAL

GREAT HALL

MASARYK HALL

LAMPORT STADIUM

CLUB KINGSWAY

SUNNYSIDE PAVILLION

CLUB TOP HAT

MEOW

PALAIS ROYALE

EDGEWATER HOTEL

CNE COLISEUM

BANDSHELL

MUZIK

EXHIBITION STADIUM

MOLSON AMPHITHEATRE

QUEENSWAY BALLROOM

PALACE PIER

MIMICOMBO ROLLER RINK

BRANT INN

NRG

COPPS COLISEUM

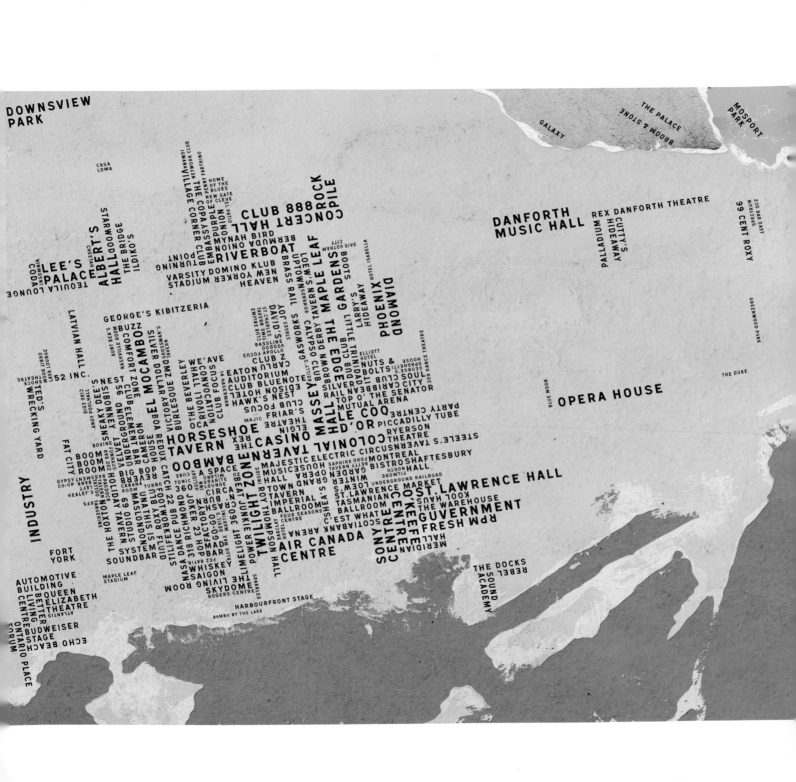

December 31, 1999, and January 1, 2000, Air Canada Centre

INTRODUCTION

*T*he *Flyer Vault: 150 Years of Toronto Concert History* has been a long time coming. Although I saw the Supremes at the O'Keefe Centre when I was 11, my first real rock show was Jefferson Airplane at the same venue in the spring of 1970. In the years since those first two shows, I have seen easily 2,000, maybe even 3,000 concerts. From the start, I kept a handwritten list of every show, noting the date, venue, and name of each artist in the order they appeared onstage.

Over the years I would hear about shows that happened before my time, such as Cream at Massey Hall, Led Zeppelin at the Rock Pile, and festivals such as the Rock and Roll Revival, which featured the Doors and John Lennon at Varsity Stadium, all of which I had missed by just a year or two. By the time I was 15, I was writing for rock and

July 5, 1987, Kingswood Music Theatre

roll magazines and eventually I became an ethnomusicologist and a professor of music. My interest in all things popular music continued to expand both forward and backward in time.

Several years ago I began to try to document all the shows from the 1960s that occurred before I started going to concerts. This led back into the 1950s, and eventually, given my disparate tastes in music and what I do in my professional life, I kept going farther back in time, curious about whether heroes of mine, such as John Coltrane, Hank Williams, Bessie Smith, and Sister Rosetta Tharpe, had ever played Toronto.

In the meantime, on his own life path, Daniel Tate was working the street team beat for a local concert company from 1995 to 2005 and started collecting flyers and posters. Daniel eventually accumulated a collection of several thousand flyers, storing them in a bin at his parents' home. Twenty or so years later, he started the well-known Instagram account The Flyer Vault, where he posted some of the gems in his collection along with contextual commentary about each respective show.

ATLANTIS

presents

Thursday November 4th

All Ages (liquor with ID)
8pm to 3am

DJ TIM (Utah Saints)
DJ E!N
John Aquaviva (Plus 8)
Ambient C
Dr Trance

Location:
The Opera House
735 Queen St East at Broadview

INFO: 760-3185

TICKETS at TICKETMASTER (870-8000)

TORONTO
Play De Record • 357a Yonge St • 586-0380
Traxx • 427 Yonge St • 977-4888
X-Static • 162 John St • 599-3851
Rag Tag • Fairview Mall • 499-8366

OUTSIDE TORONTO
Word Up Fashion • Bramalea City Centre • Brampton
Record Bar • 785 Albert St • 579-2411 • Oshawa
Records On Wheels • 112 Kerr St • 844-1913 • Oakville
Lots of Discs • Unit 1, 505 The Queensway • 276-4356 • Mississauga
Full Tilt • 63 Queen S St • 567-1296 • Mississauga

November 4, 1993,
Opera House

September 4, 1999, Toronto Congress Centre

In the fall of 2017 Daniel reached out to me. I had done the research and written the liner notes for three different CD sets of George Clinton and Parliament-Funkadelic. Daniel wanted to know if I had any flyers for the group's legendary shows at the Hawk's Nest in 1969 and 1970. I didn't, but over coffee, while looking through Daniel's incredible collection on his laptop, we quickly figured out that our interests, knowledge, and individual collections dovetailed perfectly. With each of us spurring the other on, over many months Daniel's collection of posters, flyers, and concert advertisements expanded to about 8,000 items while my database of musical performances in Toronto increased at a similar rate. Daniel's earliest image was an incredible advertisement for Jenny Lind's famous performances at the St. Lawrence Hall in 1851, while I had found references to music performances by touring ensembles playing Toronto going back to 1840, a mere six years after the city incorporated. We decided that a book comprised of a number of Daniel's images combined with my contextual knowledge would be a worthwhile project. So, here we are.

While both of us have wide interests in music and music history, we decided from the start that, with the exception of Jenny Lind and the first Toronto performances by the famous African American soprano Sissieretta Jones, we were not going to include classical music in the project. What we have done is complicated and unwieldy enough. To adequately document performances of Western art music in Toronto would require a wholly separate book unto itself. We also decided to use the year 2000 as a cut-off date. Maybe in a subsequent volume we will take on the Toronto concert scene in the 21st century.

Narrowing down Daniel's collection of 8,000 images to the approximately 170 images included in this book was an extraordinarily difficult and painful task. There are hundreds of additional images we would have loved to have included. There were similar problems in writing the text (Daniel wrote the Hip Hop, Contemporary R&B, and Electronic and Dance Music chapters; I wrote all the others). The more we dug into this project, the more we uncovered; consequently, the project kept shape-shifting. New information would come to

January 15, 1998, Maple Leaf Gardens

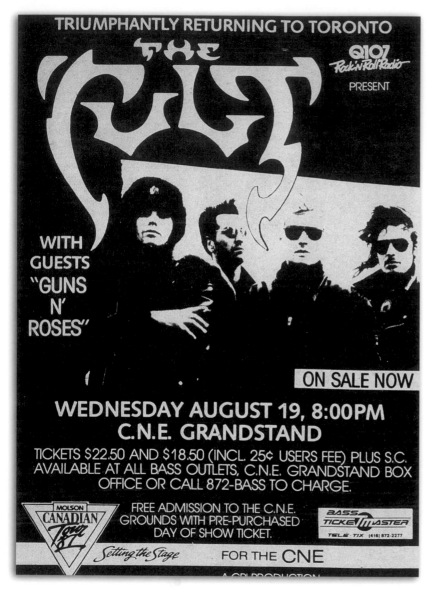

August 19, 1987, CNE Grandstand

light and we'd realize that what we previously thought were the earliest performances in a given genre or by a given artist were completely wrong and we'd have to rewrite. This was especially true the farther back in time we went.

For anything before the mid-1960s, we had to rely heavily on newspaper articles, ads, and reviews. Both the *Toronto Star* and the *Globe and Mail* are digitized. The *Star* goes back to 1894, while the *Globe* was first published in 1844. Being able to digitally search back issues of those two papers made this project possible. While we both did substantial work with microfilm copies of the now-defunct *Toronto Telegram*, *Share*, and *Contrast*, and had access to print copies of Toronto's NOW magazine, the majority of what we were able to access came from the *Globe* and the *Star*. If we had several more years and could go through every issue of the *Telegram*, the *Toronto Sun*, and earlier newspapers such as the *Toronto World* and *Toronto Empire*, I am sure we would find information and stories about concerts that we at present don't know about. So, there are bound to be things we've missed or have gotten wrong.

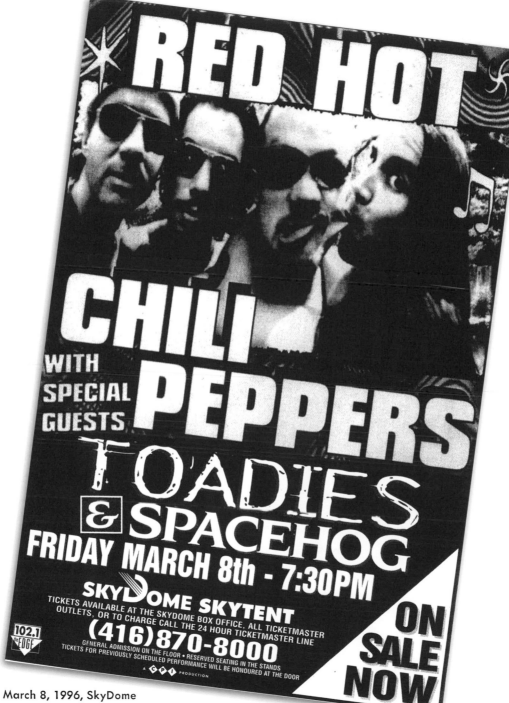

March 8, 1996, SkyDome

July 18, 1989, Horseshoe Tavern

We have organized the chapters by genre. Obviously, at times there will be overlap, so punk performances appear in both the chapter focused on punk, new wave, and hardcore, as well as in the chapter that covers the Queen Street scene of the late 1970s and 1980s. The book focuses on touring shows coming to Toronto, but we also tried to reference many, but perhaps not nearly enough, of the great local artists that have been so important to Toronto's nightlife going back to the 19th century.

At times, especially for early material, for which reviews are rare and seldom very informative and there's nobody alive who can tell us anything about the shows, the chapters can become a little bit like encyclopedia entries. And, while fascinating in terms of sheer information, these do not have as many stories as we would have liked. We tended to focus on debut performances by artists and shows that for one reason or another were exceptional. For example, we talk about the Rolling Stones' first appearances in Toronto in the 1960s, as well as the famous El Mocambo show in 1977, but we don't talk about the group's appearances in 1972, 1975, 1989, 1994, etc. If we had taken any other approach, the book would have ballooned to the point of being unpublishable.

When looking back at the wealth of information that we accumulated in researching this book, it is fascinating to see how early Toronto became one of the most important cities for touring musicians in North America, and, by extension, the world. This was largely because of the railway that connected Toronto to Detroit (beginning in 1856); in the 19th and early 20th centuries, Toronto was considered part of a Midwest circuit that included Chicago, Detroit, Cleveland, and Buffalo. In later years, when Toronto became the largest city in Canada, it served as a sort of gateway to the country. Subsequently, it evolved, alongside New York and Los Angeles, into one of the three cities in North America that bands simply *had to play*. For more than a century and a half, Toronto has been an extraordinary place to see the world's greatest musicians perform. Its history in this regard is something to marvel at.

— Rob Bowman

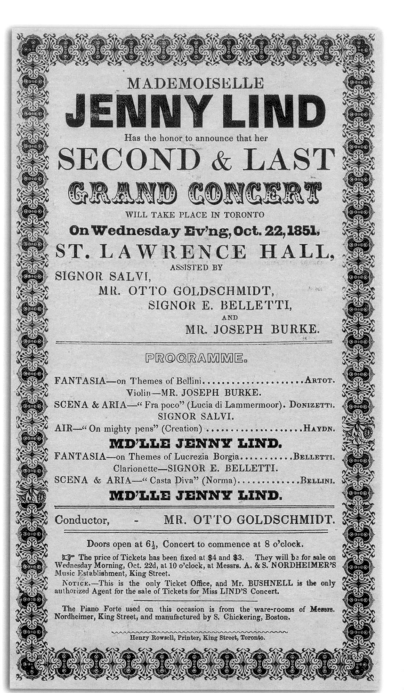

October 22, 1851,
St. Lawrence Hall

1
MINSTREL TROUPES
AND
VAUDEVILLE STARS

When Swedish soprano Jenny Lind appeared at the recently opened St. Lawrence Hall on Tuesday, October 21, 1851, it is quite likely that she was the first international star to visit the city. Toronto's population was just 30,000, the streets were not paved, and a railway had not yet been built to link the city directly to hubs in the United States. One has to assume that Jenny Lind and her accompanists arrived in Toronto by stagecoach. It is sobering to realize that just 17 years earlier the city of Toronto had been known as the town of York and that Confederation was still 16 years down the road! In light of this, the fact that the performance even happened seems like a miracle.

Born in 1820, Lind was known as the "Swedish Nightingale" and had achieved substantial fame in Europe when American impresario P.T. Barnum approached her about touring the United States. Lind only agreed to embark on such an adventurous undertaking when Barnum offered her what, for the time, was a fortune, which Lind used, not for her own gain, but to fund free schools back home in Sweden. Barnum, a promoter nonpareil, was able to generate so much publicity for Lind's performances that at many shows tickets were sold by auction.

Toronto clearly caught the fever. Lind's name appeared in the *Globe* 91 times in 1850 alone! The first mention of the tour was in March 1850, and the tour was considered significant enough that the *Globe* reviewed the opening show in New York that September. The American press dubbed the phenomenon "Lindmania," some 113 years before the advent of Beatlemania!

Lind played 93 shows for Barnum before deciding to continue the tour on her own. The Toronto show was booked under the auspices of Lind herself and, even with a steep price for the time of three dollars a ticket (this equals about $125 in 2019; well into the early 20th century, most theatres could not charge more than one dollar for a ticket to any kind of performance), was so successful that she added additional shows on the Wednesday and Thursday. For a town of just 30,000 residents, the event was talked about for years after.

In the second half of the 19th century, entertainment in Toronto consisted largely of minstrel, Wild West, and vaudeville shows. In many respects, the advent of blackface minstrel song and dance numbers by solo performers in the 1820s marked the beginning of the American music industry. A particularly ugly phenomenon, the early minstrel shows featured white men applying burnt cork to their faces so as to appear black. They would then caricature African Americans, portraying them as slow-witted and happy on the plantations, where they would sing, dance, and eat watermelon and chicken all day. As reprehensible as these shows were, they introduced African American music, albeit not necessarily in a completely authentic form, to white audiences in the north.

According to Lorraine Le Camp in her 2005 dissertation "Racial Considerations of Minstrel Shows and Related Images in

Canada," the first blackface performers to appear in Toronto came to town with the circuses. She lists such performances as taking place in 1840 (only six years after Toronto was incorporated as a city!), 1841, 1842, and 1843. Unfortunately, the venues or the exact dates of any of these performances are not known.

These were probably not the first local blackface performances. According to an article in the *Toronto Star* in June 2018, as early as July 20, 1840, Toronto's small (the black population in Toronto in 1855 was 539 residents; in 1840 it would have been considerably smaller) but obviously politically aware black populace, largely comprised of former African American slaves, petitioned city council to refuse to license circuses that included blackface performers to set up within city limits. The petition stated that such performances made "the Coloured man appear ridiculous and contemptible," and led to "contaminating the wholesome air of Our City with Yanky [*sic*] amusement of comic songs known by the name of Jim Crow and Aunt Dinah." The petition was sadly unsuccessful.

Similar petitions were submitted over the next three years, but it was only when an 1843 petition pointed out that the city of Kingston had already banned such shows, that Toronto's city council fell in line and for a short time refused to license such performances. The city's refusal to license minstrel acts, unfortunately, did not last very long.

In 1849, the Ethiopian Harmonists appeared at the Royal Lyceum on King Street (the word *Ethiopian* was commonly used by blackface minstrel troupes to try to convey the idea that they were somehow authentically representing black culture). The Lyceum was the first purpose-built theatre in Toronto, and the performance by the Ethiopian Harmonists was the debut appearance by a minstrel ensemble (as opposed to a solo performer in blackface) in Toronto. It was only six years earlier that the Christy Minstrels and the Virginia Minstrels staged the earliest concerts by full minstrel ensembles in Buffalo and New York City respectively.

Toronto was quick to embrace this new form of entertainment. In May 1850, the Nightingale Ethiopian Serenaders of Philadelphia played the Royal Lyceum (advertisements for the show stressed that the first part of the performance was in whiteface while the second and third parts were in blackface) and White's Serenaders (noted in newspaper advertisements as "Splendid Ethiopian Entertainment") came to the Lyceum in July of that year. In 1851, more than a half-dozen minstrel ensembles played at either the Lyceum or Temperance Hall.

Such performances continued unabated for the next several years at these two venues, as well as at St. Lawrence Hall, the City Theatre, the Music Hall, and Yorkville Town Hall. Notable among these were appearances by the most famous blackface minstrel troupe, the Christy Minstrels, in 1856 and 1861. The second most important minstrel troupe, the Virginia Minstrels, wouldn't get to Toronto until 1898, when minstrelsy as professional entertainment was on the wane. In 1855, Thomas "Daddy" Rice, known as the father of American minstrelsy and the actor who first developed the Jim Crow character, played the Royal Lyceum for a week. Toronto's own internationally famous blackface minstrel star, Colin "Cool" Burgess, was featured with Sam Sharpley's Minstrel Troupe at the Music Hall in November 1863.

There were also a number of performances of stage adaptations of the Harriet Beecher Stowe abolitionist novel *Uncle Tom's Cabin* in Toronto. A number of these adaptations changed the nature of the story to support slavery and were also done in blackface. The first such production in Toronto appears to have been in June 1853, again at the Royal Lyceum.

After the Civil War ended in 1865, newly freed African Americans began to form minstrel companies of their own, and quickly came to dominate the industry. While African American blackface minstrels still had to satirize aspects of black culture to appeal to white audiences, such troupes supplied a vehicle for talented black actors and singers to work in showbiz rather than to farm or work other labour-oriented jobs. It also gave them some control over the authenticity of both the music and the satire.

The earliest appearance of an African American blackface minstrel troupe in Toronto that we found took place in the year following Confederation, when an ensemble called the Georgia Minstrels performed at the Music Hall on November 21, 1868. A writer for the *Globe* seemed impressed, while his review suggested that he had seen a minstrel show before: "The musical part of the entertainment was interspersed with the usual oddities attachable to Negro music, which, of course, made the audience laugh to their heart's content."

The Georgia Minstrels returned to the city four times through the 1870s, usually performing for two or more nights at the Royal Opera House. In 1875, they were billed as "The Original Georgia Minstrels (and Brass Band) and The Great Slave Troupe and Jubilee Singers." In 1878, the advertisements for their shows mentioned that Billy Kersands, one of the most famous of all African American minstrel performers, would be appearing with the ensemble. Later in the year they returned to Toronto, billed as Callender's Georgia Minstrels. At the time, there was more than one troupe touring as the Georgia Minstrels, the word *Georgia* having become code, meaning that the ensemble was black. In 1879 the group was billed as Sprague's Original Georgia Minstrels. It was led by the great composer and bandleader James Bland, who was perhaps second only to Kersands in African American minstrel show fame.

Rivalling Callender and Sprague in the minstrel business was J.H. Haverly's many white and African American blackface touring ensembles. Modelling himself on P.T. Barnum, Haverly was a master at publicizing his troupes via hyperbolic newspaper ads and broadsides. Haverly's Minstrels, an African American troupe, first appeared in Toronto in June 1877 at Mrs. Morrison's Grand Opera House. In December 1879 he brought his white United Mastodon Minstrels to the Royal Opera House for three nights. Two months later his Genuine Colored Minstrels played the Grand Opera House. Various Haverly ensembles, including the intriguingly named Haverly Strategists, came to Toronto on a regular basis through 1905.

Other African American blackface minstrel troupes, such as Emerson's Mecatherian Minstrels and Sam Hague's British Minstrels, played both the Royal Opera House and the Grand Opera House in the 1870s and 1880s.

In December 1898, a white theatrical troupe, Primrose and Dockstader's Minstrels, appeared for three nights at the Grand Opera House. The difference in

BUFFALO BILL!

"He is king of them all."—Gen. E. A. CARR.

AT

WOODBINE PARK

Commencing This Afternoon.

3 Days, August 22, 24, and 25.

Afternoons Only.   Performance
Given Rain or Shine.

Carriages   Admitted   Free.

Buffalo Bill's

Wild West

FIRST AND LAST TIME IN CANADA.

Giving an Exact Exhibition of Western
Border Life.

The Greatest Novelty of the Century.
Gates open at 1 p.m.   Performance at 2:30 p.m.
The following are a few of the numerous FEA-
TURES:—The renowned Sioux Chief,

SITTING BULL,

and Staff. WHITE EAGLE and 52 Braves.   The
One-Legged Sioux Spy, FRISKING ELK.
The Great Markswoman from the Western Border, Miss ANNIE OAKLEY.   Largest HERD OF
BUFFALO ever exhibited.   Great Indian Buffalo
Hunt, known as "The Surround."   The Phenome-
nal Boy Shot, JOHNNY BAKER.   Cowboy Kid,
SET CLOVER, the unequalled Cowboy Shot,
shooting at marbles. half-dollars, and nickels.
MUSTANG JACK, the Champion Jumper, jump-
ing over a horse 16½ hands high.   BUFFALO BILL
will shoot at clay pigeons from traps; also with
revolver, rifle, on foot and on horseback, at full
speed, at glass balls.   BUCK TAYLOR, King of
the Cowboys, in novel equestrianism and lassoing
wild cattle, and riding bucking horses wilder than
ever.   YELLOW HAND'S DEATH by Buffalo
Bill.   Grand BATTLE SCENES similar to
Fish Creek, Cut Knife, and Batoche.
Music furnished by the famous Cowboy Band.
We fulfil every promise.   CODY & SALSBURY.
Admission, 50c.   Children, 25c.   Grand Street
Parade to-day at 10 a.m.

August 22, 24, 25,
1885, Woodbine Park

the minstrel shows put on by black and white performers is easily gleaned from the following sentence in the *Globe*'s review where they commended the performance of "Mr. George Primrose in his watermelon song, in which four pickaninnies gave a laughable cakewalk."

Primrose and Dockstader's Minstrels came back to Toronto in December 1899. By 1903 the duo had split up and Lew Dockstader returned to town with "his Great Minstrel Company" to play the Princess Theatre at the end of the summer. Dockstader would return to the Princess Theatre several times through 1909. Given that Torontonians bought tickets to see touring troupes on a regular basis for 60 years, clearly the city's residents were more than a bit taken with blackface minstrelsy.

Tony Pastor is often considered the grand master of vaudeville largely due to his famous 14th Street Theatre in New York City. He brought his first vaudeville troupe to Toronto in 1875, playing two nights in July at the Grand Opera House. The ad for the performance read "Tony Pastor with His Traveling Company with 10 different acts." The acts referred to would have included comedians, jugglers, musicians, dancers and various novelty specialties.

In addition to vaudeville, Wild West shows were quite popular. Just as minstrel shows purported to give their audiences a sense of what life was like in the southern United States for African Americans, Wild West shows promised their audiences that they would provide a portal into life in the rugged southwest. One of my favourite advertisements from the period is for Buffalo Bill's Wild West Show, which came to Woodbine Park for three days in August 1885. The ad proclaims that this is the first and will be the last time the show will come to Canada and that the show will provide patrons with "an Exact Exhibition of Western Border Life — The Greatest Novelty of the Century." It goes on to list among its "numerous features" a "renowned Sioux Chief."

Some 41 years after Swedish soprano Jenny Lind had delighted Torontonians, in September 1892, the famed African American soprano Sissieretta Jones, a.k.a. "The Black Patti," sang at the Auditorium (formerly Shaftesbury Hall on Adelaide West). In 1897 she returned on two separate occasions to play the Toronto Opera House and the Grand Opera House.

Bob Cole wrote the first full-length musical comedy written and performed exclusively by black Americans, which hit a New York stage in 1898. While there were only a total of eight performances at the Third Avenue Theatre in NYC, the show played for a week that year at the Toronto Opera House and came back for another week at the same venue in 1900. In 1907 and 1908 two more musicals written, directed, and performed by African Americans, Bert Williams and George Walker's *Abyssinia* and *Bandana Land*, each played the Grand for a week.

In 1899, Canadian brothers Jerry and Mike Shea opened the first Shea's Theatre on the east side of Yonge Street between Adelaide and King. The Sheas would later build a second theatre, known as Shea's Victoria, at Richmond and Victoria in 1910, and four years later would open Shea's Hippodrome on the west side of Bay, just north of Queen. With a capacity of 3,200 (some sources say 2,600), the Hippodrome was the largest movie palace in Canada and one of the largest in the world. All three of

February 22–27, 1897, Grand Opera House

the Shea's buildings presented vaudeville shows and eventually movies.

For years, the three Shea's theatres, along with the Princess Theatre, the Grand Opera House, the Majestic Music Hall, and eventually Loew's Theatre, presented some of the biggest stars in vaudeville. Ontario native May Irwin had first appeared onstage in New York in 1877 at the Metropolitan Theatre. Having worked for Tony Pastor for many years, she initially became famous for her acting and comedic abilities. By the 1890s she had become a recording star, best known for singing "coon shouting" songs, her biggest hit being "The Bully Song" (also known as "Bully of the Town"). By 1896, she appeared in her first silent film, *The Kiss*. Considered somewhat risqué at the time, it was the first film to actually feature a couple kissing.

Irwin first appeared in Toronto in 1897 at the Grand Opera House in what was billed as "Her Greatest Comedy Success," *Swell Miss Fitzwell*. Irwin was a white singer who specialized in singing ostensibly black material, leading the ads for the show to loudly proclaim "Hear her Negro songs. The best Toronto has ever had." Among the list of songs she was to sing was "Pickaninny

Lullaby" and "Honey on My Lips." Irwin would subsequently take the show to New York where she played the Bijou Theatre. She would return to Toronto in April 1905 where she appeared in another comedy, *Mrs. Black Is Back*, at the Princess Theatre.

During the first two decades of the twentieth century a who's who of star comedians, singers, and actors appeared in Toronto's vaudeville palaces. Comedian, actor, and part-time juggler W.C. Fields took the stage at Shea's Theatre in 1901. Sophie Tucker, dubbed "The Last of the Red Hot Mamas," brought her comedic, vocal, and acting skills to the Majestic Music Hall in October 1909. In March 1910, Shea's Theatre staged an incredible show featuring Al Jolson (in blackface), Hilda Thomas and Lou Hall, Smith and Campbell, Harry De Coe ("The Man with the Table and the Chairs"), Les Trombetta ("a Parisian Dancing Novelty"), Marcel and Boris ("Equilibrists, in Original Work"), and what was called the Kinetograph, which would show "all new pictures" (e.g., silent films). The special extra attraction was "Jos. Hart's Bathing Girls."

The biggest-selling black recording artist of the first two decades of the 20th century,

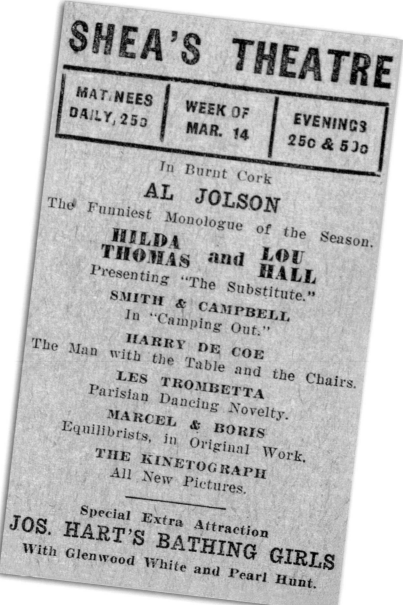

March 14, 1910, Shea's Theatre

January 8, 1946,
Massey Hall

Bert Williams, came to the Princess Theatre in March 1912 as part of the Ziegfeld Follies. Amazingly enough, the ad simply read "A Perfect Cast and 75 Ziegfeld Beauty Girls."

In November of that year, Eddie Cantor, playing the blackface character "Jefferson," appeared in a vaudeville show at Shea's Theatre. Marion Harris, who came to fame in 1916 as a white woman singing blues- and jazz-inflected material, and was often billed as "Queen of the Blues," appeared at Shea's in June 1919. Irving Berlin appeared in Toronto that same year as part of the Ziegfeld Follies.

A bevy of the biggest recording stars of the early part of the century, including Billy Murray and Canadian Henry Burr, appeared at Massey Hall in 1920 in an incredible evening featuring eight artists who recorded for the His Master's Voice record company. Also on the bill were the outstanding banjo player Fred Van Eps, the Sterling Trio, and the Peerless Quartet. The latter two ensembles featured Burr as well as other singers on the bill, such as Albert Campbell. Collectively, this concert was probably the most star-studded pop music concert ever to be staged in Toronto up to that point.

Although vaudeville packages started to die out in the 1920s due to the popularity of "talking pictures," as late as 1929, a show featuring film actress Dolores Costello, tap dancers Buck and Bubbles, comedians George Burns and Gracie Allen, and the Lee Twins & Co (advertised as "nine stepping beauties") appeared in a revue entitled "Rhythmic Dance Divertissements" at Shea's 3,200-seat Hippodrome.

The legacy of vaudeville-influenced shows continued through the 1930s, when headlining jazz stars such as Louis Armstrong, Cab Calloway, and Duke Ellington would come to town for a week as the star attraction on a bill that was typically comprised of four or five lesser acts that included dancers and comedians. More often than not, a movie was also thrown into the mix. This combination of movies and live performances would continue into the late 1950s at venues such as the Casino Club, located on Queen at Bay.

December 3–10, 1951, Loew's Uptown

FIRST APPEARANCE IN CANADA !

Shaftesbury Hall !

TWO GRAND CONCERTS.

BENEFIT OF FISK UNIVERSITY,

1871. NASHVILLE, TENN. 1830. BY THE

Jubilee Singers !

ORIGINAL COMPANY,

MONDAY EVENING, OCT. 18TH.

AND

FRIDAY EV'G., OCT. 22D, 1880.

"I NEVER SO ENJOYED MUSIC."—*Spurgeon.*

Admission, 50 cents. Reserved seats, 75 cents. Diagram at Nordheimer's Music Store on and after Wednesday, 13th inst.   1356

October 18, 22, 1880, Shaftesbury Hall

2

Jubilee, Spirituals, and Gospel

In 1845, escaped slaves who had fled to Canada via the Underground Railroad built the British Methodist Episcopal Church at 94 Chestnut Street, near Dundas and Bay Streets. Slavery had only been abolished in the British Empire 12 years earlier. This church, seating about 200, was the site in 1873 of the first advertised performances by a touring black religious group. Although it had only been eight years since the end of the Civil War, the Plantation Jubilee Singers from New Orleans performed at the Chestnut Street church on November 3. The term *jubilee singers* in the 19th and early 20th centuries was used by groups whose repertoire largely consisted of spiritual songs. The word *jubilee* refers, of course, to New Year's Day 1863, when the Emancipation Proclamation became law and all African American slaves were officially declared to be legally free.

The *Globe* reported that "this band of singers should be heard by all who wish to hear genuine samples of the sacred songs which made music in the cornfield in those days where the plague spot of slavery was as yet unblotted from the land."

The group performed for the next two nights at Temperance Hall, located on Temperance Street between Bay and Yonge, south of Richmond Street. Apparently, the concerts were part of a tour designed to raise money to build a church back in New Orleans.

Six years later, Rev. Walter Hawkins and his Troupe of Jubilee Singers performed at the same church on Chestnut. Hawkins was from southwestern Ontario and had led jubilee groups in the area since 1869. His programs were often combined with introductory remarks before each song in which he spoke about the inhumane world of slavery.

After the Civil War, one of the most pressing problems for newly freed slaves was education. A number of black colleges were quickly established, beginning in 1866 with the Fisk Free Colored School (later Fisk University) in Nashville, followed by the Hampton Institute in Hampton, Virginia, which opened its doors in 1868. Not surprisingly, these colleges were in dire need of funds for everything from books to desks to housing for their students. In 1871, led by the school's treasurer and music director, George L. White, the Fisk Jubilee Singers began a tour to raise money for the college. They were extraordinarily successful, raising $140,000 ($4 million in 2019 dollars) in their first three years of touring. By April 1873 they were in Great Britain performing for Queen Victoria.

Word of the Fisk Jubilee Singers' success quickly spread to the handful of other newly formed black colleges. Several of them, including the Hampton Institute, formed their own jubilee ensembles, which also toured to raise money for their respective schools. The Hampton Jubilee Singers performed at Toronto's Music Hall June 1 and 2, 1874, singing "slave songs of the south, plantation songs, and sacred melodies." Their performance was presented under "the Distinguished Patronage of their Excellencies the Earl and Countess of Dufferin." Two months later, an ensemble referred to as the Hampton

Colored Students performed "Slave Songs of the South" at the Horticultural Gardens on the site of Toronto's first public park, what is now Allan Gardens (renamed in 1901 after the donor of the land, former mayor George William Allan). The park and pavilion had been built just 14 years earlier. One assumes that this was the same group that performed at the beginning of June.

In February 1877, a group billed as the Original Nashville Coloured Jubilee Singers performed at the Royal Opera House. On April 27, another jubilee group was at the Grand Opera House. Jubilee singing was clearly a very popular form of entertainment for Torontonians in the last quarter of the 19th century!

The Fisk Jubilee Singers finally made it to Toronto in October 1880, playing on the eighteenth and twenty-second at Shaftesbury Hall (located at Queen and James Streets by Old City Hall). By this time they were no longer formally associated with Fisk University. Instead, they were touring privately under the leadership of their original director, George L. White.

They were so successful that they came back to the Hall for two more shows on November 8 and 9. On the ninth, the *Globe* reported, "The pieces were for the most part the sacred plantation melodies which they sang with as much verve as the slaves would have done a quarter century ago in Louisiana, but with more taste and artistic appreciation of their real beauties." Amongst the spirituals the group performed were "Steal Away," "The Band of Gideon," and "The Gospel Train." The *Globe* review noted that "by special request the company sang 'John Brown's Body,' which no one can hear them sing without emotion."

Four days later the group was performing at the Horticultural Gardens Pavilion. Less than a year earlier, a new, bigger and better pavilion had been built, modelled on the Crystal Palace in London, England. Unfortunately, in 1902, the new pavilion was destroyed by fire.

Approximately 1,800 people per night attended the Fisk Jubilee Singers next performances in Toronto on October 6–8, 1881, at the Horticultural Gardens Pavilion. They came back less than two weeks later and performed again at the pavilion on the twenty-second. To the eternal shame of the city, four Toronto hotels refused the group accommodation due to their skin colour, prompting a number of editorials in the city's newspapers, some of which encouraged boycotts of the offending hotels.

The Fisk Jubilee Singers, now under the leadership of Frederick J. Loudin, were back twice in 1882 and three times in 1883, splitting their performances between Shaftesbury Hall and the Horticultural Gardens Pavilion. In 1884, Loudin took the Fisk Jubilee Singers on a six-year tour to Great Britain, Australia, and Asia. Soprano Maggie Porter Cole and her husband, tenor Daniel Cole, broke away from Loudin's group and formed an ensemble they confusingly called the Original Fisk Jubilee Singers. This group performed eight times in Toronto between October 20 and December 12, 1884, seven times at Shaftesbury Hall and once at the Horticultural Gardens.

After a five-year break, the group returned and was evidently much less popular, playing smaller venues such as the Western Congregational Church on January 4, 1889, the Association Hall (later the YMCA Hall) on Yonge Street the next day, and then in December at the Carlton Street Methodist Church. Additional performances by the Fisk Jubilee Singers occurred in at least five different churches in the 1890s. In 1898, Fisk University began sponsoring a jubilee group again and, of course, took back the name the Fisk Jubilee Singers. This group appeared in Toronto a handful of times in the 1920s and '30s, including a particularly memorable performance April 22, 1926, at Massey Hall.

A number of other jubilee groups performed spirituals in Toronto in the late 19th century. On November 1, 1880, just days after the first Fisk Jubilee Singers performance in Toronto, the Hamilton Jubilee Singers performed at the Academy of Music. According to the *Globe*, the venue was "crowded to the doors" and the group received "hearty applause." The performance was part of a Temperance League meeting. Jubilee groups from both southern Ontario and the United States, including Hamilton's Canadian Jubilee Singers, the O'Banyoun Jubilee Singers (who were also from Hamilton), St. Catharines' Ball Family Jubilee Singers, and the Tennessee Jubilee Singers, commonly performed at Canadian Temperance League meetings over the next few decades, at local churches, the

Association Hall, the Shaftesbury Theatre, and Massey Hall.

In August 1881, the Louisiana Jubilee Singers performed for three days at the Horticultural Gardens as part of a production of the play *Uncle Tom's Cabin*. In 1884, the Tennessee Jubilee Singers performed as part of Miller's Uncle Tom's Cabin company at the Royal Museum (located at Bay and Adelaide) and Montford's Museum. The Royal was renamed Montford's Museum when it was taken over by a new owner. At the time, dime museums were multi-purpose entertainment facilities, often displaying curios of various kinds on one floor and offering lectures and musical or theatrical performances on another. The idea of the dime or dime-store museum was started by P.T. Barnum in New York City in the late 1830s.

May 1884 saw a Canadian group from St. Catharines, the Ball Family Jubilee Singers, led by patriarch Rev. Richard Ball, sing at the Queen Street Baptist Church. A year and a half later, the Mississippi Jubilee Singers gave a "Grand Thanksgiving Jubilee" concert at Temperance Hall. Even more interesting, perhaps, was the March 19, 1887, performance by the New Orleans University Singers

April 13–15, 1926,
Massey Hall

for asylum patients in Toronto. Eight days later, this group, billed as the New Orleans Jubilee Singers, delighted audiences at the Horticultural Gardens.

The first appearance in Toronto by Hamilton's O'Banyoun Jubilee Singers in

March 1888 at Shaftesbury Hall is significant in that the group had been formed in Halifax in the early 1860s, before the end of the Civil War, years before the advent of the Fisk Jubilee Singers. This suggests that the first touring and performing jubilee groups may have been assembled by former slaves in Canada. (Thanks to Dr. Jesse Feyen for his research on this group.)

There were numerous performances by jubilee groups throughout the 1890s and into the 20th century. In 1894 and 1895 there were two notable performances by African American vocal ensembles that may or may not have included spirituals. On September 7, 1894, the Virginia Quarette sang what was advertised as "plantation melodies" at the Queen's Hotel as part of the entertainment at a banquet held by the Mutual Reserve Fund Life Association. It would be fascinating to know what they sang that night.

A year later, from September 30 through October 5, the Jefferson Sisters, advertised as former slaves who had worked on Thomas Jefferson's plantation, sang "plantation melodies" in a production called "Slave Life Before the War" at the Crystal Theatre in the Eden Museum. Located at 91–93 Yonge Street, the Eden Museum burnt down in 1897. In 1899, a new building was constructed on the site and christened the Shea Theatre after co-owners and brothers Jerry and Michael Shea. As was the case with white audiences in the northern United States, Torontonians clearly had a fascination with black culture at large and what life was supposedly like when slavery reigned in the southern states.

Jubilee singers continued to make appearances in Toronto well into the 20th century. The Carolina Jubilee Singers and the Virginia Jubilee Singers could be found performing in Toronto in the 1930s, and as late as the 1950s the Eureka Jubilee Singers of Chicago performed here.

Movie star and classically trained singer Paul Robeson, billed as the "Great Negro Baritone" and presented by I.E. Suckling, first performed in Toronto at Massey Hall on November 21, 1929. As usual, his repertoire that night included a number of concert spirituals. Robeson came back to perform in 1935 at the Eaton Auditorium (now the Carlu at Yonge and College). Linking his socialist views with Toronto's left-leaning

MANAGEMENT - - - I. E. SUCKLING
195 Yonge Street   Ad. 0345

THURSDAY
THE GREAT NEGRO BARITONE
PAUL
ROBESON

In a program of Negro Music, who, early
this month, "sold out" Two Recitals in Five Days at Carnegie Hall, N.Y.,
and who, this past summer, "sold out" Two Recitals in Royal Albert Hall,
London (capacity 8,000).

"I have heard all the great singers of our time. No voice has ever moved
me so profoundly with so many passions of thought and emotions."—
James Douglas in "The London Daily Express."

Seats now at Massey Hall—1.00, 1.50, 2.00—Tax (10%) extra.

November 21, 1929, Massey Hall

Jewish labour movement, one of Robeson's most memorable Toronto performances was on December 3, 1949, when he appeared with the Toronto Jewish Folk Choir at Massey Hall.

The first gospel performer (as opposed to spiritual or jubilee ensemble) to perform in Toronto was Sister Rosetta Tharpe who tore the roof off of Shea's Hippodrome, giving four performances a day during the week of March 11, 1940, on a bill with Cab Calloway, Chu Berry, and Cozy Cole. The first gospel group to come to Toronto was the New York–based Southernaires, who performed at Massey Hall in 1942 and two years later returned for a show at the Eaton Auditorium. The latter was a fundraising concert organized by the Toronto African Methodist Church. What is particularly interesting about the Southernaires' performances in the early 1940s is that, although these were the first concerts by an American gospel group in Toronto, the group is just a footnote in gospel history, recording a few records for Decca in 1939, but none that sold in substantive numbers. Despite achieving little success as recording artists, the Southernaires first appeared on radio in

October 1930 in New York City. Over the next several years, their radio appearances became increasingly popular. From 1933 through 1943 they performed in a dramatic radio series called *The Little Weatherbeaten Whitewashed Church*, which was syndicated across the United States.

Torontonians probably heard this show via Buffalo station WEAF, or perhaps it was picked up by a local station. In either case, it must have been through radio that the Southernaires acquired a big enough following in Toronto to play Massey Hall. They would come back to Eaton Auditorium one more time in 1947. That same year the obscure Cleveland Colored Quartet performed at the Crusaders Church.

The Wings Over Jordan choir also played Toronto in the mid-1940s, appearing at Massey Hall March 24, 1944. Led by Glenn T. Settle and based in Cleveland, Ohio, the Wings Over Jordan choir were huge radio stars, beginning national broadcasts in the United States in 1938 that were also heard in Canada. They were the first important gospel choir. Sporting 17 singers at their Massey Hall show, this would have been a fantastic concert to see. In what was typical of the time, the *Globe and Mail* reviewer wrote a factual but understated review, commenting, "They confine themselves to spirituals and many in the audience were doubtless surprised at being asked to stand for the Bendictioa when the concert was at the end. Since Negroes, for the most part, take their religion joyfully, there was no lack of buoyancy in the program.… The expression they put into 'Little David' and 'Standing in the Need of Prayer' was inspiring."

While Toronto was never a centre for African American gospel music tours until recent times, there were a few interesting and notable gospel performances in the second half of the 20th century that are worth pointing out. On Tuesday, March 15, 1949, the massively popular Golden Gate Quartet made their first Toronto appearance (despite being recording stars as early as 1933). The occasion for their Toronto debut was the second annual variety night put on by Variety Village to raise money for disabled children. The quartet was featured at the Odeon Cinema on a multi-act bill that included Pearl Bailey, Lorne Green, jugglers, a classical soprano, and the movie *The Passionate Friends*. As the show was a charity event, tickets were a whopping (for the time) five dollars, and interestingly enough were sold at the three most elite hotels in the city: the Royal York, the King Edward, and the Prince George. Variety Village clearly knew where moneyed Torontonians spent their time! The Golden Gate Quartet returned to play a week in December 1949 at the legendary Casino Club at Bay and Queen.

One of the odder performances by a black gospel group in Toronto occurred in 1951 when the Charioteers performed at a Toronto Maple Leafs game at Maple Leaf Gardens. Over the course of their career, the Charioteers performed both secular and sacred material. Unfortunately, there is no extant review to let us know what they might have performed that night at the Gardens.

Gospel superstar Mahalia Jackson first played Toronto in February 1956. Jackson's greatest recordings, such as "Move on Up a Little Higher" and "What Can I Give," were cut between 1947 and 1952 for Apollo Records. Given that Apollo was a small independent label that was marketed nearly exclusively to African Americans and had limited distribution, most Torontonians

International Artists presents

MAHALIA JACKSON

World's greatest Gospel Singer

MASSEY HALL **TOMORROW** 8.30 P.M.

Tickets now on sale at the Box Office

February 21, 1956,
Massey Hall

would not have been aware of Jackson's vocal prowess prior to her signing with Columbia Records in 1954. With the promotional acumen of Columbia behind her, Jackson sold out Massey Hall, returning numerous times over the years to the venerable Shuter Street concert hall, including performances in 1956, 1957, 1959, 1961, and 1963. While none of the hard-singing postwar male gospel quartets seem to have performed in Toronto in the 1940s and 1950s, the great Clara Ward Singers, who first came to fame in the late 1940s, played for two weeks at the recently opened O'Keefe Centre in February 1963, third on a bizarre bill that included Jack Benny and Jane Morgan.

Riding the mainstream success of his arrangement of an 18th-century hymn, "O Happy Day," which sold over two million singles in 1969 and reached number four on the pop charts in the United States and number two in Canada, Edwin Hawkins headlined an "All-Star Gospel Sing Out" at the CNE Grandstand on August 29, 1971. Atypical of gospel performances, the evening featured an interracial bill that included the Oak Ridge Boys and the LeFevres.

While Edwin Hawkins was riding high on the pop charts, Andraé Crouch and the Disciples were waxing their first recordings for Light Records. Crouch helped found the Contemporary Christian Music genre, bridging white and black gospel music. On May 25, 1974, Andraé Crouch and the Disciples, together with the Archers, performed at what was advertised as a "Big Jesus Music Festival" at Varsity Arena.

Micah Music, run by Karen and Oswald Burke, who would later found the Toronto Mass Choir, promoted a number of gospel concerts in the 1980s and early 1990s. Among their more notable shows were the Richard Smallwood Singers and Thomas Whitfield at Convocation Hall and Commissioned at Minkler Auditorium, both in the late 1980s, and BeBe and CeCe Winans in August 1992 at the Ontario Place Forum.

Harbourfront dabbled a bit in black gospel. In early July 1990, on the main stage, the venue hosted one of the great gospel stars of all-time, Shirley Caesar, plus the legendary gospel quartet the Fairfield Four, the Mass Choir of the Toronto Association of Gospel Music Ministries, and Zimbabwe's Machanic Manyeruke.

The final truly extraordinary Toronto gospel concert of the 20th century by an American superstar was the May 1995 appearance of Kirk Franklin and the Family at the Queensway Cathedral. Meanwhile, the homegrown Montreal Jubilation Gospel Choir and Toronto Mass Choir would both appear many times in the city throughout the 1980s and 1990s, typically bringing the house down during every performance.

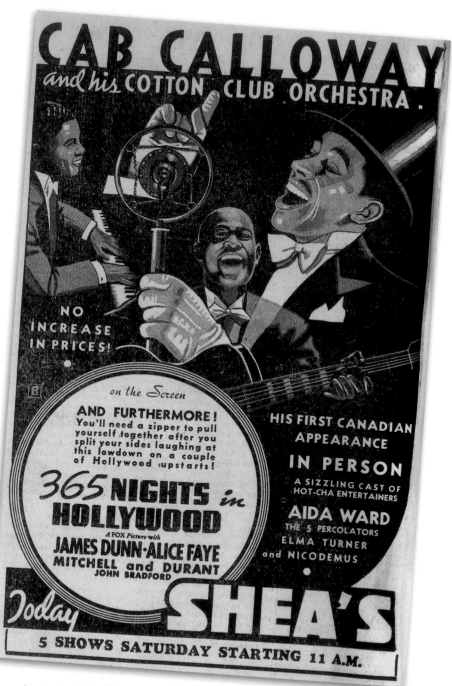

December 3–8, 1934, Shea's

3
JAZZ

As the 19th century was coming to a close, ragtime was taking North America by storm. Commonly played by piano "professors," the musical style gained prominence in mid-1890s compositions by Ernest Hogan, Ben Harney, and Scott Joplin. Given that ragtime was a more syncopated version of the popular march music of composers such as John Philip Sousa, it is not surprising that dance bands across the United States and Canada began to incorporate rag numbers and the rag style of playing into their performances. In New Orleans, where rhythms were always more syncopated than in the rest of the continent, musicians such as the legendary Buddy Bolden, and eventually King Oliver, Kid Ory, and Louis Armstrong, began to take the rag style of syncopation and apply it to semi-improvised arrangements of blues, pop tunes, and, yes, ragtime compositions. In the process, what we know as New Orleans jazz was born.

While both ragtime and jazz were created by black Americans, given the racial attitudes of the day, the first jazz recordings were by a group of white New Orleans musicians working under the sobriquet the Original Dixieland Jazz Band. Led by cornetist Nick LaRocca, the group recorded their first 78 rpm record, *Livery Stable Blues*, backed with Dixieland Jass [*sic*] Band One-Step, in New York City February 26, 1917. Eight weeks later, the record was being advertised in the *Globe and Mail* as being for sale in Toronto.

Toronto was clearly smitten with this new music. In September, the *Globe* ran an advertisement with the heading "Edison Concert Re-creation Program" (Edison was one of the early manufacturers of phonographs). The event was to be held in "the Edison tent just beside the art galleries" in both the afternoon and evening. Among the records being played in this public demonstration of the wonders of the phonograph was *Canary Cottage* by another white jazz band that recorded in New York City, the Frisco Jass [*sic*] Band.

A black jazz band wouldn't get to record until 1921, when New Orleans trombonist Kid Ory cut two sides in San Francisco. In 1923, King Oliver's Creole Jazz Band, featuring Louis Armstrong, would be the first African American band to make a series of recordings. Cut in Chicago, the Oliver records are widely considered the definitive New Orleans jazz recordings of the day.

Unfortunately, none of the early jazz greats toured much beyond New York and Chicago, and none played Toronto. The first so-called jazz musician to come to Toronto was the white pop bandleader Paul Whiteman, who, typical of the times, was billed as "The King of Jazz" despite playing mostly arranged, at best slightly syncopated, jazz-tinged music. As early as the summer of 1921, Whiteman's recordings were being advertised in Toronto. In 1923, he presented a nine-piece "Romance of Rhythm Orchestra" at Loew's Yonge Street (now the Elgin Theatre), co-billed with a silent movie entitled *Hearts Aflame*. It doesn't seem that Whiteman himself came to Toronto, as the orchestra was under the direction of Alex Hyde.

Whiteman finally made it to Toronto in 1924, appearing at Massey Hall with a

25-piece orchestra on May 30 and 31 and again on October 1. He sold out every show and received rave reviews in the newspapers. In May, Whiteman billed his show as "An Experiment in American Music." The *Globe*'s correspondent was clearly impressed, writing that Whiteman "sets out to bridge the gap between 'jazz' and music of the better sort, eliminating the blatant vulgarity of the older 'jazz' which made it distasteful to musicians of taste." The clearly stuffy scribe went on to note that "even the drummer and traps, that one expects to go needlessly hysterical, had the deportment and austerity of a concert master."

Bing Crosby sang for a short period with Whiteman, but did not play Toronto with him. Crosby first came to town as a member of the Rhythm Boys in October 1930, when they appeared in the "Green and Gold Revue" along with Al Mitchell and his Syncopators and pop singer Lillian Roth at the Greater Imperial at Yonge and Dundas. During their week-long run, the Rhythm Boys played in a midnight benefit concert on October 15 along with 19 other artists, who were then playing the Imperial, the Princess, Shea's Hippodrome, and

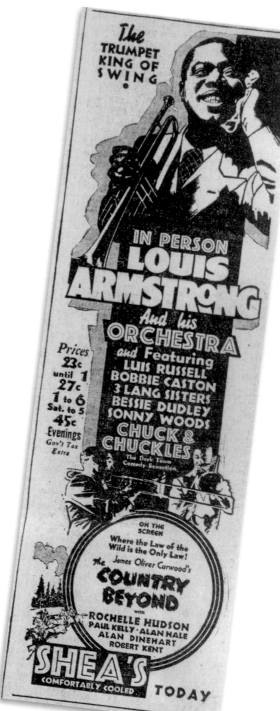

June 27, 1936, Shea's

the Embassy Club, for the Federation of Community Service. Nineteen years later, Crosby's heir, Frank Sinatra, would pack Mutual Arena for two shows.

Arguably the first black American jazz musician to play Toronto was Eubie Blake, who, along with Noble Sissle, had written a hit Broadway show called *Shuffle Along*, in which they both starred. While there was a plot to the show, it mainly served as a framework to showcase jazz-inflected music and dance. *Shuffle Along*, with Blake and Sissle front and centre, played a week at the Royal Alexandra Theatre in late September 1923. It was so successful that it was brought back for two more week-long runs at the Princess Theatre in January and October of 1924. In April 1925, Blake and Sissle's second all-black Broadway show, *Chocolate Dandies*, played for a week at the Princess.

Duke Ellington and his Cotton Club Band were the second African American jazz musicians to appear in Toronto, coming to the Imperial (now the Ed Mirvish Theatre) for a week at the end of June 1931. Alongside Ellington, the movie *My Past* was screened, and a "musical" by the Imperial Concert Orchestra, as well as an organ interlude by Horace Lapp, were featured. Ellington would be a regular attraction in Toronto for the next several decades.

Beginning October 15, 1932, the famed New York big band leader Fletcher Henderson came to Shea's Hippodrome, billed as being direct from Connie's Inn, "the hottest spot in Harlem." During what the newspapers described as the "vaudeville portion of the show," the Four Cossacks, comedian Bobby Pinkus, and Will J. Ward ("music & comedy chatter") provided additional entertainment. The *Globe* wrote that Henderson is "one of the first of his race to organize and popularize a band specializing in the musical rhythm which is now generally supposed to be symbolic of Harlem," while the *Star* reviewer opined, "As usual, these sons of Harlem pep it up in real style and the tunes are catchy."

After Henderson's successful run, Shea's began to feature a number of American jazz greats, with Cab Calloway appearing in 1934 and 1935, Jimmie Lunceford in 1935, and Louis Armstrong (billed as "The Trumpet King of Swing") and Fats Waller in 1936.

A particularly exciting year for Toronto jazz fans was 1938. Chick Webb and his Savoy

Swing Orchestra featuring Ella Fitzgerald rocked the Brant Inn in Burlington on July 1, giving local jazz fans their first taste of perhaps the greatest jazz singer ever. Claude Hopkins played the Palais Royale on the Lakeshore in August, and in November the venerable Duke Ellington made his fifth appearance in Toronto, playing Maple Leaf Gardens with Ivie Anderson and Dolores Brown. (Ellington's second appearance was at the CNE in 1934.) Tickets were a dollar, and part of the evening's festivities included a jitterbug contest presented by the Lion's Club of Toronto to support work on behalf of underprivileged boys. The Ellington performance at the Gardens was the first large-scale popular music concert in Toronto and was certainly the first time popular music was featured at the Gardens.

The swing years from 1935 to 1945 were good for Toronto jazz fans. White bands such as Benny Goodman's and the Harry James Orchestra were regular visitors. Count Basie, Bob Crosby, Charlie Barnet, Louis Armstrong, Louis Prima, and Duke Ellington all played one-nighters at the Palais Royale, while Glenn Miller and Ellington played similar one-offs at

July 8–9, 1949, Mutual Arena

PALAIS ROYALE

The Sepia Swing Sensation

COUNT BASIE

and his ORCHESTRA.

ONE NITE ONLY
THURS., FEB. 16

Tickets if Purchased Before Feb. 16:
Ladies, 50c;   Gentlemen, $1.

Prices on Date of Engagement:
Ladies, 75c;   Gentlemen, $1.25.

February 16, 1939,
Palais Royale

the Mutual Arena. Meanwhile, Lucky Millinder and Fats Waller came to Shea's Hippodrome for a week at a time, as did vocal ensembles such as the Andrew Sisters and the Mills Brothers. Cab Calloway played Maple Leaf Gardens in 1941, and, as the war came to an end, a flood of jazz shows came to the Gardens, featuring mostly white artists such as Gene Krupa, Charlie Spivak, and Woody Herman. Krupa appeared May 1, 1945. The *Globe and Mail* described the concert as follows: "Four thousand of the happiest hepcats in human imagination, some of them draped in really zooty suits, were on hand to drink in the music of Gene Krupa, the hottest drummer this side of Darkest Africa."

Louis Jordan made one of his two Toronto appearances at Club Top Hat in 1943, playing for a week and a half in April. Jordan had left the Chick Webb band in 1938, and by the time he appeared at Club Top Hat, he was leading a jump blues band that was riding high on hit songs such as "What's the Use in Getting Sober (When You Gonna Get Drunk Again)," "The Chicks I Pick Are Slender and Tall," and "Five Guys Named Moe."

WEDNESDAY NOV. 23RD.

TICKETS NOW SELLING! AT INFORMATION DESKS OF EATON'S and SIMPSON'S
JESS APPLEGATH — BIRKS ELLIS RYRIE — HEINTZMANS — GEO. WALLACE

Extra! JITTERBUG CONTEST BIG PRIZES!

DANCING TO DUKE EIGHT TO ONE A.M.

ONE DOLLAR PER PERSON

THE IDOL OF TWO CONTINENTS
Duke ELLINGTON
AND HIS FAMOUS ORCHESTRA
WITH IVIE ANDERSON and DOLORES BROWN
Presented by the LION'S CLUB of TORONTO
TO SUPPORT WORK ON BEHALF OF UNDER PRIVILEGED BOYS

MAPLE LEAF GARDENS

Duke Ellington dance tickets on sale at all branches of United Cigar Stores.
ALL SEATS RESERVED.

November 23, 1938, Maple Leaf Gardens

While swing music was flourishing, in the early 1940s a new, radical style of jazz evolved in New York City called bebop. Its leading practitioners were alto saxophonist Charlie Parker, trumpeter Dizzy Gillespie, pianists Thelonious Monk and Bud Powell, and drummer Kenny Clarke. The first chance Torontonians got to hear this music was when an unbilled Thelonious Monk accompanied Coleman Hawkins for two weeks in April 1944 at Club Top Hat. The first featured bebop artist to play Toronto was Dizzy Gillespie who played the Queensway Ballroom (which would shortly change its name to the Palace Pier)

at Lakeshore West and Humber on March 24, 1945. On November 14 of that year, Charlie Parker played Massey Hall along with Slam Stewart, Trummy Young, Erroll Garner, and Hal West. The review the next day in the *Globe and Mail* barely mentioned Parker, focusing on Erroll Garner instead.

Parker would return to Massey Hall in April of 1948 as part of the first of Norman Granz's Jazz at the Philharmonic tours. Other jazz notables on the bill were Sarah Vaughan, Red Rodney, Flip Phillips, Dexter Gordon, Barney Kessel, Duke Jordan, and Howard McGhee.

Perhaps the most legendary jazz show in Toronto's history, however, occurred

April 7–14, 1943, Club Top Hat

at Massey Hall in May 1953 and featured Parker, Gillespie, bassist Charles Mingus, pianist Bud Powell, and drummer Max Roach. This was the one and only time that these five musicians would ever play together. The evening was organized by the New Jazz Society of Toronto, headed by Dick Wattam. With some members literally still in high school, the young enthusiasts got into a car, drove to New York, and proceeded to sign up the five musicians individually to play the show. (Parker was tracked down at a music store on Broadway!) The ads for the concert simply said "Jazz Festival" and listed the names of each of the performers.

Unfortunately, Wattam and company had never promoted a show like this before and failed to take into account that the world heavyweight boxing match between Rocky Marciano and Jersey Joe Walcott was being shown on television that night, which meant a lot of people stayed home glued to their television sets. In between the two halves of the concert, the band and much of the audience went across the street to the Silver Rail to watch the fight.

While estimates range, it is safe to say that somewhere between 600 and 1,100 tickets

Jazz Festival

DIZZY GILLESPIE • CHARLIE PARKER
BUD POWELL • MAX ROACH
• CHARLES MINGUS

Plus

CBC All-Stars • 17-Piece Orch. led by Graham Topping
MASSEY HALL—TONIGHT—8:30 P.M.

Tickets NOW at all agencies and Premier Radio

May 15, 1953,
Massey Hall

were sold, while Massey Hall's capacity was about 2,750. The result was that there was not enough money to pay the musicians. Incensed, Charles Mingus took the master tapes that the New Jazz Society had made of the concert and released them on his and Roach's Debut label (Parker had to be listed as Charlie Chan on the original issue due to other contractual obligations). Mingus titled the album *Jazz at Massey Hall*, in the process making Massey Hall famous the world over.

Ironically, the *Star* didn't bother to review the show, while the *Globe* praised Bud Powell and the opening 17-piece local ensemble led by Graham Topping, but expressed disappointment with Parker's and Gillespie's performances.

Perhaps the greatest Canadian jazz musician ever, pianist Oscar Peterson, made his

August 6–13, 1951,
Elliott Hotel

Massey Hall debut in March 1946. Two months later, fans of the Dixieland revival could go to the Eaton Auditorium to hear New Orleans musicians Sidney Bechet, the DeParis Brothers, and stride pianist James P. Johnson. Perhaps the second-greatest stride piano player was Willie "The Lion" Smith, who appeared at the Colonial Tavern for a week in early 1951.

Throughout the 1950s, '60s, and into the '70s, Toronto was a regular touring stop for virtually all forms of jazz. In 1947 the Colonial Tavern was bought by Goody and Harvey Lichtenberg, who promptly initiated a jazz policy by hiring African Canadian pianist Cy McLean and his Rhythm Rompers. McLean reigned nightly at the club for the next several years. In 1950, the Colonial started bringing in artists such as Red Norvo, Sidney Bechet, and Helen Forrest for a week at a time. The week of December 28, Dizzy Gillespie appeared at the Colonial. On tenor saxophone was John Coltrane. This would be one of possibly two times that Coltrane, perhaps the greatest saxophone player in jazz history, ever played on a Toronto stage during his all-too-brief life.

From August 11 to 16, 1952, Billie Holiday played what would have been a fabulous week at the club. The previous August she had played a week at the Elliott Hotel at Church and Shuter Streets. Earl "Fatha" Hines, Dave Brubeck, Duke Ellington, Chet Baker, Dinah Washington, Louis Jordan, Sarah Vaughan, Ella Fitzgerald, Max Roach, Cab Calloway, Gerry Mulligan, George Shearing, and eventually avant-garde jazz musicians such as Thelonious Monk, Ornette Coleman, and Rahsaan Roland Kirk would work the Colonial into the early 1970s. At that point, the interest in mainstream jazz was waning and the Colonial started booking soul, blues, and eventually rock bands.

One of the most infamous weeks at the Colonial had to be December 1–6, 1969, when Miles Davis took the stage nightly four months after he had recorded his game-changing *Bitches Brew* album. Accompanying Davis was saxophonist Wayne Shorter, drummer Jack DeJohnette, and keyboard wiz Chick Corea. With *Bitches Brew*, Miles had fully embraced playing funk and rock-infused electric music. Many jazz critics and fans saw such a move as heresy.

The *Globe and Mail* reviewer was clearly one such critic, writing, "For the most part this is wind, rushing stuff, like the thundering charge of a cattle stampede — exhilarating to some ears perhaps, but not the kind of thing I could stay with for very long."

Jazz would clearly never be the same.

The Town Tavern, located at 16 Queen Street East, was also active in bringing in jazz from March 1955 forward. Like most clubs of the era, they usually booked artists for a week at a time. Miles Davis played for a week beginning November 28. John Coltrane was playing with Miles at the time, but for the Town Tavern gig Miles was listed as fronting a quartet, which means that Coltrane may have stayed back in New York for the week. Unfortunately, neither the *Globe and Mail* nor the *Toronto Star* reviewed the show. Over the next 15 years the Town featured such stellar artists as Oscar Peterson, Dakota Staton, Erroll Garner, the Modern Jazz Quartet, Ahmad Jamal, Carmen McRae, Lester Young, Coleman Hawkins, Herbie Mann, Stan Getz, Phineas Newborn, Lambert, Hendricks and Ross, Art Blakey, Horace Silver, Jimmy Smith, and between

Opening Tonight
MILES-DAVIS
QUARTET
RECORDING ARTISTS
Town Tavern

Saturday Matinee 3 to 5 p.m.
• Reserve now for Christmas
and New Year's

November 28, 1955,
Town Tavern

A particularly interesting jazz-related show rolled in to Massey Hall April 26, 1954. Billed as a "Mambo Rumba Festival," over the course of the evening, Tito Puente, the Joe Loco Quintet, Myrta Silva, Mercedita Valdés, and Miguelito Valdés turned Toronto on to the best of Latin jazz.

Miles Davis first came to Toronto in 1950, third on a bill headlined by Billy Eckstine and George Shearing at Mutual Arena. After playing the Town Tavern in 1955, he returned two years later as part of a package show at Massey Hall billed as "Jazz for Moderns." On Thursday July 24, 1959, he appeared at the CNE on the second day of what was billed as the First Canadian Jazz Festival. Although John Coltrane was in Davis's band at the time, for some unknown reason Jimmy Heath took his place from July 5 to August 15, so Toronto jazz fans did not get a chance to hear Coltrane at the festival!

Ten years later, as described above, in December 1969, Miles played for a week at the Colonial Tavern. Unbelievably, on the final night of his stand, the Kinks were playing a few doors north at Le Coq d'Or. What a night! Davis's shows at Massey Hall in December 1970 (with Sonny Greenwich

August 12 and 17, 1957, Billie Holiday, accompanied by pianist Mal Waldron and Toronto's own Archie Alleyne on drums.

In the 1950s the Casino Club also contributed to making Toronto a jazz-rich city. Located on the northwest corner of Queen and Bay, the Casino had an eclectic booking policy, bringing in pop, R&B, country, and jazz acts. Ella Fitzgerald and Louis Armstrong were among the latter artists to play the club.

March 9, 1950, Casino

January 2, 1951,
Casino

and synth pioneers Syrinx opening up) and in January 1974 were mind-melting electronic affairs that permanently changed what jazz could and would be. Fusion groups following in Davis's wake, including Weather Report and Return to Forever, were regular visitors to Toronto over the ensuing years. The January 26, 1973, jaw-dropping display of technical virtuosity that occurred at Convocation Hall during the Mahavishnu Orchestra's first visit to Toronto has to be the most memorable of all jazz fusion concerts in Toronto.

In 1956, Doug Cole bought a restaurant at 260 Dundas Street East called George's Spaghetti House. He opted to keep the name of the venue and eventually started featuring jazz acts six nights a week. Moe Koffman was in charge of the booking and over the years the club featured most of Canada's finest jazz musicians, including Don Thompson, Rob McConnell, and Koffman himself. In 1971, Cole opened a second club, Bourbon Street, at 180 Queen Street West. Bourbon Street tended to book American artists for one-week stints, with backing provided by a Toronto house band. Notable artists to play there in the 1970s included Mary Lou Williams, Maxine Sullivan, Al Hibbler, Zoot Sims, Jim Hall, and Paul Desmond. The latter two artists also recorded live albums at Bourbon Street. For a time in the early 1980s, Cole ran a third jazz club called Basin Street, located above Bourbon Street.

One of the great little-known jazz shows in Toronto's history ran for the week of March 20–25, 1961, at the O'Keefe Centre. Advertised as "Impulse: A New Jazz Review," the show featured the first of only two Toronto performances by the incomparable Nina Simone, perhaps the only appearance by Nigerian drummer Olatunji and his Drums of Passion who for this performance included Yusef Lateef, dancer Carmen de Lavallade, and the Maynard Ferguson

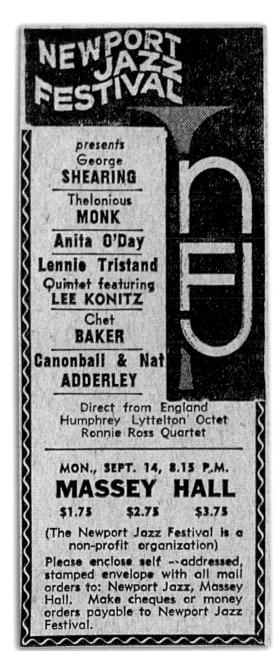

September 14, 1959, Massey Hall

March 20–25,
1961, O'Keefe
Centre

1980s, three of the most memorable nights featuring Sonny Rollins, Charles Mingus, and Pharoah Sanders.

In the late 1950s, the jazz world in New York City was turned on its head as musicians such as pianist Cecil Taylor, alto saxophonist Ornette Coleman, and keyboardist and cosmic bandleader Sun Ra began to break away from standard notions of melody, harmony, and form, each in their own unique way. What some called the Avant-Garde and others called Free Jazz, by the 1960s was often referred to as "The New Thing." It would not be until December 1970, when the Town Tavern booked Ornette Coleman for a week, that Toronto got to hear any of this new music performed live.

Ornette returned to Toronto to play the Colonial in May 1973, which happened to be the first jazz show I went to. The evening was so outside the norm that I felt as if I had left the planet. A month later, multi-reed player Anthony Braxton played the Music Library on Avenue Road, just north of St. Clair. Cecil Taylor would finally make his Toronto debut in October 1975 as part of an incredible series of concerts at York University. York's Burton Auditorium only

Orchestra. Early ads for the show listed Art Blakey and the Jazz Messengers and the Gil Evans Orchestra. Reviews seem to indicate that Blakey didn't make the gig, however, and between March 1 and 4, Evans was replaced by Maynard Ferguson.

The El Mocambo occasionally featured touring jazz artists in the 1970s and early held 600 people, and tickets were mostly sold in advance via an arts subscription series that included theatre and dance performances, as well as music. The majority of people who bought tickets through the subscription series wouldn't have known who Taylor was. That night they were in for a shock. The music was so intense that half the audience walked out; ironically, 200 or 300 fans were outside wanting to buy tickets, but were not allowed to do so because the show was sold out!

Bill Norris, who was involved with *Coda* magazine, Sackville Records, and the jazz record store on Dundas Street East, staged an unbelievable series of avant-garde jazz shows at a small venue called A Space on Nicholas Street, just west of Yonge. Norris would fly the artists to Toronto to record an album for Sackville Friday night and/or Saturday afternoon and then have the artists play A Space on Saturday night and Sunday afternoon. Tickets were three dollars, and the artists he booked included the *crème de la crème* of the contemporary avant-garde scene, including Roscoe Mitchell, Anthony Braxton, Julius Hemphill, Dollar Brand (later Abdullah Ibrahim), Hamiet Bluiett, and Oliver Lake.

As Norris's efforts were winding down, Gary Topp and Gary Cormier, collectively known as the Garys, began booking shows at the New Yorker Theatre in 1976 and 1977. In between bringing the Ramones, John Cale, Lightnin' Hopkins, and Talking Heads to town, the Garys booked Carla Bley's Big Band into the New Yorker. In 1978 they moved their operation to the Horseshoe Tavern, where they brought Sun Ra to town three times in that first year, as well as booking Cecil Taylor, Anthony Braxton, and Carla Bley. When they moved to the Edge in 1979 and 1980, they continued bringing in cutting-edge jazz artists such as Archie Shepp and Anthony Braxton. The 1970s and early 1980s were an extraordinary period for adventurous avant-garde jazz in Toronto.

By the 1990s, aside from local players, the jazz concert scene had considerably waned, although every year it is propped up by the Beaches International Jazz Festival and the Toronto Jazz Festival. The latter was founded in 1987, originally under the name DuMaurier Jazz Festival. For 10 days each summer, the city features a wealth of jazz artists while remaining pretty quiet for the rest of the year.

February 14, 1969, Massey Hall

4
THE
BLUES

On August 10, 1920, Mamie Smith stepped to the microphone at Okeh Record's studio in New York City and proceeded to sing a composition by Perry Bradford entitled "Crazy Blues." While white singers such as Marion Leonard had been recording blues compositions for a few years as part of their "a-bit-of-everything" pop recording careers, the importance of the Smith record cannot be overemphasized.

Blues was probably developed in the southern United States in the 1890s by the first generation of African Americans born outside of slavery. In that same decade, ragtime, jazz, barbershop harmony singing, and Pentecostal gospel music also first emerged. Composer and society bandleader W.C. Handy recalls hearing blues played by a solitary man using a slide on a guitar at a railroad station in Tutwiler, Mississippi, in

LOEW'S YONGE STREET

NOW PLAYING--Noon to 11 p.m.

Betty Compson

IN

"The Bonded Woman"

■ ■ ■ ■ ■ ■ ■ ■ ■

VAUDEVILLE

Program Headed by

Mamie Smith

and Her

"Jazz Hounds"-

Also Other Attractions

■ ■ ■ ■ ■ ■ ■ ■ ■

Special Feature Picture

The Burning of Smyrna

October 22, 1922,
Loew's

sheet music form with the publication of "The Memphis Blues." It was Handy's compositions, such as "St. Louis Blues," that brought the folk genre to white singers in the pop mainstream and eventually opened the door for Mamie Smith's moment of glory in 1920.

By the time he had acquired fame as a composer, W.C. Handy performed very rarely and does not appear to have ever performed in Toronto. Given that the city had a population of only 500,000 in the early 1920s and was pretty lily white, it is quite amazing that within two years of recording "Crazy Blues" Mamie Smith appeared onstage October 22 at Loew's Yonge Street (now the Elgin Theatre). The billing for the show read "Mamie Smith and her Jazz Hounds, Other Vaudeville Artists plus the films *Bonded Woman* and *Pardon My Glove.*" The other vaudeville artists included on the bill were the typically eclectic comedians and acrobats, as well as a clarinet/accordion duo. Topping things off was an instructive playlet entitled *How to Make Love.* As was typical for vaudeville-style revues, shows ran continuously from noon to 11:00 p.m. The reviewer from the *Globe*

1903. A year earlier, Ma Rainey encountered a woman who taught her a blues song while Rainey was travelling and performing as part of a tent show. Rainey soon thereafter incorporated the woman's song into her stage performances, while by 1912 Handy had codified the blues in

January 29, 1958,
Eaton Auditorium

didn't have a lot to say, writing only that "Mamie Smith and her jazz band, the headline vaudeville act, had original syncopated melodies."

It would appear that Mamie Smith was the only classic/vaudeville blues singer to play Toronto during the 1920s and '30s. Given that radio was in its infancy in the early 1920s, few Torontonians would have had the chance to even hear these artists. Further, classic blues singers such as Bessie Smith and Ma Rainey had unlimited work in the States for largely African American audiences in the major cities in the north as well as every little hamlet in the south. Crossing the border to play Toronto probably never entered either the artists' or local promoters' thoughts.

The type of blues that W.C. Handy and Ma Rainey recalled hearing in the first years of the 20th century were what would become known as country blues, typically featuring a solitary male singer accompanying himself on guitar. At times, a second guitarist would be added and/or the male singer would also play harmonica with a wire rack around his neck. This style of music was also recorded by male singers accompanying themselves on piano and by small string or jug bands. While more than 10,000 blues records were issued between 1925 and 1940 by such giants as Blind Lemon Jefferson, Charley Patton, Skip James, Son House, Blind Willie McTell, and Robert Johnson, many of these musicians rarely if ever travelled out of the south (although Robert Johnson *did* make it to Detroit and supposedly crossed the border into Windsor). No country blues musicians played Toronto until after the Second World War.

The first example of a pre-war country blues musician playing Toronto occurred after the end of the war when Josh White, billed as a "Minstrel of Work Songs, Blues and Ballads," opened the Musical Arts series at the Eaton Auditorium on October 17, 1946. The somewhat obscure Josephine Premice performed Haitian songs and dances to open the show. Tickets ranged from $1.50 to $3.00. By this point, White had reinvented himself, changing the style he had used when recording in the late 1920s and 1930s for a primarily African American audience into a more folk-oriented style that was much more palatable for left-leaning white liberals. He had recently had success on Broadway and was by the early 1940s a full-fledged participant in the folk revival, recording as a part-time member of Pete Seeger's Almanac Singers. On his own he recorded the politically charged albums *Southern Exposure: An Album of Jim Crow Blues* and *Chain Gang*, as well as a cover of Billie Holiday's "Strange Fruit" just a few years earlier. At the same time he had a massive hit with "One Meatball," which allegedly was the first million selling record by a black male artist.

The *Globe and Mail*'s reviewer did not seem too impressed with White's Eaton Auditorium debut, writing, "Intonation means nothing in this new concert art. The voice is allowed to skid from any lower note to a higher one and produce a more or less steady tone at any point within a half-tone of the one aimed at. In some cases the voice doesn't even try to get on pitch." The reviewer clearly knew very little about African American musical aesthetics at large and blues music in particular. White would return in 1949 to play the Casino Club at Queen and Bay, as well as perhaps a dozen more times before his death in 1969. In the 1960s he typically played Yorkville coffee houses such as the Penny Farthing.

November 21–26, 1977, Colonial

Sonny Terry and Brownie McGhee similarly reinvented themselves in the postwar period, becoming central to the white-centred folk revival. Terry first played Toronto in 1958 on a bill with Pete Seeger. Two years later, with McGhee, he performed at Ascot Hall at Keele Street just north of Annette. The little-remembered Ascot was probably the first venue to feature blues performers from the United States on a semi-regular basis. In the early 1960s, in addition to Sonny Terry and Brownie McGhee, John Lee Hooker and Jimmy Reed also played the Ascot. In 1966, Howlin' Wolf, with Toronto's City Muffin Boys opening up, played a Jewish labour hall and activist centre called the Labor Lyceum on Spadina at St. Andrew. Wolf would later play the Riverboat in Yorkville, before becoming a regular at the Colonial Tavern and then the El Mocambo, where he continued to appear until his death in 1976.

While Pinetop Smith had recorded the first piano boogie-woogie record in 1928, the boogie-woogie craze didn't really start until John Hammond included Meade Lux Lewis, Albert Ammons, and Pete Johnson in his first "Spirituals to Swing" concert in December 1938. It took a while, but Meade Lux Lewis and Pete Johnson made their only Toronto appearance in April 1952 at Massey Hall, in a show that included jazz virtuosos Art Tatum and Erroll Garner.

On a separate front, pre-war blues great Lonnie Johnson struck postwar gold in 1948 with the R&B hit "Tomorrow Night." He played Toronto for the first time in May 1965, booked into the Yorkville club the New Gate of Cleve. While allegedly only four people showed up on the first night, things got a little better over the weekend, and a month later he was booked into a second Yorkville club, the Penny Farthing. Impressed with the more welcoming racial attitudes he found in Toronto, Johnson decided to move here, opening his own Yorkville club, Home of the Blues, in 1966. While Home of the Blues quickly failed, Johnson gigged regularly in the city over the next three years until he was hit by a car in March 1969. Suffering a post–car accident stroke, he would sing on a Toronto stage just one more time, in February 1970, performing at Massey Hall with an emotional Buddy Guy, who had grown up idolizing Johnson. Guy and local Toronto blues rock band Whiskey Howl were opening up for Memphis great Bobby "Blue" Bland's first ever Toronto show, some 20 years after he cut his first record.

In 1967, African Canadian entrepreneur Howard Matthews took over George's

Kibitzeria, located at 338 Huron Street, north of Harbord. Lonnie Johnson was a regular at the club, often playing in the early evening from six to nine. On the weekends Matthews brought a host of blues greats to the city in 1968 and early 1969, including Sunnyland Slim, Willie Dixon, Jesse Fuller, Reverend Gary Davis, Bukka White, and Roosevelt Sykes.

By the second half of the 1960s, British rock bands such as the Rolling Stones, the Animals, the Yardbirds, and Cream had created a white rock audience eager to hear the postwar blues icons that had influenced Mick Jagger, Eric Burdon, and Eric Clapton. When the Masonic Temple, located at the corner of Yonge and Davenport, became Toronto's premier rock and roll venue under the name the Rock Pile, it is not surprising that blues greats John Lee Hooker, Albert King, B.B. King, and Muddy Waters were also booked there.

In February 1969, Richard Flohil brought B.B. King to Massey Hall. While King had been recording R&B hits since "Three O' Clock Blues" in 1951, this was his first Toronto performance, and Flohil was taking

June 23–28, 1969, Colonial

a gamble. He ended up making a $700 profit that night and B.B. returned a few months later to play the Rock Pile.

While the Rock Pile did not last, quite quickly the Colonial Tavern picked up the

Fall/Winter 1974,
El Mocambo

blues mantle. Having opened in 1945 as a jazz mecca, in 1969 the owners started mixing in blues with their jazz offerings, bringing in artists such as James Cotton, Muddy Waters, Albert King, and John Lee Hooker for a week at a time in 1969 alone. For the next several years the Colonial became a second home to Muddy, Howlin' Wolf, T-Bone Walker, John Hammond, Hooker, and many others. In 1972, the legendary El Mocambo began to compete with the Colonial, bringing in Otis Rush for a week that November. That fall the club also booked local blues artists such as King Biscuit Boy and the Downchild Blues Band. In January 1973, Hound Dog Taylor made his first Toronto appearance at the El Mo, followed by James Cotton and Freddie King in May, Howlin' Wolf in June, Luther Allison, T-Bone Walker, and Big Walter Horton in July, and Mighty Joe Young, Buddy Guy and Junior Wells, Son Seals, and J.B. Hutto in August. Albert Collins made his Toronto debut under the neon palms in November 1973.

Grossman's Tavern, at Spadina and Cecil Street, didn't book touring bands, but proved to be a very important locale for homegrown blues bands. The club opened as a cafeteria in 1943 and began to book jazz bands when it acquired a liquor licence in 1948. In 1969, Downchild Blues Band got its start as the house band at Grossman's. Led by guitarist Donnie Walsh, Downchild was the first important Canadian blues band and served as the inspiration for Dan Aykroyd and John Belushi's Blues Brothers. The late 1960s and early 1970s were an extraordinary time to be a blues fan in Toronto.

In the late 1970s and for part of the 1980s, the Ontario Place Forum served as a home for some of the biggest blues stars, such as B.B. King, but it was Derek Andrews's work as the booker at Albert's Hall that revived the blues scene in Toronto in a big way. From December 1981 through 1985, Andrews brought in a who's who of contemporary Chicago blues artists, including the only Toronto appearances by Lefty Dizz, Eddie Kirk, Eddy Clearwater, and Queen Sylvia Embry, alongside bigger names such as Otis Rush, Buddy Guy, Junior Wells, Otis Clay, Rockin' Dopsie, and Etta James. Unbelievably, for most of Andrews's time at Albert's Hall, there was

June 1983, Albert's Hall

no cover charge! Over roughly the same years, the Hotel Isabella on Sherbourne Street was bringing in blues artists such as Archie Edwards, Sunnyland Slim, Elizabeth Cotten, and Phil Guy, as well as booking local blues acts such as Chuck Jackson and the Cameo Blues Band.

Perhaps the most legendary Toronto blues gig from the early 1980s was Stevie Ray Vaughan's debut show at the El Mocambo in July 1983, shortly after he'd turned down a chance to tour with David Bowie that summer. The show is often listed as occurring on July 11 due to a fake poster created in the 1990s. The gig actually occurred on Wednesday, July 20, the El Mo ad simply listing that date as featuring a "special guest artist." What is little known is that Vaughan had actually made his Toronto debut four days earlier, opening up for a sparsely attended Steppenwolf show at the CNE Bandshell. In 1991, a DVD of Vaughan's El Mocambo show was released.

The early 1990s were a bit sparse for touring blues acts coming to Toronto, but in 1995 Downchild Blues Band bassist Gary Kendall took over the booking of the Silver Dollar. Located on the west side of Spadina a few doors north of College, the Dollar had originally opened on New Year's Eve 1958 and served as the cocktail lounge of the Waverly Hotel. Over the years, the venue had been used for a variety of purposes, but under Kendall's guidance the Silver Dollar became Toronto's last blues mecca, featuring seminal artists such as Byther Smith, R.L. Burnside, Billy Boy Arnold, and the last Toronto performance by the great Bobby "Blue" Bland.

"My most vivid memory was an incredible solo he played during 'Voodoo Chile,' all while beads of sweat ran down his nose and splattered across his fretboard and pickups. Transfixed on playing, he didn't seem to notice or perhaps care! Will never forget it. Miss him so much."

— Pat Valente
(Stevie Ray Vaughan, Concert Hall, June 1983)

October 13, 1962, Massey Hall

5
COUNTRY

Toronto is commonly thought of as a city of immigrants, and, in fact, the extraordinary amount of immigration that the city has experienced is one of the primary reasons that it has blossomed into one of the great cities of the modern world. While not thought of as immigrants in the typical sense, for decades Toronto experienced a steady influx of migrants from both the east coast specifically and rural and small-town English-speaking Canada in general. By and large, at least until the 1960s, the majority of these migrants were country music fans.

Country music evolved out of the Anglo-Saxon ballad and rural dance music traditions brought to North America from the United Kingdom. With the beginning of radio in the early 1920s, various talented locals from the southern United States could be heard fiddling or singing on 15-minute radio segments, usually early in the morning as farmers were rising to start their workdays. By 1923, country music began to find its way onto 78 rpm records, creating the genre's first national stars in Jimmie Rodgers and the Carter Family by the end of the decade. Rodgers died of tuberculosis in 1933 and the Carter Family didn't tour outside of the south. Consequently, neither act graced Toronto's stages until a revised version of the Carter Family played Massey Hall as part of a Grand Ole Opry package tour in October 1963.

Nonetheless, Torontonians were clearly listening to the music as is evident from newspaper ads promoting new record releases by a wide variety of country artists in both the *Star* and the *Globe* in the 1920s. By December 1933, cowboy songs were being featured on Toronto radio shows. The two most famous country barn dance radio shows — Shreveport's Louisiana Hayride and Nashville's Grand Ole Opry — began showing up in Toronto radio listings in 1937 and 1939 respectively. The first country star to appear in Toronto was Hollywood's singing cowboy Gene Autry, who performed as part of a Wild West Rodeo at CNE Coliseum, held November 14–16, 1940. The other major singing cowboy star of the era, Roy Rogers, appeared with his horse Trigger on what was billed as the "Wildest Show on Earth: Texas Rodeo" at Maple Leaf Gardens for a week in May 1944. Autry came back for another week at the Gardens in May 1946, accompanied by what was advertised as "daring cowboys and cowgirls, outlaw horses and wild steers." Interspersed with Autry singing such chestnuts as "You Are My Sunshine" and "South of the Border" were "crack bronco-busters, calf-ropers and steer wrestlers" and Autry's horse, Champion Jr., who "showed great showmanship in a series of marches, waltzes and shimmies."

Fans of the latest country music genre, honky-tonk, would have been in ecstasy over the appearance of Hank Williams and the Drifting Cowboys on October 27, 1949, at the Mutual Arena. The ads touted Williams as being "Direct from Nashville," playing in what was billed as a "Monster Square Dance/Modern Dance." Earlier that

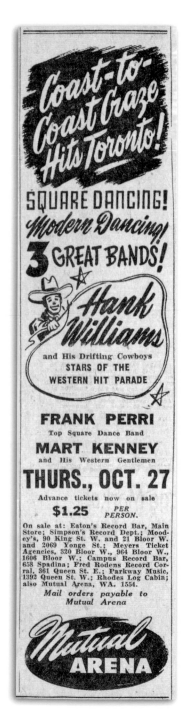

October 27, 1949,
Mutual Arena

month the *Toronto Star* had mentioned that the square dance phenomenon was sweeping the country and that with the Hank Williams show Torontonians would get to finally experience what a square dance was like. The opening acts that night were local musicians Mart Kenney and his Western Gentlemen and Frank Perri and his band. The price of admission was $1.25. Only a single ad ran in both the *Star* and the *Globe*, so the show must have been largely promoted via country radio and/or handbills on telephone and hydro poles. Unfortunately, none of the city's newspapers deigned to review the dance and so we are unlikely to ever know how many fans turned up or what the evening was like when perhaps country's greatest star ever played in Toronto.

Honky-tonk was still popular in the city when Tex Ritter lit up the stage at the Mutual Arena in June 1950. Again, there were no reviews in the city's papers.

Ever since the autumn of 1925, Nashville's Grand Ole Opry had been the symbolic home of country music. Originally a weekly radio show broadcast in front of a live audience, after the Second World War, the

TONITE
2 BIG SHOWS 7-9 p.m.
IN PERSON!
FRED RODEN Presents
HANK SNOW
AMERICA'S GREATEST
CANADA'S OWN
FOLK SINGER
GRAND OLE OPRY
SHOW FROM NASHVILLE
TICKETS NOW
FRED RODEN'S OR
MUTUAL ARENA Box Office
Adults $1.50 Tax Incl.
Children 50c Under 12
Mutual Arena

March 18, 1952,
Mutual Arena

harmonica wizard Wayne Raney, as well as Red Garrett, Stan Cardinal, and the Tennessee Pioneers. Tickets for the show were a mere $1.25.

The Frizzell show was a great success and helped generate a wave of country tours coming through Toronto. On February 21, 1952, Cowboy Copas played Massey Hall, and just under a month later, Canadian-born expat Hank Snow came to town as part of what was billed as the "Grand Ole Opry Show" to play two concerts at the Mutual Arena. That November, banjo player and comedian Grandpa Jones and Ramona hit the city as part of yet another Opry tour, this time playing two shows at Legion Auditorium at 22 College Street. In January 1953, Ray Price "and his Grand Ole Opry Troop" also performed at Legion Auditorium.

With the rock and roll phenomenon still a couple of years away, country music remained very popular in Toronto in the early 1950s. The ever-eclectic Casino Club booked Tex Ritter for a week in February 1953. That same week the Gene Autry Show, including the Hoosier Hot Shots and the Melody Ranch Stars,

Opry expanded its empire by sending out tours that were, in many respects, modelled after the earlier vaudeville bills featuring a variety of artists that included at least one comedian. In 1951 an Opry tour featuring the great honky-tonk singer Lefty Frizzell came to Massey Hall. Also on the bill was performed at Maple Leaf Gardens. While in town, Autry graciously took the time to visit young patients at the Hospital for Sick Children.

By 1955 the El Mocambo was experimenting with booking country acts, regularly featuring the Sons of the Purple Sage for two or three weeks at a time. Twenty years later, the El Mo would be bringing in neo-Western Swing acts such as Asleep at the Wheel. One of the oddest country bookings in the 1950s occurred in April 1956 when the Colonial Tavern briefly departed from its jazz policy, presenting a "Big Western Show" starring Elton Britt, Mime Roman, Texas Jim Robinson, and wacky country guitar wizard Zeb Turner.

Johnny Cash made the first of dozens of appearances in Toronto at the Casino Club August 18–23, 1956. The following April the Casino brought in Hank Snow for a week, and in October 1957 the Casino presented a "Grand Ole Opry Jamboree" featuring Roy Acuff, the Smoky Mountain Boys, June Webb, Pat and His Jug Band, Bashful Brother Oswald, and, as a special added attraction, the Wilburn Brothers. Now, that would have been a happening show.

The Palace Pier picked up on Torontonians' love of country music when an Opry Show featuring Johnny Cash, Roy Acuff, the Wilburn Brothers, and June Webb took the stage in February 1958. Two months later, smooth country crooner Jim Reeves also played the Palace.

The year 1959 was significant for country music fans in Toronto. In July, Conway Twitty played a week at the Colonial Tavern. Even more significantly, the Horseshoe Tavern on Queen Street presented its first American touring star, Sun Records artist Marvin Rainwater.

The next June (1960) Johnny Cash came to town, and for two nights in October Massey Hall hosted the "Rani Ghar Country and Western Music Festival," featuring Stoney Cooper and Wilma Lee, Minnie Pearl, the Clinch Mountain Clan, Ray Price and his Cherokee Cowboys, Grandpa Jones, and Crazy Elmer. Interestingly enough, although the show was at Massey Hall, which has numbered seats and rows, the tickets were general admission. Rani Ghar was short for the Rani Ghar Grotto, which, curiously, is an order of the Masons. Apparently, in Toronto, they were very actively

September 3, 1956, Casino

promoting country shows to raise money for their charitable activities!

Grand Ole Opry shows continued to hit town on a regular basis into the early 1960s. Red Foley and Roy Acuff headlined what was billed as the "Grand Ole Opry Combined with the Ozark Jubilee" show. It took place at Massey Hall November 3 and 4, 1961, with two evening shows and a Saturday matinee. Roy Acuff, as per usual, served as MC, played the violin, ukulele, tambourine, and a yo-yo. For most in attendance the highlight was when Acuff balanced his fiddle on his nose.

November 1, 1958, Massey Hall

In 1962, Patsy Cline made her only Toronto appearance a mere five months before she was killed in a tragic plane crash. The occasion was another Opry show at Massey Hall, featuring, in addition to Cline, Minnie Pearl, Leroy Van Dyke, Hank Locklin, George Hamilton IV, the Louvin Brothers, Stoney Cooper and Wilma Lee, comic Rufe Davis, and the Clinch Mountain Clan. The ensemble played three shows on October 13 at 2:30, 7:00, and 9:15 p.m. A reviewer for the *Globe* described Cline as follows: "Swathed in blue and gold brocade with a blonde wig, she sent her potent voice swooping into all the Moorish crannies of the hall." The latter, of course, was a reference to the Moorish arches that decorated the upper walls of Massey Hall.

In September 1964, a "Country and Western Festival with stars from the Grand Ole Opry" swung into the Hall for another three-shows-in-one-day gig, this time featuring Hank Williams Jr., Bill Anderson, rockabilly chanteuse Wanda Jackson, Bobby Bare, banjo player and comedian Grandpa Jones, and Melba Montgomery. Jackson stole the house with her fifties rockabilly hit

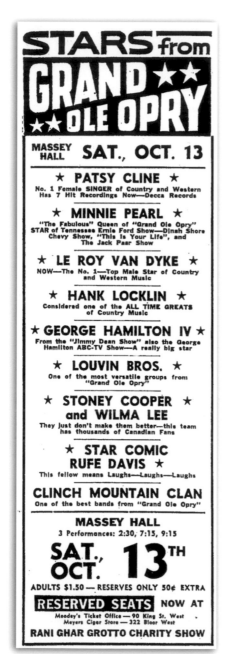

STARS from GRAND OLE OPRY

MASSEY HALL   SAT., OCT. 13

★ **PATSY CLINE** ★
No. 1 Female SINGER of Country and Western
Has 7 Hit Recordings Now—Decca Records

★ **MINNIE PEARL** ★
"The Fabulous" Queen of "Grand Ole Opry"
STAR of Tennessee Ernie Ford Show—Dinah Shore
Chevy Show, "This Is Your Life", and
The Jack Paar Show

★ **LE ROY VAN DYKE** ★
NOW—The No. 1—Top Male Star of Country
and Western Music

★ **HANK LOCKLIN** ★
Considered one of the ALL TIME GREATS
of Country Music

★ **GEORGE HAMILTON IV** ★
From the "Jimmy Dean Show" also the George
Hamilton ABC-TV Show—A really big star

★ **LOUVIN BROS.** ★
One of the most versatile groups from
"Grand Ole Opry"

★ **STONEY COOPER** ★
and WILMA LEE
They just don't make them better—this team
has thousands of Canadian Fans

★ **STAR COMIC**
RUFE DAVIS ★
This fellow means Laughs—Laughs—Laughs

CLINCH MOUNTAIN CLAN
One of the best bands from "Grand Ole Opry"

MASSEY HALL
3 Performances: 2:30, 7:15, 9:15

SAT., OCT. 13TH

ADULTS $1.50 — RESERVES ONLY 50¢ EXTRA

RESERVED SEATS NOW AT
Moodoy's Ticket Office — 90 King St. West
Meyers Cigar Store — 322 Bloor West

RANI GHAR GROTTO CHARITY SHOW

October 13, 1962,
Massey Hall

"Let's Have a Party." Ray Smith played the Embassy Club at Bloor and Bellair in September 1964. Over the next several years the Embassy would bring in a number of country musicians.

In 1962 Ann Dunn converted a bowling alley on Dovercourt just north of College into the city's first after-hours country club. Originally constructed in 1914 as a dance hall for soldiers billeted in Toronto during the First World War, the building was converted back into a dance hall by Dunn, who renamed it the Matador after its Alhambra-like arched ceiling. Open from 12:30 a.m. to 4:30 a.m. on Fridays and Saturdays, the Matador officially served only hot dogs, soft drinks, and coffee and typically featured local country music bands, who most often took the stage around 2:00 a.m. Audiences routinely would pack the classic oak sprung dance floor.

Leonard Cohen was a family friend of Dunn's and came by the club a number of times, eventually writing his 1992 classic "Closing Time" about the Matador and shooting a video for the song at the venerable club. The video for k.d. lang's hit single "Crying" was also shot at the Matador. Over the years, country stars such as Ian Tyson, Loretta Lynn, Dottie West, and Bobby Bare graced the Matador's stage. The legendary back wall was signed over several decades by icons such as Joni Mitchell, Conway Twitty, Leonard Cohen, Charley Pride, Roy Rogers, and Johnny Cash. Other fondly remembered country and western after-hours clubs included the Golden Guitar and Aunt Bea's Nashville Room on Spadina, south of College. The latter was opened in 1965 by Beatrice Martin, who was the hostess at the Horseshoe for 11 years. Located two flights up, the room had a large dance floor, and every weekend night through the early 1970s the club was open from 1:00 a.m. to 5:00 a.m., and was typically packed with around 250 patrons. Perhaps the most exciting night at Aunt Bea's occurred September 13, 1969, when Jerry Lee Lewis dropped by after finishing his set at the Toronto Rock 'n' Roll Revival festival at Varsity Stadium and proceeded to play unannounced for several hours.

Johnny Cash continued to be a regular visitor to the city, playing Massey Hall every year from 1962 through 1965. By 1965, the Canadian National Exhibition (CNE) began presenting country music shows. On August 22 that year the CNE advertised an "All Star Hootenanny" with Johnny Cash, the Statler Brothers, the Common Folk, the York County Boys, and Klaas van Graft and his orchestra under the direction of Ellis McLintock. Earlier that summer, on June 27, a "Country Music Spectacular" took place at the old Maple Leaf Stadium on Lakeshore just west of Bathurst, featuring the first Toronto appearance by Buck Owens in addition to performances by Webb Pierce, Minnie Pearl, Billy Walker, Connie Smith, and MC "Cousin Bill" Bessie. There were shows at both 2:30 and 8:00 p.m.

The Horseshoe Tavern, located on Queen Street just east of Spadina, opened in 1947 and was the second establishment in the province to obtain a liquor licence. The main room was lined with cheap plywood panelling and black-and-white pictures of country stars from the past. The club would book touring artists in for a week at a time and, like the Colonial, there was a Saturday afternoon matinee that underage patrons could attend if they sat on the diner side of the room. I don't know how many young people were hip to country, but at least one, Toronto

It's the Rave of Toronto!

You and your friends are cordially invited to the newly opened Horseshoe Tavern, where the delicious food and distinctive atmosphere is second to none.

Sunday Dinner served from 2 to 8 p.m.

TORONTO'S FINEST EATING PLACE

HORSESHOE TAVERN

368-370 QUEEN STREET WEST at SPADINA

For Reservations, Phone HARRY—WA. 0838

December 10, 1947, Horseshoe

class to the core, the Horseshoe's audience consisted of a lot of Maritimers, as well as tourists from small Ontario towns such as Timmins, Sudbury, and Sault Ste. Marie. From 1963 through the end of 1966, the house band at the Horseshoe was the Blue Valley Boys featuring Johnny Burke, Dick Nolan, Roy Penney, and Bunty Petrie. The majority of the band members were from Newfoundland, and they brought with them the East Coast style of country music to the delight of all the expat Maritimers who made up the majority of the Horseshoe's patrons. In 1967, Al Hooper's Blue Diamond Show Band took over as the house band at the 'Shoe. Hooper, a New Brunswick native, made a deal with Horseshoe owner Jack Starr in which his band would headline one week a month and would also open up for (and often also back up) visiting American and Canadian artists for the other three weeks. While Starr booked many Nashville country stars into the 'Shoe, he also brought in an extraordinary number of small-time Canadian country artists, most of whom are now long forgotten.

One of the more auspicious dates at the Horseshoe was Monday, June 3, 1968, when

musician Alec Fraser, certainly was, and he fondly recalls how much he learned from watching and listening to house guitarist Roy Penney at those matinees.

In the 1960s the Horseshoe became a major force in country music in Toronto, bringing in artists such as Willie Nelson, the Carter Family, Bill Anderson, Carl and Pearl Butler, Tex Ritter, Ernest Tubb, Charley Pride, Ferlin Husky, Conway Twitty, Little Jimmy Dickens, Waylon Jennings, Dottie West, and Stonewall Jackson. Working

Waylon Jennings became the first of the country music outlaws to play Toronto. According to Al Hooper, Jennings's band was arrested at the border when they were caught with a substantial amount of marijuana hidden in their amplifiers. Jennings, though, was allowed into the country. From Monday to Wednesday that week he played the Horseshoe with the Blue Diamond Show Band backing him up. On the Thursday morning he was able to bail out his band, which included a clean-shaven, short-haired Willie Nelson on bass. Nelson and company accompanied Jennings for the last three nights of his stint at the Horseshoe.

There was next to no newspaper coverage of any of these country shows. While the papers were happy to take the ad money for country gigs, they didn't see the music as generally worth reviewing. Most Toronto country fans got their news about shows and their daily fix of country from the early 1960s on through Richmond Hill's 50,000-watt radio station CFGM. Musician Doug Browne remembers that in the 1970s and early 1980s CFGM did a weekly radio show from Minkler Auditorium at Seneca College that was called "CFGM's Opry

June 3–10, 1968, Horseshoe

North." The show featured local and big name Canadian talent as well as the occasional visiting American artist.

In late 1968, Stompin' Tom Connors, wearing his trademark battered black cowboy hat, performed at the Horseshoe for the first time. Connors was, for the most part, unknown at the time. But as a populist who wrote fun, sometimes silly singalong songs about the lives of common people, revolving around hockey, harvesting tobacco, and growing potatoes, while referencing places such as Sudbury, Kirkland Lake, Saskatchewan, and Tillsonburg, he quickly found a loyal audience among the Horseshoe regulars. While he would sing, Connors continually stomped his cowboy boot on the back beat on a half-inch plywood board with his left foot. Typically, wood chips would go flying throughout the show and by the end of the night the board had a hole in it. In 1971 Connors recorded his *Live at the Horseshoe* album that included, of course, "The Horseshoe Hotel Song," and in 1973 he filmed most of *Across This Land with Stompin' Tom Connors* at the 'Shoe. Connors became synonymous with the club, at one point playing a record-setting 25 straight nights there.

On February 4, 1972, Stompin' Tom graduated from the Horseshoe to play Massey Hall. While the hall was not quite sold out, Connors went down a storm. Jack Batten crowed in the *Globe and Mail* that, "Connors showed himself to be … a Canadian nationalist, right up there with Walter Gordon and Jack McClelland." Overtime, Connors's audience broadened to include a massively wide range of young and old, rural and urban Canadians. His recording "The Hockey Song" virtually became a second national anthem.

In addition to establishing his club as a shrine to country music, in the 1960s and early 1970s Horseshoe owner Jack Starr would regularly send dozens of patrons on organized bus tours to Nashville. He knew his audience well and these trips proved to be a very popular money-maker for the club.

The O'Keefe Centre also presented country shows in the 1960s. Opened in 1960 at Yonge and Front Streets, by 1966 the O'Keefe was presenting Johnny Cash and the Eddy Arnold Show with Boots Randolph and Leroy Van Dyke. In 1969, Cash had grown so popular that he headlined Maple Leaf Gardens, his show at that time featuring Sun Records label-mate and the writer of "Blue Suede Shoes," Carl Perkins. Cash would return to the Gardens many times over the next several years.

On March 1, 1969, nascent concert promoter Michael Cohl brought Buck Owens into Maple Leaf Gardens. Unfortunately, Cohl did not sell enough tickets to fill the floor and was unable to pay Owens his guarantee. Gardens owner Harold Ballard agreed to loan Cohl $20,000 to cover Owens's fee, on the condition that Cohl would take on Ballard's son, lawyer Bill Ballard, as his partner. Thus was born Cymba Productions, which eventually morphed into Concert Productions International (CPI). Several years later, Cohl became the most powerful concert promoter in the world, promoting worldwide tours by the Rolling Stones, Pink Floyd, David Bowie, and U2.

On April 9, 1972, Massey Hall presented a show headlined by Lynn Anderson and featuring the holy trinity of the country music outlaw fraternity: Johnny Paycheck and the Cashiers, Waylon Jennings, and Willie Nelson. December 6, 1975, brought Dolly Parton to town for the first time, with two shows at Massey with Johnny Paycheck and Narvel Felts also on the bill. It is odd to think that this show occurred just four days after Bob Dylan's Rolling Thunder

November 2, 1969, Maple Leaf Gardens

Revue had left town. I wonder how many people went to both the Parton and Dylan shows? I would guess very few.

SEE STARS AT THE O'KEEFE

SEE STARS AT THE O'KEEFE

The MAC DAVIS Show
Special guest star **DOLLY PARTON**
'Reigning queen of country music'
Time Magazine
June 27 - July 2
Mon. - Thurs. 8:30 p.m.
Fri. & Sat. 6:30 and 9:30 p.m.
Tickets $5 - $12.50
O'KEEFE CENTRE
Front and Yonge Sts., Toronto, Ontario M5E 1B2 (416)363-6633

June 27–July 2, 1977,
O'Keefe Centre

By 1976, the Horseshoe stopped booking country shows on a regular basis, with one major exception. Starting December 5, 1977, for two weeks, a Horseshoe regular over the past few years, Ottawa native Sneezy Waters, brought his stage show into the declining bar. Written by National Film Board director Maynard Collins, *Hank*

Williams: The Show He Never Gave was originally conceived for film before Collins, with the help of University of Ottawa theatre professor Peter Froehlich, adapted it as a play. Originally staged in Ottawa, Waters proved to be brilliant playing the role of Hank Williams and the show was consequently booked into the Horseshoe.

Hank Williams died in the back of a limousine filled with pills and booze on his way to a New Year's Eve gig in Canton, Ohio, on December 31, 1952. The premise of the play is that, while he was lying in the back of the car going in and out of consciousness, Hank was thinking of the show he was going to give to ring in the New Year. For the staging of the play, all signs of life past 1953, such as the bar's televisions, were removed. Suitably tacky New Year's Eve decorations were strewn everywhere and the band members had their hair done and were dressed in the same garb favoured by Hank Williams and the Drifting Cowboys.

During the two sets, Waters would sing about 20 of Williams's classic songs, but unlike the real Hank Williams, he delivered several monologues between songs, excoriating his first wife, talking about teenage alcoholism, about growing up in Alabama, lamenting that the New York Giants had once again beaten the Brooklyn Dodgers (appropriately before singing "You Win Again"), his battles with the Grand Ole Opry, flashbacks to playing revival tents, his problems with drinking and drugs, and spirituality and death. Waters, à la Williams, performed as if he was drunk the whole night and, per instructions from director Froehlich, did not engage with the patrons. Amazingly enough, the audience participated every night anyway, some heckling Williams as they might have in real life, others requesting songs, all of which Waters/Williams ignored as if he was the real Hank Williams. The second act was a "harrowing portrayal of Williams's utter disintegration," leaving many audience members with tears in their eyes.

In 1978, Waters relayed to *Globe and Mail* reporter Dane Lanken, "We've gone to pains to create the illusion that it's Hank on stage, but it's more of an interpretation than an impersonation. That's at least partly because Hank didn't say anything about himself, he didn't talk. We've got to interpret what we know of the character from his songs mostly.

Hank was in very bad shape toward the end, drinking steadily and taking pills and not eating, but we've tried to give him dignity. He was a drunkard but a gifted drunkard and people loved him, really loved him."

The show was brilliant, got great reviews, and came back to play the Horseshoe for the two weeks in December 1978 that followed the Garys' final weekend of punk and alternative shows, The Last Pogo and The Last Bound Up. *Hank Williams: The Show He Never Gave* would be reprised for a 10-day run beginning November 11, 1982, at the Bathurst Street Theatre and then again in April of 1992. The latter performance contained more anger, as Waters had met country star Minnie Pearl several years after his Horseshoe shows. Pearl told Waters that the last time she saw Hank Williams, "He was about as dignified as a wounded animal. He was under a table crying and they were trying to get him onstage." Waters was outraged at the state Williams had been reduced to and felt that this anger came out in the way he portrayed Williams's character onstage.

In the 1980s, with no other club picking up the slack, country shows were generally limited to big stars playing large venues such as Massey Hall, Maple Leaf Gardens, the CNE Grandstand, as well as the occasional all-day country music affair such as "Summer Country '87," staged at Molson Park in Barrie and featuring Hank Williams Jr., Gary Morris, Dwight Yoakam, the Good Brothers, and Highway 101. With country music going ever more mainstream, Garth Brooks took over the CNE Stadium on September 3, 1992.

An exception was late October 1984, when Albert's Hall brought to town for the first time the pride of Consort, Alberta, Kathy Dawn Lang, better known under her stage moniker, k.d. lang. Partway through the week, on November 1, the *Globe and Mail's* Liam Lacey declared, "There is probably no better performer in Canadian music right now than k.d. lang, the Alberta punk queen." Just a few weeks prior to the gig, most Torontonians had never heard of her, but by week's end, dozens of people were being turned away. Declaring a psychic connection to Patsy Cline (her band was cheekily called the Reclines), lang paradoxically sported a punk haircut, "old-fashioned metal-frame glasses [without actual glass in them!], and cut-off cowboy boots with work socks rolled down around her ankles." Running around the stage, in and out of washrooms, lang described her style to *Maclean's* as a "hootenanny wingding Daddy-O of a good time." While lang's ersatz look and performance style certainly brought her attention, it was her heart-tearing voice that ultimately turned heads at Albert's Hall and that quickly turned her into a country superstar. By 1987 she would be headlining Kingswood Music Theatre at Canada's Wonderland.

Nearly as exciting as k.d. lang's first appearance in Toronto was Gary Topp's decision, seven years after his last punk show featuring a performance by X at Lee's Palace, to bring the Dixie Chicks to Massey Hall on April 22, 1999, to promote their *Wide Open Spaces* album. This was the first theatre tour by one of the most exciting new groups in all of popular music. Topp had seen them on TV, was struck by how outside the mainstream they were, and went after them with a vengeance. The show was a slow seller, but by the day of the concert Topp had managed to sell it out. Unbelievably, the show was not reviewed in either of the city's main newspapers.

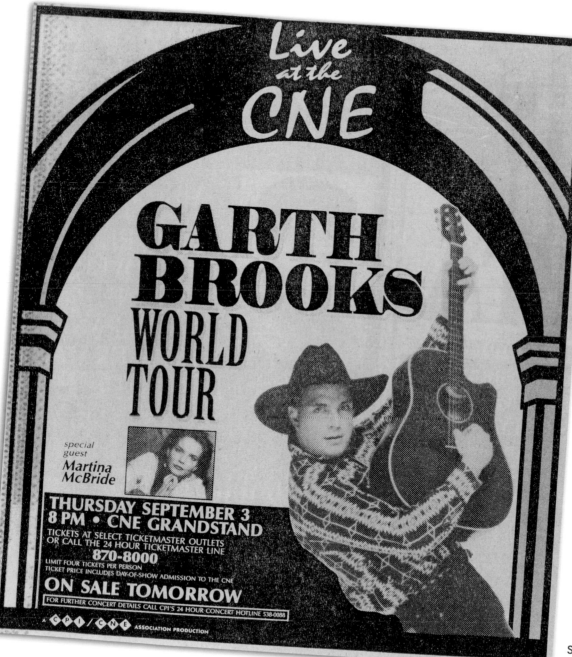

September 3, 1992,
CNE Grandstand

February 6, 1965,
Massey Hall

6 FOLK

When most people think of folk music and Toronto, they tend to focus on the hothouse of activity that was Yorkville in the 1960s, when more than a dozen coffee houses and clubs were nurturing local talent while booking a who's who of touring American folk and blues artists. While that was indeed a halcyon period in this city's glorious music history, professional folksingers actually began coming to Toronto nearly two decades earlier.

The first performance by a touring folksinger was Richard Dyer-Bennet's October 25, 1945, appearance at the Eaton Auditorium (now the Carlu). Dyer-Bennet was a contemporary of Woody Guthrie, Lead Belly, Burl Ives, Pete Seeger, and Josh White and started out performing at the

Village Vanguard and other New York City nightclubs in the early 1940s. After playing concerts at Town Hall and Carnegie Hall in New York in 1944, impresario Sol Hurok signed him up for a series of national and international tours. That is undoubtedly how he made his way to Toronto in the autumn of 1945, billed as "The Twentieth Century Minstrel in a program of Ballads and Folk Songs." He came back to the Eaton Auditorium in October 1949 along with dance satirist Iva Kitchell.

The Eaton Auditorium was the site of numerous classical, jazz, and folk concerts throughout the 1940s and '50s. In the 1940s Josh White, who had first recorded back in 1927, reinvented himself and his repertoire for the white folk revival, often performing with Pete Seeger in the Almanac Singers. He first came to Toronto as a solo artist on October 17, 1946, playing the Eaton Auditorium. His performance was advertised as being by a "Minstrel of Work Songs, Blues and Ballads." Actress and singer Josephine Premice, performing Haitian songs and dances, shared the bill.

Burl Ives was 41 when he came to Toronto to perform for a week at the Casino Club in October 1950. Ives had started his career as an itinerant folksinger in the 1930s before finding work in both Hollywood features and on Broadway. In the early 1940s, as was the case with Josh White, Ives had performed at times as part of the Almanac Singers, and in 1947 he scored his first radio hit with an old minstrel song titled "Blue Tail Fly."

On June 13, 1953, the man who had almost single-handedly kick-started the folk revival, Pete Seeger, played what was billed as "The Third Annual Peace Picnic" at Exhibition Park. On January 29, 1954, he came back to play a Folk Song Festival at an unnamed auditorium at 85 Christie Street. Seeger returned a few months later, on September 15, to play two shows at the First Unitarian Church. The afternoon show was geared toward children; the evening show included folk songs for all ages.

Seeger had been a member of the band the Weavers, who enjoyed big hits in the early 1950s with their version of Lead Belly's "Goodnight, Irene" and the South African song "Wimoweh." After members of the group were listed in *Red Channels* as having communist affiliations, Decca

August 1949, Casino

Records deleted their entire catalogue in 1953. Unable to get concert bookings, the group broke up. Reuniting in December 1955 to play Carnegie Hall, the Weavers decided they wished to carry on, but were still having problems getting booked in the United States.

Vanguard Records released the Carnegie Hall concert as an LP in April 1957. On the first day of that month the Weavers embarked on their comeback tour, with Massey Hall being the first stop. Reflecting the group's penchant for singalongs, the notice in the *Globe and Mail* that day read, "Part of the concert may involve audience participation. Seeger is said to have magical powers in persuading the stub-holders to sing out freely in their cracked tenors and scratchy sopranos."

The Weavers show was promoted by a fascinating woman named Vivian Stenson. Born in 1926 in Wales, Stenson had immigrated to Canada and was at the time working at the CBC. "It starts with Edith Fowke," Stenson recalled in 2016. "She taught at York University and she had a program on the CBC about folk songs. I was helping her with translations from Hebrew when she said to me the Weavers were coming [back] together, and even though they were persona non grata in the States, they could work here. But nobody would book them. So I said 'I will.' I had never done that before. I was rising to the occasion. So I hired Massey Hall, I got people around me to work on posters and what have you, and brought in the Weavers. That was my beginning. I walked around Massey Hall thinking, 'I own this place tonight.'"

In October and again in November, Stenson brought African American songstress Odetta to Eaton Auditorium for her first Toronto appearances. Over the next few years, until she moved to New York City in 1961, Stenson brought a host of folksingers to Toronto, presenting John Jacob Niles giving an outdoor performance at Casa Loma and Tom Lehrer, Julian Bream, Larry Adler, Theodore Bikel, Richard Dyer-Bennet, Laurindo Almeida, Salli Terri, and Josh White at the Eaton Auditorium. She also booked Guy Carawan, of the Highlander Folk School, into the Museum Theatre at the Royal Ontario Museum. Stenson brought the Weavers back to Massey Hall in March 1959 and again in May 1960, and in

October 1959 she promoted the Kingston Trio's first Toronto show at the same venue. Stenson was a pioneering woman in what was generally a man's world of concert promotion.

After Stenson left Toronto, various promoters, including Marty Bockner, continued to bring in folk artists to Massey Hall. In 1961 Theodore Bikel played there in May while the Kingston Trio filled the hall in November. In March 1962, the Weavers made one final appearance at Massey followed on November 9 by Joan Baez's first performance at the storied hall. Beginning in November 1962, Peter, Paul and Mary would be regulars at the hall. Interestingly, their first appearance in the city occurred four months earlier when they played for a week in early August at the O'Keefe Centre as a featured act in comedian Jack Carter's revue.

The commercial end of the folk music spectrum was so successful that in the fall of 1963 Massey Hall announced a series of folk concerts to run from September 26, when the New Christy Minstrels were scheduled to play, through to a performance by the Chad Mitchell Trio on March 1, 1964. In between, the Clancy Brothers with Tommy Makem, the Brothers Four, and the Rooftop Singers each headlined shows at the hall. On April 18, 1964, Oscar Brand, Jean Carignan, the Couriers, the Fernwood Trio, Al Cromwell, Malka and Joso, and Gordon Lightfoot all played Massey Hall. This would mark the first appearance for Lightfoot at Massey. Three years later, in May 1967, he would begin his storied yearly multiple-night run of shows at the hall, eventually playing Massey more than 175 times over the course of his career.

In 1961, Orillia native Ruth Jones founded the Mariposa Folk Festival. Although not a strictly Toronto-based event, the festival has significant ties to the city. For the first three years the festival was held in Orillia, but in 1964 it moved to Toronto, where it was staged at Maple Leaf Stadium. That year Buffy Sainte-Marie and Gordon Lightfoot were among the featured performers. From 1965 through 1968 the festival was held at Innis Lake, but returned to Toronto in 1969, where it found a home on the Toronto Islands. It stayed on the Islands through 1979. During its tenure in Toronto, the festival featured performers such as Joan Baez, Joni

Mitchell, James Taylor, John Prine, Steve Goodman, Bonnie Raitt, Bukka White, Bruce Cockburn, Murray McLauchlan, the McGarrigle Sisters, and the debut performance of Sweet Honey in the Rock.

A year before the first Mariposa festival, Yorkville Avenue, a small street just north of Bloor, became the epicentre of Toronto's coffee house scene. With the drinking age at the time being 21, coffee houses that sold espresso and desserts, and provided chess boards and music became very popular with those unable to get in to the local bars. The roots of the Yorkville coffee house scene go back to 1955.

The first coffee house that featured folk music in Toronto was the Concerto Café, located at 89 Bloor Street West, at Bellair. The venue was opened by two gay men, former British intelligence officer Claude Dewhurst and Hungarian-born Irving Bolgar. By June 1955, Greg Curtis was singing folk songs at the Concerto. The coffee house was successful enough that in September, Dewhurst and Bolgar decided to open a second venue, The Concertino Café at 32 Avenue Road, a few doors down from Yorkville Avenue. In 1956, Denys

Sterio and her husband purchased the Concertino, renamed it La Coterie, and featured folk music in the early part of the evening and jazz after midnight. For all intents and purposes, these were the first folk clubs in Yorkville. Greg Curtis was often described in newspapers at the time as Toronto's first professional folk singer. As late as 1963 he could be found playing at the Gate of Cleve in the heart of Yorkville.

Two other early Yorkville coffee houses were Werner Graeber's 71 Club, and John McHugh's Half Beat. McHugh would open a second club, the Penny Farthing, in 1963 at 112 Yorkville, booking such future and present folk icons as Joni Mitchell (born Joan Anderson, it was at the Farthing that she met her husband-to-be Chuck Mitchell), Lonnie Johnson, José Feliciano, John Lee Hooker, Josh White, Bonnie Dobson, and Ramblin' Jack Elliott.

Interestingly, in 1967 the club hosted a session in which two British expats, John Norris and Dick Flohil, gave a talk on what the ads referred to as "Negro music." Given how many blues and jazz musicians had regularly played Toronto over the years, it seems odd and a particularly late 1950s/

RIVERBOAT

COFFEE HOUSE

134 YORKVILLE AVE. 922-6216

EVERY NIGHT
(EXCEPT MONDAY)
8 p.m. – 3 a.m.

TUES., MAY 25th, to SUN., JUNE 6th
ANITA SHEER
"SHINDIG STAR"

TUES., JUNE 8th, to SUN., JUNE 20th
GORDON LIGHTFOOT
"I'm not saying..."   "For loving me..."
WARNER BROS. RECORDING STAR

May–June, 1965,
Riverboat

early 1960s British thing to do to have two collectors/enthusiasts explain the history of the music at a club.

The Purple Onion was located at 35 Avenue Road, right at the corner of Yorkville. Started by four Ryerson students in their early twenties, the Onion has gone down in local lore as the site where Buffy Sainte-Marie wrote "Universal Soldier." It was also the place where Carly Simon first played Toronto with her sister Lucy as part of the Simon Sisters. The club regularly booked acts such as the Travellers, Malka and Joso, Joni Mitchell, Shawn Phillips, Carolyn Hester, Leon Bibb, Gordon Lightfoot, and the duo Sonny Terry and Brownie McGhee.

The Village Corner, owned by John Morley and Roy Davies, located at 174 Avenue Road, was the launching pad for Ian and Sylvia in 1961. Jean Redpath,

Joni Mitchell, Gordon Lightfoot, and Len Chandler also played the club in the early 1960s. The Village Corner's moniker was the rather cool "Folk singing for the discriminating folknik."

Far and away the most important folk music club in Yorkville, however, was the Riverboat. Bernie Fiedler and his wife Pat had run the Mousehole before opening the slightly larger Riverboat in October 1964 at 134 Yorkville Avenue. The club was situated downstairs and sat about 120 patrons, with the majority of the seats running down the hallway away from the stage. Brass portholes lined the walls, somehow tying into the theme of being on a Riverboat. As was the case with most of the Yorkville clubs, the Riverboat generally brought artists in for a week, and mixed blues stalwarts such as Howlin' Wolf, Buddy Guy and Junior Wells, and Sonny Terry and Brownie McGhee with a who's who of white folksingers such as Simon and Garfunkel, Arlo Guthrie, Tim Buckley, Phil Ochs (who wrote "Changes" while playing at the club), Gordon Lightfoot (who in his own words felt he had finally "arrived" when he played the Riverboat for a week in March 1965), Tim Hardin, Kris Kristofferson, Tom Rush, Janis Ian, Joni Mitchell, and Neil Young (who eventually released a live album from his week-long run in 1969 and referenced the club in his song "Ambulance Blues"). In the 1970s, the Riverboat continued apace, booking Bruce Cockburn, Murray McLauchlan, Dan Hill, John Prine, Steve Goodman, Judee Sill, Bonnie Koloc, and, for one very strange week, the Incredible String Band. The Riverboat show that I really wish I'd seen is the Staple Singers, who arrived for a week of performances in October 1967. The heady days of the Riverboat finally came to a close in June of 1978 after coffee houses become passé with the lowering of the Ontario drinking age to 18.

The most anticipated folk concerts in the 1960s in Toronto were without a doubt Bob Dylan's appearances at Massey Hall on November 13, 1964, and November 14 and 15, 1965. The concert in '64 was all acoustic. The 1965 shows featured Dylan playing acoustically for the first half and then electric in the second, backed by Toronto's legendary group the Hawks (later the Band).

Dylan's first electric gig had been at the Newport Folk Festival that summer and proved to be extremely controversial, with reports suggesting that many in the audience had loudly booed the iconic singer because they felt that playing an electric guitar was somehow heresy in the hallowed world of folk music. On the succeeding tour, Dylan and the Hawks were routinely booed by

January–February 1969, Riverboat

October 29, 1998,
Maple Leaf Gardens

booing, but according to a number of people I have spoken to over the years, while there were a few scattered boos, the majority of the sold-out crowds both nights were in ecstasy as they witnessed Dylan and the Hawks literally redefining the very possibilities of what it could mean to play popular music.

Dylan would come back to Toronto dozens of times over the years, playing mind-numbing, legendary shows with the Rolling Thunder Revue at Maple Leaf Gardens on December 1 and 2, 1975, and similarly stunning shows on his gospel tour at Massey Hall April 17–20, 1980. Much of the latter run was released on DVD in 2017 on Dylan's *Trouble No More* box set.

One of Toronto's (and now Los Angeles's) major concert promoters, Elliott Lefko, recalls a particularly important folk concert in his musical life that occurred May 27, 1973: "My memorable concert was at Massey Hall. It featured Jose Feliciano with opening act Ray Materick. I was 16. I really loved Feliciano's music and was looking forward to his singing and playing. He was great, and it was one of my first times at Massey, and that was always magic. But the big highlight was the local opener. Ray Materick came on

segments of the audience in both North America and Europe. Hawks guitarist Robbie Robertson has always claimed that Toronto was among the worst audiences in terms of

"I was 16 ... the big highlight was the local opener. Ray Materick came on stage and just blew everyone away. It's rare to see an unknown performer deliver such a strong set that made everyone there become fans instantly. He was very folky with an acoustic guitar and a raw voice and dressed all in faded denim. He had these beautiful songs that just made you smile and realize you were viewing a real star."

— Elliott Lefko,
vice-president, Goldenvoice, Toronto promoter extraordinaire
(José Feliciano with Ray Materick, Massey Hall, May 27, 1973)

stage and just blew everyone away. It's rare to see an unknown performer deliver such a strong set that made everyone there become fans instantly. He was very folky with an acoustic guitar and a raw voice and dressed all in faded denim. He had these beautiful songs that just made you smile and realize you were viewing a real star. Watching him set something off within me and I knew I wanted to be involved in a music career and that he would become famous.

"Immediately I contacted him and had him play at my high school. And within a year he had signed a record deal with Asylum Records and had a hit on the radio. Fast forward to 2010 and I was promoting a show with A-ha at Massey Hall and they needed a solo acoustic act to open. I contacted Ray, and many years later he returned to Massey to once again open a show ... and this time I was the promoter. A dream realized."

There were a few attempts at opening new coffee houses in the 1970s. The Fiddler's Green Coffee House on Eglinton Avenue opened in May 1970 and remained there

YORK UNIVERSITY THEATRE
KEELE South of STEELES

PERFORMING ARTS FESTIVAL

Feb. 16—Thursday, ART IN CANADA PANEL
Dalto Camp, Greg Curnoe, Dorothy Cameron, Theodore Heinrich.

Feb. 17—Friday, LEONARD COHEN SINGS
and the City Muffin Boys.

Feb. 18—Saturday Matinee. AN AFTERNOON OF TOTAL ENVIRONMENT
Z. Blazeje's paintings, Brian Browne Trio, Poets — Michael Collie, Keith Harrison,
Joe Rosenblath.

Feb. 18—Saturday Night, "THE ORIGINAL YORK REVIEW"

Feb. 19—Sunday Matinee, CANADIAN UNDERGROUND FILMS.

Complete series ticket;   Public $10.00   York Students $2.50
Call 635-2370

February 17, 1967, York University Theatre

until the old house it was in, which was owned by the YMCA, was scheduled to be demolished at the end of 1978. On the first Friday of 1979, Fiddler's Green opened at its new home at the Tranzac Club at 292 Brunswick Avenue, where it continued to present shows until June 1987. In addition to local musicians such as Bruce Cockburn, the club brought in touring artists such as the Georgia Sea Island Singers, Lester Flatt and Earl Scruggs's first reunion, Ramblin' Jack Elliott, the New Lost City Ramblers, Tom Paxton, Peggy Seeger, Martin Carthy, the Battlefield Band, and the High Level Ranters.

In January 1974, Ken Whiteley and Don Sedgewick opened Shier's Coffee House in the Peanut Plaza in Don Mills. For the next three years, the club booked local singers as well as the occasional touring artist such as Blind John Davis and Rosalie Sorrels before closing its doors in 1977.

By and large, the folk genre eventually became limited to festivals, although many former folksingers became successful as part of the singer-songwriter genre. A number of new singer-songwriters also began to emerge in the late 1960s and 1970s. An early example is Leonard Cohen, who played an extraordinary first performance in Toronto when he sang (rather than just read poetry) at York University Theatre on February 17, 1967, as part of a three-day arts festival. This was a full 10 months before the release of his first album! On May 22 of that year he would also play a few songs alongside Buffy Sainte-Marie at the Queen's Park Love-In.

Perhaps the most famous singer-songwriter concert in Toronto history was Neil Young's legendary performance at Massey Hall for two shows on January 19, 1971 (eventually released as a live CD). A close second would be Joni Mitchell's last tour without a band when she was supporting her *Blue* album and played Massey Hall (February 25, 1972) with Jackson Browne opening up. Since then, Toronto has hosted every singer-songwriter imaginable, from Randy Newman at Grumbles and Massey Hall in the 1970s, Joan Armatrading at Convocation Hall in the late 1970s, Tracy Chapman at the Diamond in 1988, Leonard Cohen at Massey Hall in the 1970s and '80s and the O'Keefe Centre in 1993 to Jeff Buckley at C'est What and Albert's Hall in 1994 and the Music Hall in 1995.

April 2, 1957,
Maple Leaf Gardens

7 '50s ROCK 'n' ROLL

In many respects, one might consider jump blues singer Wynonie Harris's Monday, January 10, 1949, appearance at the Eaton Auditorium as the first rock and roll show in Toronto. Although the performance was advertised as a jazz concert and Harris was co-billed with jazz tenor saxophonist Lester "Prez" Young, Harris rocked as hard as anyone. In fact, the ads for the show billed the ebullient singer as "The Good Rockin' Man" in a reference to his 1948 smash cover of Roy Brown's "Good Rockin' Tonight." Elvis Presley would cover the song six years later for his second Sun Records release. Tickets for the show were set at the interesting price points of $1.20, $1.80, and $2.40. Unfortunately, none of the Toronto papers saw fit to review the show.

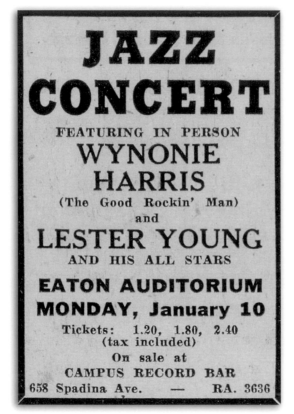

**January 10, 1949,
Eaton Auditorium**

The second rocking show in my mind would be the week honking tenor sax great Big Jay McNeely took over the Colonial Tavern in March 1953. McNeely would honk, shriek, and over-blow to the point where his sound broke up, then walk through the audience and often out the front door, creating pandemonium, trance, and ecstasy wherever he performed. That

week at the Colonial would have been absolutely insane!

A former member of the Four Aces of Western Swing, Bill Haley had begun experimenting with recording rock-oriented material as early as 1953. By the summer of 1954, he was hitting the pop charts with a sanitized cover of Big Joe Turner's "Shake, Rattle and Roll," which he quickly followed with "Dim, Dim the Lights (I Want Some Atmosphere)," "Birth of the Boogie," and "Mambo Rock." Haley's career hit the stratosphere with "(We're Gonna) Rock Around the Clock." The record had originally been released in May 1954 to moderate sales. But when the song was included in the soundtrack to the 1955 teen flick *Blackboard Jungle*, it was re-released as a single in May 1955 and promptly stormed its way to the top of the pop charts where it stayed for a full two months. Interestingly enough, Haley and His Comets' first two Toronto performances were at small venues. From Wednesday, June 1 to Saturday, June 4, 1955, they played the Colonial Tavern. (They were supposed to begin the run on Monday, May 30, but when they got an offer to perform on Milton Berle's television

June 1–4, 1955, Colonial

show, the Colonial allowed them to delay their Toronto run.) On July 25, 1955, they played a dance concert at the Palais Royale. Two months later they returned to play another week at the Colonial Tavern (September 26–August 1).

A week before Haley's appearance at the Colonial, the club brought in what was billed as a "Rock 'n' Roll Show" featuring the Three Chuckles and the Stomp Gordon Quartet. The Three Chuckles were led by Teddy Randazzo on accordion and had enjoyed a Top 20 pop hit with "Runaround" at the end of 1954. Randazzo would go on to write such hits as "Goin' Out of My Head" and "Hurt So Bad" in the 1960s.

While these early rock and roll shows are fascinating, it was in 1956 that the music took the world, including Toronto, by storm. In February 1956, the Colonial booked local band the Crew Cuts for a week backed by the Moe Koffman Sextet. The Crew Cuts were riding high with their monstrous 1954 cover of the Chords' "Sh-Boom," as well as their 1955 covers of the Penguins' "Earth Angel," Gene and Eunice's "Ko Ko Mo (I Love You So)," the Dandeliers' "Chop Chop Boom," the Nutmegs' "A Story Untold," and Otis Williams' "Gum Drop." In March, the Colonial brought the Platters (of "Only You" and "The Great Pretender" fame) to town.

Up to this point, aside from Wynonie Harris, the rock and roll acts appearing in Toronto were decidedly on the lighter side. That would change big time when a package tour featuring Little Richard, Fats Domino, Ruth Brown, the Clovers, the Cadillacs, the Turbans, Little Willie John, and Choker Campbell and His Big Band hit the Mutual Arena on April 10. Admission was a whopping two dollars! With a lineup like that, I am quite confident that any Toronto teenager who attended the show was never the same! The evening was advertised as "The Dance of the Year! Rhythm and Blues of 1956," reflecting the fact that, at the time, the terms *Rhythm and Blues* and *Rock and Roll* were somewhat interchangeable.

The day after the show, the *Toronto Star* ran an article with the rather curious headline "Jazz Review," further indicating total confusion in the mainstream media as to just what this new music was. The subheading of the article declared "1,500 Teen-Agers Squeal Mesmerized by Rhythm." The reviewer, Stan Rantin, was clearly none too impressed with the show, writing, "Walls, floor and rafters of Mutual St. arena quivered in terror last night as the Rhythm 'n' Blues Show of 1956 exploded upon Toronto.... On the whole, little of the show could be considered musical — but the crowd liked it."

The reviewer for the *Globe*, Alex Barris, was even more ignorant, proudly concluding his review by stating, "I left before Fats Domino came on, so I can't really say how he was but I am confident that I saw and heard enough to strengthen my suspicion that Rhythm 'N Blues is simply Stuff 'N Nonsense which will never replace music."

Despite how bad the writing about entertainment was in the local newspapers, the rock and roll onslaught continued when Big Joe Turner played the Palace Pier on

April 10, 1956, Mutual Arena

September 29, 1956, Maple Leaf Gardens

August 23. But the big news was the three massive package shows to take place at Maple Leaf Gardens in April, July, and September 1956. The April 30 show drew 13,000 fans and featured Bill Haley, the Flamingos, the Colts, Joe Turner, the Platters, the Drifters, LaVern Baker, Clyde McPhatter, Frankie Lymon, the Teen Queens, and Bo Diddley, all backed by Red Prysock and His Big Rock and Roll Orchestra.

The July 16 show drew about the same number of fans and was advertised as "The Top Record Stars of 1956." This concert featured Chuck Berry, Little Richard, Frankie Lymon, Carol Carr, Carl Perkins, Bobby Charles, Shirley and Lee, Al Hibbler, Della Reese, the Cleftones, and the Spaniels, this time backed by Illinois Jacquet and His Orchestra. Buffalo disc jockey George "Hound Dog" Lorenz served as the MC.

The September 29 concert was billed as "The Biggest Show of 56" and featured many of the same artists from the two earlier shows, including Bill Haley, the Platters, Frankie Lymon and the Teenagers, Clyde McPhatter, the Clovers, Ella Johnson, Chuck Berry, Shirley and Lee, Shirley Gunther, and the

Flairs, backed by Buddy Johnson with His Big Orchestra. Once again, "Hound Dog" Lorenz served as MC.

The *Star* headlined their review of the April 30 show with the hysterical line, "13,000 Almost Berzerk in Gardens Rock 'n' Roll Orgy." The review itself was straight-out racist: "Like natives at a voodoo ritual, the crowd writhed and reeled until their pent-up emotions burst the dam of reason and they clambered onto the stage and into the aisles to dance." *Toronto Star* writer Stan Rantin suggested the concert "resembled a wild west show, a jungle extravaganza and a revival meeting all rolled into one." Backstage, Bill Haley surprisingly told Rantin that this was the biggest crowd he had ever played for!

The *Star* had their regular entertainment columnist cover the July concert. In addition, the paper hired the curate of St. Timothy's Anglican Church, Rev. David McGuire, to pen a column about the show. McGuire found that "the music itself is not particularly musical in any sense of the word, except with regard to the rhythm. This aspect was exploited to the full — at the expense of everything else. To anyone

MAPLE LEAF GARDENS

SUPER ATTRACTIONS presents
The BIGGEST *Show of Stars* of '57   ALL IN PERSON

Fats
DOMINO
AND HIS
Orchestra

La Vern
BAKER

Frankie
LYMON

THAT'LL BE
THE DAY

Chuck
BERRY

Clyde
McPHATTER

THE
CRICKETS

The Spaniels   *The Drifters*

ALL IN PERSON

"DIANA"   "Mr. LEE"
PAUL ANKA   JOHNNIE & JOE + THE BOBBETTES
"OVER THE MOUNTAIN"

HAROLD CROMER M.C.   ★   Crying TOMMY BROWN

PAUL WILLIAMS AND HIS BIG ORCHESTRA

"ROCK & ROLL SHOW"
SATURDAY, SEPT. 14 — 8.00 p.m.
TICKETS NOW ON SALE
Prices: $1.00 - $1.75 - $2.50 - $3.00
Box Office Open Daily 10 a.m. to 9 p.m.

Tickets also available:
IN TORONTO—at Royal York and King Edward Hotels and
Moodey's ● IN HAMILTON—at Connaught Hotel and Maple
Leaf Ticket Agency ● IN OAKVILLE—at John Black Agency.

not particularly interested in jumping up and down, it became rather nerve-wracking." Hopefully, Rev. McGuire's nerves eventually settled down!

Rock and roll returned to Maple Leaf Gardens in February 1957 when Fats Domino, Bill Doggett, Clyde McPhatter, LaVern Baker, Chuck Berry, the Five Keys, the Moonglows, the Five Satins, Ann Cole, Eddie Cooley and the Dimples, Charles Brown, and the Schoolboys were backed by Paul Williams (of "Hucklebuck" fame) and His Orchestra. The audience topped out at about 11,000, sparking the *Star* to conclude that rock 'n' roll was dying!

On April 1, 1957, Steve Gibson's Red Caps came to the Colonial Tavern with Damita Jo, but the big show of the year was Elvis Presley's one and only appearance in Toronto on April 2. Presley played two shows that day, at 6:00 and 9:00 p.m. Surprisingly, only about 25,000 fans turned out for the two shows combined. Even more surprising was the fact that the *Globe* didn't review the concert. The *Star*'s reviewer complained that she couldn't hear a single thing Elvis said or sang during his one-hour show. Consequently, most of the commentary in

September 14, 1957, Maple Leaf Gardens

her review focused on what she termed the hysterical behaviour of Presley's adolescent female fans.

A few weeks later, Pat Boone led a rather sanitized set of pop entertainers into the Gardens on May 25, while "The Biggest Show of Stars of '57" brought the real thing back to the Gardens on September 14 in a show featuring Fats Domino, LaVern Baker, Frankie Lymon, Chuck Berry, Clyde McPhatter, the Crickets featuring Buddy Holly, the Everly Brothers, Eddie Cochran, Buddy Knox, the Drifters, Jimmy Bowen, Paul Anka, the Spaniels, and Johnnie and Joe, once again backed by the Paul Williams Orchestra. The MC this time was pioneering vaudeville dancer and comedian Harold Cromer.

Three weeks later, on October 5, 1957, the Everly Brothers returned for what was billed as a "Rockabilly Dance Spectacle" at the Palace Pier. On April 10, 1958, Carl Perkins headlined a show at the same venue supported by fellow rockabilly singers Sonny James, Buddy Knox, and Jimmy Bowen. But the two big shows of 1958 were once again held at Maple Leaf Gardens. On January 20, the Everly Brothers, the Rays, Jimmie Rodgers, Buddy Holly, Margie Rayburn, Paul Anka, the Shepherd Sisters, Danny and the Juniors, the Tune Weavers, the Hollywood Flames, Eddie Cochran, the Mello-Kings, Billy Brown, Jimmy Edwards, and Al Jones, backed by Sam Donahue and His Orchestra, shook it up for 7,000 fans. By this stage, rock and roll had become so much a part of the mainstream that neither the *Star* nor the *Globe* could be bothered to review the show.

Neither paper chose to review the April 21 show either, one that featured an extraordinary lineup, including Sam Cooke, Jimmie Rodgers, Paul Anka, Clyde McPhatter, George Hamilton IV, LaVern Baker, Frankie Avalon, the Silhouettes, the Royal Teens, the Storey Sisters, the Crescendos, the Monotones, the Playmates, Jimmy Reed, Jackie Wilson, Huey Smith and the Clowns, Jimmy Dell, and Bobby Marchan, all backed by Paul Williams and His Orchestra.

Package shows, mostly put together through American Bandstand host Dick Clark's company, continued to come through Toronto in 1959, '60, and '61. Each of these concerts reflected the general turning away from the more R&B-influenced visceral form of mid-'50s rock and roll toward the teenage pop schlock of the so-called "in-between years." In January 1959, "The Biggest Show of Stars" brought the Platters, Clyde McPhatter, Little Anthony and the Imperials, the Crests, the Cadillacs, Johnny Olenn and the Blockbusters, Fabian, Bo Diddley, the Kalin Twins, Jimmy Clanton, Duane Eddy, and Ella Johnson, backed by Buddy Johnson and His Show of Stars Band. In September the "Dick Clark Caravan of Stars" presented Paul Anka, Lloyd Price, Annette Funicello, Duane Eddy, Jimmy Clanton, LaVern Baker, the Coasters, the Drifters, the Skyliners, Bobby Rydell, and Phil Phillips.

The "Biggest Show of Stars for 1960" came to town on January 25, 1960, and featured Frankie Avalon, Clyde McPhatter, Bobby Rydell, Johnny and the Hurricanes, the Crests, Freddy Cannon, Sammy Turner, Linda Laurie, the Isley Brothers, the Clovers, Cliff Richard, and Dick Caruso, all backed by the Paul Williams Orchestra, with Harold Cromer once again serving as MC. While the format of these package shows was perfected, the actual concerts, featuring a lot of bland pop in between a few R&B artists such as the Isley Brothers and the Clovers, were less interesting and consequently were not selling out.

The astute reader might have noticed that piano-playing madman Jerry Lee Lewis did not appear on any of these package tours. Lewis would finally make it to Toronto in January 1961, when he played a three-week run at the Yonge Street club Le Coq d'Or. Bo Diddley also became a regular in Toronto clubs in the 1960s, playing the Edison Hotel, the Concord Tavern, the Embassy Tavern, and Le Coq d'Or a number of times over the course of the decade.

The most interesting development in the world of rock and roll in Toronto in the late 1950s was the arrival of Ronnie Hawkins and the Hawks. The earliest ad we could find for Ronnie Hawkins was for a gig at the East York Arena on July 17, 1959. Over the next 20 plus years a plethora of incredible musicians would pass through his group, including all five members of what would become the Band, as well as members of Crowbar, the Full Tilt Boogie Band, and King Biscuit Boy. It is not an overstatement to suggest that the arrival of Hawkins transformed the very shape that rock and roll would take in Toronto in the 1960s.

The 1961 to 1963 version of the Hawks, which included Robbie Robertson, Levon Helm, Rick Danko, Richard Manuel, and Garth Hudson, influenced every important 1960s rock and roll musician in the city.

For a brief period at the end of the 1960s, there was a revival of interest in 1950s rock. The Toronto Rock and Roll Revival Festival at Varsity Stadium in September 1969 featured Chuck Berry, Little Richard, Bo Diddley, Jerry Lee Lewis, and Gene Vincent alongside the Doors and John Lennon (the promoters had also tried to get Creedence Clearwater Revival). And for two nights in May 1972, Bill Haley, Chuck Berry, Jackie Wilson, Ben E. King, Bo Diddley, and the Drifters played Massey Hall for teenagers too young to have experienced the music the first time around and for those in their late twenties and early thirties wishing to relive their youth. The formula was successful enough that two similar packages played Maple Leaf Gardens in October 1972 and May 1973, the latter including the great Roy Orbison.

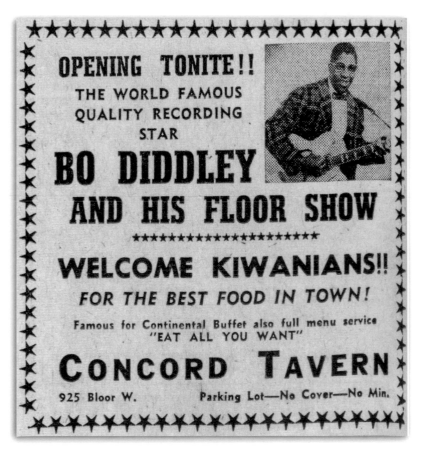

July 3, 1961, Concord Tavern

May 3, 1969, Maple Leaf Gardens

8 CLASSIC ROCK

One of the most significant events in Toronto concert history was the Beatles' appearance at Maple Leaf Gardens on September 7, 1964. The four lads from Liverpool played two shows that day, as they did on both of their return visits to Toronto in late summer of 1965 and 1966. Each of their three Toronto visits turned the city's media and fans on their heads as is evidenced by the fact that the day after their September 1964 appearance, the *Globe* ran a whopping 15 articles about the show. Typical of every Beatles appearance in Toronto, the reviewers spent most of their column inches writing about the screaming adulation the group received from their rabid fans. One of the *Globe*'s writers felt a need to state unequivocally, "Four Beatles

September 7, 1964, Maple Leaf Gardens

can't out-vocalize a Maple Leaf Gardens full of youngsters braying their adoration."

Of the other British invasion acts, only the Rolling Stones, Gerry and the Pacemakers, the Dave Clark Five, and Herman's Hermits were big enough to play the Gardens. Gerry and the Pacemakers were the first to follow the Beatles, headlining a bill at the arena that included Billy J. Kramer and the Dakotas on November 1, 1964. The Dave Clark Five came through twice, November 2, 1964, and November 23, 1965. Herman's Hermits first came to Toronto August 6, 1966, when they headlined a show with the Animals, Toronto's the Five Rogues, and the Spastiks at Maple Leaf Stadium, which was located at Bathurst and Lakeshore before it was demolished in 1968. The *Star*'s Marilyn Beker was particularly impressed with Five Rogues lead singer George Olliver.

In August 1967, the Hermits performed at the Gardens. What was significant about the latter show is that the Blues Magoos and the Who opened for them. Only 3,000 fans turned up. Ralph Thomas of the *Toronto Star* noted that rock shows at the Gardens had been bombing for at least a year at this point. Thomas thought that the Who was the best act on the show but that they suffered from atrocious sound. He concluded his discussion of the group's set, "So, the big excitement of the evening turned out to be not the Who's music but it's by now famed destruction of instruments at the end of its set. The four Who set off smoke bombs, smashed an amplifier, tore their drum set apart and demolished a guitar." The article was accompanied by a photo of the Who destroying the stage, captioned

"I saw the Beatles' first Toronto concert in 1964 at Maple Leaf Gardens and was lucky enough to see them again in 1965 and 1966. The first year I screamed, the second I cried, and the third I listened. As their songwriting matured, so did I."

— Martha Johnson, lead singer, Martha and the Muffins

"Before heading home, we phone my mother to see if there is anything she needs us to pick up. Frantically, she says, 'I've been trying to find you. Phone Uncle Max. He has an extra ticket for tonight's Beatles concert for Marilyn' … I get to sit beside my very proper, formal uncle, who's wearing a suit, of course … as I scream my head off watching my idols sing. Didn't hear a word or a chord. Didn't matter."

— Marilyn Tate (The Beatles, Maple Leaf Gardens, September 7, 1964)

"IN SENSATIONAL FINALE, THE WHO DESTROY ITS EQUIPMENT." What the adolescent screaming Hermits' fans felt about the Who can only be imagined.

The Rolling Stones also made three visits to Maple Leaf Gardens in the 1960s, in April and October of 1965, and again in June 1966. Local band David Clayton-Thomas and the Shays opened the April 1965 show; Patti LaBelle and the Blue Belles and the Vibrations supported the Stones in October 1965; while the Rogues, the Ugly Ducklings, the McCoys, the Standells, and the Trade Winds opened up the June 1966 performance. Newspaper accounts seem to suggest that the Stones' audiences were smaller than the Beatles' (11,000–13,000 vs. 16,000) but their fans were apparently more unruly.

Famed promoter Gary Topp was at the first show: "In 1964, while studying in Rochelle Bernstein's backyard as 1050 CHUM blasted on the transistor, I heard the Rolling Stones for the first time. 'Not Fade Away,' HOLY SHIT!!!

"So, there I am, 19 years old, at my first arena rock show with my cousin, Ronnie. It's April 25, 1965, at Maple Leaf Gardens. I loved the Stones and their rhythm and blues garage sound, their anti-establishment shit-disturbing, filthy, ugly, sexy image, and their wild anti-Beatles performance.

"I joined the Stones' fan club, which got us 11th-row-centre seats on the floor. Only about 11,000 in attendance, the place was sweaty with anticipation. There were a ton of opening groups in typical soul revue fashion. I think Cannibal and the Headhunters and the Paupers were two. Who can remember when all you wanted was the Stones?

October 31, 1965, Maple Leaf Gardens

"Fave CKEY DJ Dave Mickie was the MC. He urged the crowd to move their seats a little closer. The aisles and rows disappeared. Chaos was evident as the Stones hit the stage. World War Three had ignited. It got hotter and sweatier. The flash bulbs were popping. Everyone surged the stage, arms flying, screaming. The police and medics were busy. Brian beautifully ambiguous, maracas Mick as James Brown, stone cold Bill, Charlie coolly keeping the beat, and Keith prancing around. They went through their hits like a tornado. Then they were gone behind the curtains. It had been a dangerously delightful, mesmerizing, deafening, explosive, surreal 10-song happening. It was a riot, and a real riot it was. My ears rang for days. Ronnie and I still rave about it."

At their June 29, 1966, appearance, the show was halted when the Stones were in the midst of playing "Satisfaction" as a particularly besotted fan elected to start climbing down the netting from the balcony rail about 25 feet above the stage behind the Stones. The lights were immediately turned on in the arena, the Stones stopped playing and the girl broke free from a policeman holding onto her. The crowd gasped as she fell into the arms of a Constable Hughes who had started climbing a stage curtain to reach the girl. While he was successful in stopping the girl from falling to the stage, the curtain eventually ripped and he ended up falling eight feet into the arms of waiting officers. One officer summed the incident up as follows: "The beat got into her brain and she went haywire." Incident over, the Stones finished playing "Satisfaction," the lights went up and while the crowd screamed for more, the Stones were headed to the airport to catch their flight for the next night's show.

Arthur Zeldin, reviewing the show for the *Star*, wrote that "Jagger is a phenomenon of utter sexuality, beyond simple distinctions of maleness and femaleness. He moves without mind or will, as if he were plugged in directly to an electric outlet. With each twitch of his wiry body, each part of his puffy lips, each chord of that sad and unspeakably urgent music, his audience melted further into a screaming pulp."

The only other major rock act to come to town in 1965 was the rather tame Beach Boys, who played Maple Leaf Gardens with

Sonny and Cher, J.B. and the Playboys, the Big Town Boys, and Little Caesar and the Consuls opening on September 5. The Beach Boys would come back to the Gardens with Chad and Jeremy, the Ugly Ducklings, and the Last Words in November 1966. Both times they could barely fill half the auditorium. Two of the three other major rock concerts of 1966 were by the Lovin' Spoonful, who appeared at Massey Hall in May and at Maple Leaf Gardens in December (aside from Dylan's electric show the previous November, the May show is arguably the first rock show to be held at Massey Hall). The third major 1966 show was one of the oddest rock concerts in Toronto history, with the Byrds playing for 30 minutes at Varsity Stadium on June 22, 1966, after a professional soccer game between the Hamilton Primos and the Toronto Italia Falcons.

CHUM-AM and the "After Four" section of the *Toronto Telegram* sponsored the "Toronto Sound Showcase" on September 24, 1966, at Maple Leaf Gardens. Fourteen of the city's most popular groups, including the Stitch in Tyme, Bobby Kris & the Imperials, RK & the Associates, the Big

September 5, 1965, Maple Leaf Gardens

"CKEY DJ Dave Mickie was the MC. He urged the crowd to move their seats a little closer. The aisles and rows disappeared. Chaos was evident as the Stones hit the stage. World War Three had ignited. It got hotter and sweatier. The flash bulbs were popping. Everyone surged [toward] the stage, arms flying, screaming.... They went through their hits like a tornado. Then they were gone behind the curtains. It had been a dangerously delightful, mesmerizing, deafening, explosive, surreal 10-song happening.... My ears rang for days. Ronnie and I still rave about it."

— Gary Topp, promoter, half of the legendary duo the Garys (The Rolling Stones, Maple Leaf Gardens, April 25, 1965

Town Boys, Susan Taylor and the Peytons, Little Caesar and the Consuls, the Secrets, Luke and the Apostles, the Paupers, the Last Words, the Trip, the Spastiks, the Five Rising Sons, and the Ugly Ducklings, played from 10:00 a.m. until midnight. Ticket prices were $2 with all the proceeds going to charity. While the event was under attended, it served as a clarion call with regard to the level of great rock music happening in Toronto at the local level.

Aside from the Herman's Hermits gig, the few rock concerts in Toronto in 1967 reflected the beginnings of the 1960s counterculture. In February, New York City's the Fugs, famous for their taboo-challenging lyrics, came to the University of Toronto's Convocation Hall as part of "Perception '67." Staged by artist Michael Hayden, Perception '67 was a happening primarily designed to simulate a hallucinogenic drug experience. In June, Tommy James and the Shondells came to the Gardens, as did the Mamas and the Papas (on Canada Day), but the big rock show of the year was Jefferson Airplane's free concert at Nathan Phillips Square, which took place on Sunday, July 23 in front of some 40,000 fans. Luke and the Apostles and Spring Garden Road opened. The free concert was San Francisco promoter Bill Graham's idea and was designed to help generate interest for a week of gigs (July 31–August 5) at the O'Keefe Centre featuring the Airplane, the Grateful Dead, and Luke and the Apostles.

As was the case in most large North American cities, the number of rock shows increased exponentially in Toronto in 1968 and 1969. Frank Zappa and the Mothers of

May 24, 1969,
Rock Pile

March 29, 1970,
O'Keefe Centre

February 23, 1969, Rock Pile

Invention first performed at Convocation Hall in January 1968 before coming back to the Rock Pile (also spelled Rockpile and Rock-Pile on some posters) in '69. By 1970, Zappa was an annual visitor to Massey Hall before graduating to Maple Leaf Gardens on a double bill with the Mahavishnu Orchestra in 1973.

The 1968 Convocation Hall show was part of what ads in the *Varsity* listed as a "U.C. Festival: Babel: Society as Madness and Myth" that ran from Wednesday, January 24 to Sunday, January 28. The five day event was what in sixties parlance was termed a "happening." The first two nights were listed as multimedia shows titled "Americrap" and "Society as Propaganda." On Friday night there was a film festival while something called "Babel: Environment in Refectory" ran Saturday and Sunday from 11:00 a.m. to 11:00 p.m. The Mothers of Invention closed the festival Sunday night at Convocation Hall. Apparently it was future premier Bob Rae who booked the Mothers.

The band performed against a white backdrop, which Convocation Hall adorned with white balloons. To complete the "white" theme, the Mothers poured "shaving cream in every possible orifice in the huge organ at the front of the hall." The *Globe and Mail*'s Marilyn Beker was none too impressed, complaining how Zappa "played with dolls, lifted skulls out of a brown box … threw Crazy Foam at the audience, smashed toy cars, pounded a pick into a clothing store dummy, and made obscene gestures." She went on to opine, "There was none of the Mothers' versatility, none of their way-out driving sound. There was just too much fooling around." To cap the evening off, when various audience members began to request songs from the group's first two albums, "Zappa had the Mothers play them all at once!"

Jimi Hendrix, the Doors, and the Who all visited Toronto in both 1968 and 1969. All three bands played their initial Toronto gigs as headliners at the CNE Coliseum in early 1968. The Who show was promoted by Russ Gibb, the owner of the Grande Ballroom in Detroit. Given that the MC5 were the house band at the Grande, it is not surprising that they made their first Toronto appearance opening for the Who.

On June 5, 1968, Cream made their one and only Toronto appearance at Massey Hall. Rush bassist Geddy Lee recalls being absolutely gobsmacked by the band's power and musicianship that evening. In the fall of 1968, the Fugs visited Massey Hall, Donovan played Varsity Stadium, and the Young Rascals were at Maple Leaf Gardens.

From September 1968 through late 1969, the Rock Pile at 888 Yonge Street (at various times known as the Masonic Temple, Club 888, and the Concert Hall), presented a who's who of up-and-coming rock artists, including Blood Sweat and Tears, Country Joe and the Fish, Procol Harum, Jeff Beck, the Chambers Brothers, the MC5, Frank Zappa and the Mothers of Invention, Spirit, Family, Jethro Tull, the Butterfield Blues Band, the Grateful Dead, Ten Years After, the original Fleetwood Mac, and, on New Year's Eve 1969, Alice Cooper.

The Who played two shows at the Rock Pile on Pete Townshend's birthday, May 19, 1969. Toronto's Leigh Ashford opened. Unfortunately for Toronto audiences, the Who cut short the length of their set to fit both shows into the one night. Despite playing most of their then-new "rock opera" *Tommy* in most cities, at the Rock Pile they played a mere five songs totalling 14 minutes from their opus. The mini-TOMMY set climaxed with the single "Pinball Wizard," but entirely omitted the "We're Not Gonna Take It" and "See Me, Feel Me" sections.

Two of the most memorable Rock Pile gigs were the appearance of British eccentric the Crazy World of Arthur Brown on April 13 and June 1, 1969. Supported by Vincent Crane dressed in a white gown with angel wings whaling on a Hammond B-3 organ (later of Atomic Rooster) and Carl Palmer's extraordinary drumming (later of Emerson, Lake, and Palmer), Brown was supporting his solitary North American hit "Fire." At the first show Brown's accompanists came onstage followed by a spinning wheel of paper through which Brown made his grand entrance. His 45 minute set closed with flames shooting out of his headdress much to the amazement of the assembled throng. In between, he masqueraded as the Pope and Jesus Christ. That night there was also a power failure, which drummer Carl Palmer compensated for with a Herculean 10-minute drum solo.

Early on in the Rock Pile's history, the promoters advertised for high school reps. Ken Stowar, now the manager of community radio station CIUT-FM, was then going

May 17 & 19, 1969,
Rock Pile

to Markham District High School. He got the gig as the Markham District rep for the Rock Pile, which meant every week he hitchhiked from Markham down to the club, picked up flyers for that weekend's show and put them up at his high school. In return, he got in free to every show. What an incredible gig.

`On February 23, 1969, the Mothers of Invention played two concerts at the Rock Pile. According to Ritchie Yorke, "The first was innocuous, but at the second show a former member of the group simulated sexual intercourse with a girl who turned out to be his wife, then for a finale turned his back and dropped his trousers. Rock Pile manager Rick Taylor, 24, didn't like it, but he didn't try to stop it. 'Are you crazy, man? Just picture me trying to stop it in front of 2,000 fans.'"

Far and away the most important Rock Pile concerts were Led Zeppelin's gigs February 2 and August 18, 1969. Zeppelin played two shows on both visits, effectively bankrupting the Rock Pile in August when their manager, Peter Grant, demanded extra money before he would allow the band to take the stage. At the time, Zeppelin had just released their second album and were quickly becoming an

arena-size band. Much to Peter Grant's chagrin, Rick Taylor and John Brower, who ran the Rock Pile, had negotiated the August gig when they first booked them as relative unknowns in February, forcing them to play a small venue for relative little money. Grant was not happy, especially when he saw several thousand fans lined up to get in to both shows.

Grant was a former bouncer/strongman in the U.K., and at six feet and 300 plus pounds, liked to be intimidating. According to the late Nash the Slash, in between shows, Grant demanded extra money or he said Zeppelin would not play. When Rick Taylor produced the contract, Grant's response was to simply rip it up. While Grant and Taylor were shouting at each other, the Rock Pile's stage manager, D.D. Hill, went out back and removed the distributor cap from the band's equipment truck and hid it in a garbage bin out back. Proud of himself, he came back in and hollered to Rick that Zeppelin weren't going anywhere. It was a pretty aggressive confrontation that ultimately ended up with Taylor forking over additional money. The Rock Pile was already under financial stress. The Zeppelin show was held August 18, and the venue had not hosted a touring act since the Grateful Dead's appearance July 8. Peter Grant's actions effectively put the nail in the coffin of the club. Although a Jethro Tull show had previously been listed for a few weeks after the Zeppelin gig, it appears that the show was cancelled. Local blues greats McKenna Mendelson Mainline played four shows the week after Zeppelin and then there was nothing until Alice Cooper closed the venue on New Year's Eve.

While all the drama was going on inside, future Rush member Geddy Lee was waiting patiently outside the venue along with his bandmates Alex Lifeson and John Rutsey. As was the case with many, Led Zeppelin's first album had changed Geddy's life and he desperately wanted to see the show. The problem was that he didn't have enough money for a ticket.

"This required drastic measures," recalled Geddy in spring 2019, "and so I took the typewriter that my grandmother had bought me for my birthday and ventured down to Church Street and pawned it in one of the shops that dotted that street. Success. I guiltily accepted the money and went straight out to buy my ticket for the show that was now being referred to as 'Mighty Monday.'

"We lined up extra early for the 8:00 p.m. general admission show and we ended up in the second row, right in front of Jimmy Page ... effin amazing! The band floated onto the stage and started rippin' into a killer version of the old Yardbirds classic 'Train Kept a Rollin'. They were super loud, and the summer heat kept rising in that old Masonic Temple and the crowd was so seriously jacked and stomping that I remember little bits of plaster falling from the ceiling of the place. They literally brought down the house! The unforgettable birth of heavy rock as far as my bandmates and I were concerned. I left the show breathless and ecstatic, and it wasn't until the next day that I started trying to figure out how the hell I was going to get my typewriter out of hock before my mom found out!"

In November, Zeppelin played two more shows, this time at the O'Keefe Centre. They returned to Toronto to play Maple Leaf Gardens in 1971, and then, for some reason, the band skipped the city on their 1972, '73, '75, and '77 tours.

After their Rock Pile show, the Who played the CNE Coliseum for a second time in October 1969. They would then skip Toronto

April 7, 1968, CNE Coliseum

for a number of years, finally returning in 1975 to play Maple Leaf Gardens.

A second rock venue, the Electric Circus, had a brief run from January 23, 1969, through June 1970. Toronto guitar slinger Paul James recalls that the Circus "was a bunch of rooms you wandered through with lots of black lights and fluorescent, trippy posters. Wavy mirrors distorted the way you looked. [It was] a place to go to when you were young and high and [it] was designed for tripping on drugs."

A sister club to a New York City venue of the same name, the circular walls in the main room were painted white and made of cement, which meant that the acoustics were terrible. The Circus brought Procol Harum, Jeff Beck, Free, the Faces, the Chamber Brothers, Savoy Brown, Chuck Berry, Mountain, Country Joe and the Fish, the Flying Burrito Brothers (one of Gram Parsons's last shows with the band), and Alice Cooper to the city. Chicago Transit Authority also played the Electric Circus. According to Wayne Thompson, who booked the gig, between the time the show was booked and the concert date arrived, the band was sued in the United States and had to change their

July 2, 1971,
St. Lawrence Market

name to Chicago. Since the show was in Canada and posters had already been printed, the gig went ahead as Chicago Transit Authority. Not that it mattered. Only a handful of people turned up. The Procol Harum show at the Electric Circus was their second visit to Toronto (they had played the Rock Pile in October 1968). It was scheduled for Tuesday, February 16, 1969.

Unbelievably, Janis Joplin played two shows at the O'Keefe and the MC5 were at the Rock Pile that same night. The *Globe and Mail* reviewer managed to catch the first Procol show, which was marred by equipment problems, a half-filled O'Keefe Centre for Joplin's 6:30 show, and then the final set by the MC5. What a night that would have been!

The Electric Circus booked a pretty steady lineup of touring and local artists through August 1969. At that point they ran into financial problems. In October they attempted to draw an audience by offering underground films. A month later, they were trying to work out a deal with creditors to avoid bankruptcy. They were initially successful and by the following April were once again booking in touring artists such as Taj Mahal, the Faces, the Flying Burrito Brothers, and Mountain (the latter was described by many Facebook posters as one of the loudest shows EVER). Alas, by June they had shut down.

The May 3, 1969, Jimi Hendrix Experience show is one of the more famous concerts in Toronto history. Flying into Toronto, Hendrix's bags were searched and a small quantity of heroin was seized. While Hendrix would eventually be found innocent, a pall hung over his head and the concert at Maple Leaf Gardens that night. Although Hendrix played spirited versions of a few of his hits, such as "Fire" and "Purple Haze," he spent much of the 70-minute show playing extended blues jams and looking both subdued and pensive. Hendrix had previously headlined the CNE Coliseum supported by Soft Machine and Toronto's the Paupers. His first Toronto gig, though, was a little-known appearance as a sideman with Wilson Pickett at Club 888 (the same building that became known as the Rock Pile a few years later) on Yonge Street in May 1966.

In late 1969, with both the Rock Pile and the Electric Circus undergoing financial difficulties, the Hawk's Nest above Le Coq d'Or brought in some very interesting rock shows. Teegarden and Van Winkle played the club November 14 and 15, Spooky Tooth played November 16, Keith Emerson's the Nice appeared there November 23, while the Kinks played their first Toronto show at the small club on December 6. (That same night, Miles Davis was finishing a six-night stand at the Colonial Tavern!) After Christmas, the Dutch group Golden Earring played three nights at the Hawk's Nest, December 26–28. Dave Edmunds's group Love Sculpture appears to have been the last touring rock band to play the club. They performed their only Toronto shows January 2–4, 1970. Local R&B great Eric Mercury headlined the Hawk's Nest the following week as the club once again focused on soul, R&B, and local acts.

On October 3, 1969, Johnny Winter played Massey Hall with Toronto's Whiskey Howl opening up. This was just the third rock show ever held at Massey Hall. In 1970, Massey began to be rented regularly by promoters for rock shows; the Band, Santana, the Byrds, the Mothers of Invention, Leonard Cohen, and Van Morrison would all play Massey in 1970 alone.

Jefferson Airplane, Steppenwolf, and Three Dog Night all performed at the O'Keefe Centre in 1970, the Airplane show being their last visit to this city and one of the most intense psychedelic shows Torontonians ever experienced. Some audience members report having out-of-body experiences that night. Melinda McCracken in the *Globe and Mail* was especially taken by the group's surreal light show, writing, "Glen MacKay's Headlights … have evolved and are now devastatingly beautiful and more sophisticated than any light shows seen in Toronto thus far. The lush density of coloured images superimposed to give the illusion of several depths at once. The pinwheels, colour separated films, the overhead oil projections all have much more colour and variety now and are essential to the Airplane's performance."

Another highlight in 1970 was the September 19 show at Maple Leaf Gardens with R&B singer Wilbert Harrison and Booker T. and the M.G.'s opening for Creedence Clearwater Revival (CCR). Harrison, supporting his hit single "Let's Work Together," was a one-man band, singing while playing guitar, bass drum, cymbals,

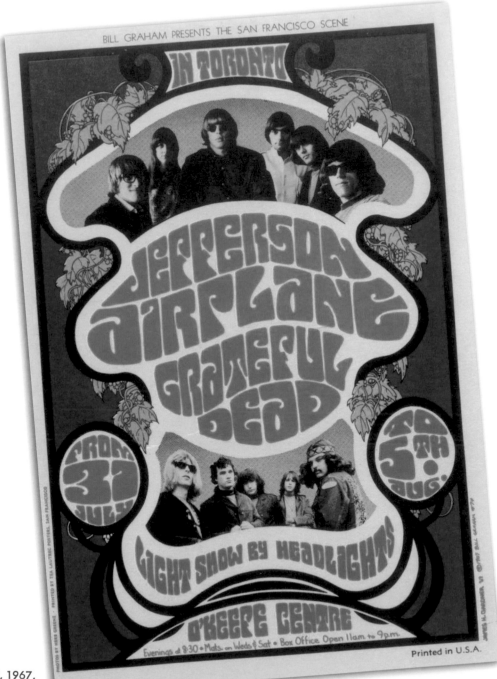

July 31–August 5, 1967,
O'Keefe Centre

and tambourine at the same time, something few Toronto audiences would have ever seen. The appearance by Booker T. and the M.G.'s was the only time the fabled Stax Records house band played Toronto in their original incarnation. According to the *Globe and Mail*, Creedence's performance was "para-religious."

In the early 1970s, a number of progressive rock shows came to Toronto. Aside from the rather milquetoast Moody Blues, the first big prog show of any consequence was when Emerson, Lake, and Palmer played Lamport Stadium on August 12, 1971, with Flower Travellin' Band and an acoustic Bob Seger opening up. The show went several hours late as the promoter had failed to pay for insurance prior to the opening of the gates. Flower Travellin' Band had moved to Toronto from Tokyo in December 1970 just after having recorded their seminal *Satori* album. Mixing heavy metal with Indian modal scales and Japanese kodo drumming, they were both exotic and extraordinary. They stayed in Toronto through March 1972 before returning to Japan.

Procol Harum also became a regular visitor to Toronto. King Crimson, Mark II featuring Boz Burrell, Mel Collins, Ian Wallace, and Robert Fripp, opened up for Procol in November 1971 at Massey Hall playing a mind-melting set in support of their *Islands* album. After the show, an article appeared in one of the Toronto dailies saying that the management at Massey Hall was thinking of banning rock shows if audiences didn't stop smoking during them. The fear was that Massey was made of wood and could easily burn down. A month later they decided things were okay, but insisted promoters pay for 15 policemen at every show to help control gatecrashing.

Crimson returned to Massey for incendiary gigs in 1973 and 1974 (eclectic folk-rock/prog band Strawbs were the opening act at the 1973 show). At the latter show, Robert Fripp took great exception to a fan who shouted "whoo" in the middle of a quiet solo, berating him from onstage against drummer Bill Bruford's sage advice. On June 4, 1972, Jethro Tull brought their *Thick as a Brick* show to Maple Leaf Gardens (the *Globe* reviewer referred to Tull's 1972 *Thick as a Brick* show as "brain-rattling stuff"). They were followed that Halloween night by Yes, who was touring their *Close to*

Concert Productions
International presents

LOU REED

The Berlin Show

QUADRAPHONIC SOUND
AT MASSEY HALL
NOVEMBER 29, 1973
SHOWTIME 8:30 P.M.
TICKETS
$4.95, $5.50 & $6.05
Tickets available at all TICKETRON
Outlets (A&A Downtown, Bloor, New-
tonbrook) and Music World Stores in
Yorkdale, Fairview and Scarborough.
Also Salsberg's Ticket Service, 279 Col-
lege St.

November 29, 1973, Massey Hall

the Edge album. The J. Geils Band and Joe Mendelson opened up.

Through the 1970s Toronto would remain a strong city for prog rock groups, with Yes, Emerson, Lake, and Palmer, and Jethro Tull regularly returning to the city and the Electric Light Orchestra (ELO), Genesis, and Supertramp each playing Massey Hall once or twice before moving up to Maple Leaf Gardens and/or CNE Stadium. On March 11, 1973, Pink Floyd made their only Toronto appearance with their original lineup, playing *Dark Side of the Moon* using quadrophonic sound at Maple Leaf Gardens. It was a stunning display of where progressive rock might go and marked the moment that Pink Floyd became one of the biggest bands in rock history.

Genesis's first Toronto show was opening up for former Velvet Underground lead singer Lou Reed at Massey Hall on April 9, 1973 (Reed came back to Massey in November of 1973). The Velvet Underground had played McMaster University in Hamilton on November 12, 1966, as part of the Andy Warhol Exploding Plastic Inevitable multimedia happening. They played Toronto once only, at the June 1969 Toronto Pop Festival at Varsity Stadium.

Other classic rock acts, such as Neil Young (most notably with Crosby, Stills, and Nash on a very rainy September 2, 1974, at Varsity Stadium with the Band and Jesse Colin Young opening up), the Faces, and the Rolling Stones, made Toronto a regular stop on their tours. Young's fall 1978 concert premiered most of the songs that he would later release on the *Rust Never Sleeps* album, including "My My, Hey Hey (Out of the Blue)." Few people know that the next day he quietly booked a studio in Yorkdale and attempted to record a number of songs for the album. Not feeling the vibe, after putting about 45 minutes of music on tape, he called off the session, walked out, and left the two-inch 24-track tape behind.

One of the greatest shows of the early 1970s was when David Bowie performed his *Diamond Dogs* show at the O'Keefe Centre in the summer of 1974. For its time, the show was a stunning theatrical spectacle sporting a massive post-industrial stage with Bowie at times literally being flown out over the audience to sing songs such as "Space Oddity." The next time Bowie came to Toronto it was

for the stripped down *Station to Station* tour at Maple Leaf Gardens in 1976. He returned to the Gardens again in 1978 for the transcendent *Heroes* show. It would be five years before Bowie toured again. On September 3 and 4, 1983, he brought his Serious Moonlight tour to Exhibition Stadium.

Van Morrison also played memorable shows in Toronto in the 1970s, first at Massey Hall in 1970. He then returned with a small string section for a show at Convocation Hall on the *It's Too Late to Stop Now* tour. In 1974 he came back for a third time, playing the Maple Leaf Gardens concert bowl in October 1974 with the Persuasions opening. After a four year hiatus, he performed two shows at the O'Keefe Centre in October 1978 on his *Wavelength* comeback tour. At one later Massey Hall show, he stormed off after 55 minutes, angry at a fan in the first balcony. When he was finally coaxed back onstage, he played a 60-minute encore, at one point going into a trance reciting the words "Louis Prima" over and over. At the *Wavelength* show in 1978, he recited what seemed to be phone numbers as he tried to bring the spirit down.

The Stones played, perhaps, the most infamous show in Toronto rock and roll

June 16, 1974,
O'Keefe Centre

history when they performed their first club gigs since the early 1960s at the El Mocambo on March 4 and 5, 1977. The gigs were scheduled because the Stones needed to record additional material for their next album, *Love You Live*. Kept secret from virtually everyone, the club was booked the whole week by April Wine, who was coincidentally recording their own live album. Radio station CHUM-AM ran a contest for fans to win tickets for the April Wine gigs. Meanwhile, CHUM-FM ran a contest to win a chance to go to a party with the Rolling Stones, who were allegedly in town to record a new studio album. The Stones contest was a ruse, as the winners had no idea that what they were actually going to do was go to the El Mocambo to see the band play live. Complicating matters, Keith Richards had been busted for possession of heroin at the Harbour Castle Hotel on February 28.

The Stones were supposed to play their first El Mo show on Thursday, March 3, but when Mick Jagger's daughter Jade got sick, he cancelled and flew to New York, returning the next morning. At this point the gig was still a secret. When the band did finally take the stage on Friday night, audience members, including this author, were treated to an astonishing show, with the Stones reaching back to their earliest days to play songs such as "Route 66," "Little Red Rooster," and Bo Diddley's "Crackin' Up" alongside their requisite hits of the time such as "Brown Sugar" and "Jumpin' Jack Flash." Prime Minister Pierre Trudeau's wife, Margaret, had been hanging out for

> "I was there! Yes, Booker T and the MGs were Neil Young's backing band. Chris Cornell had recently cut all of his hair off, so it was a great shocker for everybody. Pearl Jam nearly incited a riot by instructing the audience in the stands to rush down to the floor to join everyone else ... To see a show at that venue was a piece of Canadian rock and roll history, as it was scheduled to get torn down...."
>
> — Premadasa Gangadeen (Neil Young, with Pearl Jam and Soundgarden, Exhibition Stadium, August 18, 1993)

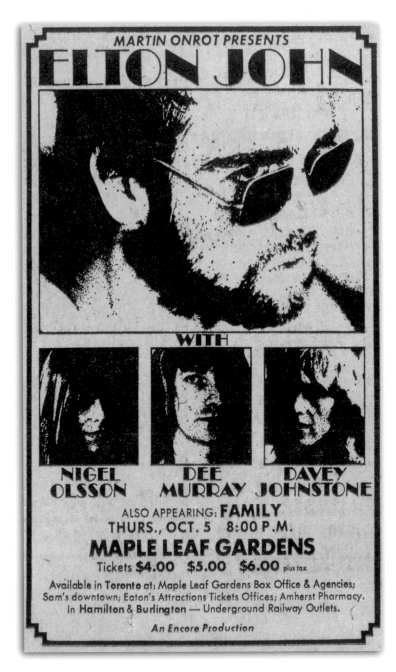

October 5, 1972, Maple Leaf Gardens

much of the week with Ronnie Wood and attended the Friday night show complete with an RCMP escort.

While the Stones were on stage Friday, word quickly got out about the event on Toronto radio. Not surprisingly, Saturday was absolute mayhem, with thousands of people on the street outside the tiny club hoping against all odds that they might be able to get in. Despite some local mythology, the Stones gig was never advertised at all, let alone under the name the Cockroaches. While only about 360 people saw the Stones each night, over the years hundreds more have claimed that they were there.

Part of the resolution of Keith Richards's heroin bust was that Richards would play a benefit show for the Canadian National Institute for the Blind (CNIB). As a result, Toronto got lucky once again as the Stones played two one-off gigs in 1979 at the 4,500-seat Oshawa Civic Auditorium on April 22. Richards originally planned to play one show at Maple Leaf Gardens, but it was unavailable. Two shows were then tentatively scheduled at Varsity Arena, but for some reason a permit could not be obtained in time for the concert, so it was moved to

Oshawa. Opening up for the Stones were the New Barbarians, a group led by Ronnie Wood but also including Keith Richards, bassist Stanley Clarke, Faces' keyboard player Ian McLagen, the Meters' drummer Zigaboo Modeliste, and the Stones' sax player Bobby Keys. This was the Barbarians' first show on their one and only tour. To the delight of many, the Stones' portion of the show opened with just Mick and Keith on acoustic guitar performing Rev. Robert Wilkins' "Prodigal Son" for the only time ever on a Toronto stage.

In the first half of the 1970s, there were a few new artists who eventually became subsumed under the classic rock mantel. Elton John was the first of these artists. There was talk of John coming to play the Imperial Theatre in late 1970, but it would be two more years before he made his Toronto debut, in October 1972. By that point, John was in the middle of his sixth North American tour in two years, as he dominated rock radio with hits such as "Your Song," "Tiny Dancer," "Levon," "Rocket Man," and "Crocodile Rock." He easily sold out Maple Leaf Gardens and delivered a show that was part Liberace spectacle and part rock

December 21, 1975, Seneca Field House (date incorrect on ad)

"The week of the show ... a Division Bell blimp flew all over the city. I was hyped beyond belief. When the show rolled around, it was everything I imagined and more. This experience changed my life, and birthed my appreciation of music and live music ..."

— Jeff Brandman
(Pink Floyd, Exhibition Stadium, July 5, 1994)

and roll throw-down. John would return to Toronto many times, usually playing the Gardens and later the Air Canada Centre. His solo piano show in October 1979 at the O'Keefe Centre was particularly special.

The Eagles were initially supposed to debut in Toronto May 29, 1973, at Massey Hall, with Spooky Tooth opening up. But they cancelled that show. They finally made it to town four years later, on March 30, 1977, when they sold out Maple Leaf Gardens.

In their original incarnation as a blues band led by Peter Green, Fleetwood Mac first played in Toronto at the Rock Pile in 1969. By the mid-1970s the band had changed most of its personnel and its sound. Led by Stevie Nicks and Lindsey Buckingham, the Fleetwood Mac of *Rumours* fame first played the city on July 4, 1977, with a show at CNE Stadium in front of some 60,000 fans. Boz Scaggs, riding high on the *Silk Degrees* album, and Kenny Loggins opened up.

Bruce Springsteen first played Toronto on the *Born to Run* tour December 21, 1975 (the ads for the show listed the date initially as December 27), taking the stage at the Seneca College Field House. The show was originally booked into Convocation Hall, but when it sold out, it was moved to Seneca. Despite a bitterly cold evening in a snow-covered city, over 3,000 fans were on hand for one of the greatest shows Toronto ever witnessed. Springsteen's next appearances here were at Maple Leaf Gardens in 1977 and 1978. Since then, he has played the city numerous times at various venues, including a solo gig at Massey Hall, Air Canada Centre (now Scotiabank Arena), and the SkyDome (now Rogers Centre).

One of the most legendary gigs by an artist now considered part of the classic rock canon was U2's debut appearance at the El

Mocambo on December 9, 1980. This was the day after John Lennon was shot, which made it amazing that anybody at all went out to see a show. But U2 was preceded by rave reviews in the British music papers, tempting several hundred fans to turn up. Amazingly, their first album would not be released for another two weeks. The *Globe and Mail*'s pop critic, Alan Niester, headed to the show still reeling from Lennon's death. The band's performance lifted his spirits as he thought U2 was "one of the most vital and interesting bands" he had seen in the past few years. As he saw it, the four Irishmen, aged 18 to 20, played "ethereal, progressive music that isn't restricted to any set styles." He concluded his review by presciently stating that "U2 could well be the Led Zeppelin of the eighties."

September 3, 1983,
Exhibition Stadium

August 23, 1980, Mosport Park

9
Music Festivals

$\mathcal{E}$xactly what constitutes a music festival is not very well defined. Some are multi-day events while others last one day only; some are annual events while others are one-offs; some occur in multiple venues while others are mounted in a single stadium or field. Most are genre-focused at least in terms of the name of the festival (although jazz, blues, and folk festivals these days routinely include a plethora of non-jazz, blues, or folk artists!); most are held in large, often outdoor venues to accommodate an audience commensurate with both the economics and the appeal of a multiple-artist bill. Sadly, many events are called festivals but in reality are simply concerts with four or five artists playing short sets in a single evening.

FIRST CANADIAN JAZZ FESTIVAL

JULY 22-25 Grandstand C.N.E. Grounds
TORONTO, CANADA.

PERFORMANCES GO ON RAIN OR SHINE

4 Evening Concerts at 8.30 p.m.	3 Afternoon Concerts at 2.30 p.m.
Reserved Seats 2.65, 3.75, 4.85	General Admission $2.20

Wed. July 22—Count Bassie Orch; The Four Freshmen; Dizzie Gillespie 5; Gene Krupa 4; Peterson 3.

Thurs. July 23 — Count Bassie Orch; Miles Davis 6—Cannonball Adderly; Modern Jazz Quartet; Lambert - Hendricks - Ross; Sarah Vaughan.

Fri. July 24—Dave Brubeck 4; Ahmad Jamal 3; Stan Kenton Orch; Buck Clayton; Vic Dickenson; Pee Wee Russell; Bud Freeman; Jimmy Rushing; Marian McPortland; Sarah Vaughan.

Sat. July 25—Louis Armstrong All Stars; Barbara Carroll 3; Coleman Hawkins; Moe Koffman 4; Mike White 6; Roy Eldrige.

Thurs. Aft., July 23 — Maynard Ferguson Orch.; Toshiko 3; Georgie Arthur 5; Ron Collier 5; Max Roach 5; Ben Webster.

Fri. Aft., July 24—The Jazz Messengers; Ruby Braff 4; Peter Appleyard 4; Pat Riccio 4; Phil Nimmons 9.

Sat. Aft., July 25—Leonard Feather presents the Encyclopedia of Jazz — featuring: Don Elliott; Willie "The Lion" Smith; Dick Hyman; and many other great jazz artists.

Co-sponsored by King Edward Sheraton Hotel and George Wein, Director Newport Jazz Festival.

Free transportation to C.N.E. Grounds for registered guests of the King Edward Sheraton Hotel

KING EDWARD SHERATON HOTEL
TORONTO, CANADA

July 22–25, 1959, CNE

Toronto has had more than its fair share of great festivals over the years. With the exception of the Mariposa Folk Festival, in the 1960s most of the earlier gatherings were one-offs. Beginning in 1987, with the debut of both the Toronto Jazz Festival and Edgefest, there have been a number of annual events, including Lollapalooza, Vans Warped Tour, and Sno-Jam.

The granddaddy of non-classical music festivals in North America is the Newport Jazz Festival, established in Rhode Island in 1954. Programmed by George Wein, Newport was an annual event that brought together a who's who of jazz artists for three days every summer. The Newport Folk Festival followed in 1959, and, like the jazz festival, became the most important folk event of the calendar year, with single performances at any given festival being the turning point in a number of artists' careers.

The first notable Toronto music festival was billed as "The Canadian Jazz Festival." It consisted of seven concerts and a panel discussion. The concerts were held at the CNE Grandstand over four days from July 22 to 25, 1959. Drawing on the Newport brand, the festival ads crowed, "Direct from the

Newport Jazz Festival featuring American and Canadian artists," before listing the acts that had been booked. The lineup was extraordinary, featuring everyone from Miles Davis, Dizzy Gillespie, and Dave Brubeck to Sarah Vaughan and Count Basie. Among the Canadian contingent were Oscar Peterson, Peter Appleyard, and Phil Nimmons. The first evening was sponsored by the Canadian Mental Health Association.

One of the most interesting aspects of the Canadian Jazz Festival was that on Friday morning at 11:00 a.m. there was a panel discussion at the King Edward Hotel (which co-sponsored the festival along with George Wein) entitled "Jazz Festivals and their value" with Father Norman O'Connor (the "Jazz Priest"), moderator John Lewis (of the Modern Jazz Quartet), Cannonball Adderley, Jon Hendricks, Miles Davis, and Ruby Braff. I would be fascinated to know what the ever querulous Miles Davis had to say! The Canadian Jazz Festival was anticipated to be an annual event, but unfortunately it was never held again.

Just as the Canadian Jazz Festival was inspired by the Newport Festival, the Mariposa Folk Festival was clearly inspired by the Newport Folk Festival. Founded in Orillia, a couple of hours north of Toronto, by Ruth Jones, her husband Dr. Crawford Jones, her brother David Major, and Pete McGarvey, the first festival was headlined by the Travellers and featured only Canadian performers. Mariposa grew quite quickly over the next several years, with Estelle Klein taking over as artistic director in 1964. Klein developed the workshop concept, wherein performers, often from disparate traditions, would share a stage, singing songs and telling stories around a common theme. Workshops also provided a vehicle so that the audience would get to see some of the bigger name artists in more intimate settings.

Klein incorporated Indigenous performers into the festival in 1966 and was generally more interested in introducing Mariposa audiences to artists and traditions that they might be otherwise unaware of than she was in big-name performers. Nonetheless, Mariposa is noted for astonishing performances by bluesmen such as Mississippi John Hurt, Reverend Gary Davis, Son House, and Bukka White, the surprise performances of Neil Young and

Joni Mitchell at the 1972 festival (Bob Dylan also showed up and nearly performed but was ushered off the island when the excitement about the possibility of him getting onstage began to lead to potential chaos), and the debut performance of Sweet Honey in the Rock in 1975. Gary Topp and Ken Whiteley both recall the rain at the 1966 festival forcing the organizers to shut the P.A. down. Despite having no P.A., the 64-year-old Mississippi bluesman Son House sang to 6,000 rain-soaked fans. Partway through his set, Phil Ochs brought out a megaphone to help amplify House's vocals. Topp remembers that by the end of the set the power of Son House's performance had literally stopped the rain!

The Monterey Pop Festival in 1967 and the D.A. Pennebaker documentary of the festival, released in 1968, were game-changers in the world of rock. Monterey featured a stunning array of artists, including Otis Redding, Jimi Hendrix, Janis Joplin, the Who, and Jefferson Airplane, and provided the impetus for dozens of rock festivals over the next few years, the most famous being Woodstock, Altamont, and Watkins Glen. Following suit, in 1969 and 1970 Toronto rock fans got to experience five pretty incredible festivals.

The Toronto Pop Festival, promoted by Ken Walker and John Brower, was held on June 21 and 22, 1969, and presented an extraordinary array of talent. By all accounts, the then-emerging Texas blues phenom Johnny Winter stole the Saturday show (his first album had been out a mere six weeks prior to the festival), while Steppenwolf held the honours Sunday, followed closely by Blood Sweat and Tears. The show was notable for being the Band's second show ever (they had played the Fillmore West in San Francisco in April). Unfortunately, the Band had equipment problems and in general turned in a rather tepid set. Also notable was the diversity of the lineup at the festival, which included the ukulele-playing Tiny Tim, Motown's Edwin Starr, Louisiana bluesman Slim Harpo (in what was probably his one and only Toronto appearance), Chuck Berry (who received a standing ovation), Dr. John, Procol Harum, and Sly and the Family Stone (two months before their groundbreaking Woodstock performance). More surprising was the fact that Carla Thomas, backed by the Bar-Kays, and the

Velvet Underground both made their first Toronto appearances at the festival. About 50,000 fans attended over the course of the festival's two days.

Brower and Walker staged a second one-day festival at Varsity Stadium on September 13, 1969. Billed as the Toronto Rock and Roll Revival, it included every important 1950s living rock and roll star except for Fats Domino and Bill Haley. In addition to such icons as Little Richard, Chuck Berry, Bo Diddley, Gene Vincent, and Jerry Lee Lewis, the promoters had booked a handful of smaller-name acts such as Cajun fiddler Doug Kershaw, 1950s revival band Cat Mother and the All Night Newsboys, swamp rocker Tony Joe White, and up-and-coming contemporary artists Alice Cooper and Chicago Transit Authority. To dissuade scalpers, tickets were printed on official banknote paper by the Canadian Banknote Co. in Ottawa.

Scalping wasn't a problem, but a lack of tickets sales certainly was. To try to combat this rather serious issue, in late August the Doors were added to the bill as headliners. The Los Angeles–based group had been scheduled to play Maple Leaf Gardens earlier in the year (March

July 21–22, 1969, Varsity Stadium

21), but the show was cancelled after lead singer Jim Morrison was arrested in Miami for alleged indecent exposure. With ticket sales still lagging, on September 12, the day before the festival, the promoters took out an ad in the *Globe and Mail* that read "BULLETIN: TORONTO ROCK & ROLL REVIVAL. Be at Varsity Stadium tomorrow for Canada's heaviest pop happening ever. Toronto grows even bigger on the pop map with the filming of the Revival by Leacock Pennebaker, who filmed the multi-million-dollar 'Monterey Pop' and 'Don't Look Back.'"

The ad went on to promise a jam finale (which never happened), a prize consisting of a trip to see the Doors record their next album in L.A. for a lucky fan who Los Angeles–based MC Kim Fowley deemed was wearing the "freakiest gear" at the festival (this never happened), and 10-dollar bills taped under various seats. The ad also claimed that "hundreds of free albums, Toronto rock and roll revival tee-shirts and other kicky things are being GIVEN AWAY."

The ad continued: "Like excitement? How about 100 Vagabond motorcyclists escorting the Doors directly from the airport into Varsity Stadium. Like Happenings? There will be plenty of spontaneous things going down at the show; for example, such drop in guests as Rodney Biggenheimer, hip mayor of Sunset Strip in L.A.; Mick Taylor, latest addition to the Rolling Stones [who was never there]; and Screaming Lord Sutch, the freakiest pop product that Britain has produced. COME. BE A PART OF HISTORY AT THE FILMING OF ROCK & ROLL REVIVAL. IT'S ALL HAPPENING IN TOGETHER TORONTO."

While all this was going on, desperate to sell tickets to cover their costs, John Brower had made contact with John Lennon via Apple Records and had tentatively convinced him to fly over and play the show with a new group that Lennon called the Plastic Ono Band, which included Eric Clapton on guitar. With Lennon hesitating to commit, the promoters had problems convincing local radio stations that Lennon was actually going to appear until the day of the festival, when Lennon was actually on a plane heading to Toronto. They also clearly were reluctant to advertise him in the Toronto newspapers even on the day before the festival.

In the meantime, Brower had phoned Russ Gibb in Detroit, with whom he had previously promoted concerts. Gibb had a show on WKNR-FM in Detroit. He believed Brower and announced that John Lennon would be coming to Toronto for the festival. According to Gibb, the station was flooded with phone calls and presumably a number of festival attendees headed to Toronto from Detroit.

In the meantime, once Lennon was actually on the plane, the *Globe and Mail* carried a notice in the morning paper confirming that the unbelievable was indeed happening and that John Lennon would be appearing at Varsity Stadium that evening prior to the Doors' performance. The *Toronto Star* never did announce that Lennon would be there.

The gambit worked, and 20,000 fans turned up. The show proved to be an unqualified success. One of the most bizarre moments occurred when Alice Cooper threw a live chicken out into the audience whose members promptly ripped it to pieces. Lennon's set was awe-inspiring, consisting mostly of rock and roll classics from the 1950s, plus the Beatles' "Yer Blues" and Lennon's solo singles "Cold Turkey" and "Give Peace a Chance." Yoko Ono contributed an astonishing version of "Don't Worry Kyoko (Mummy's Only Looking for Her Hand in the Snow)," which the conservative Toronto media of the time predictably trashed. History would prove their take on Yoko to be both racist and artistically wrong-headed given the influence Yoko would have on numerous new wave and alternative rock bands to come.

The Doors finished the festival at 1:45 in the morning, some 14 hours after it started. They played a subdued but riveting set, concentrating on longer songs while only playing one of their hit singles, that being a sprawling 12-minute version of "Light My Fire."

There were three large rock festivals in Toronto in 1970.

"The Toronto Rock Festival" was held March 25 and 26 at Varsity Arena. With the big headliners being Canned Heat and the Small Faces (a misnomer, as they really were the newly formed Rod Stewart–led Faces playing their first ever gig in North America!), as well as a fake version of the Zombies, only 4,000 fans showed up and the promoters lost their shirts. Partway through Canned Heat's closing set, at 11:00 p.m. sharp, Varsity pulled the plug, much to the disgust of the band and those boogying in front of the stage.

Ken Walker, with his new partners George and Thor Eaton, planned what they thought would be the greatest rock festival ever when they set up Festival Express. The idea was to book a bevy of A-list rock artists and put them on a train, with concert stops in Montreal, Toronto, Winnipeg, Calgary, and Vancouver. At the end of the day, Montreal and Vancouver were cancelled, and, despite a great lineup, the other three festival stops were plagued by protests and boycotts.

The Toronto version of the festival was scheduled for June 27 and 28, 1970, at Exhibition Stadium. The admission fee was $14 in advance and $16 at the door for a two-day pass. A radical organization called the May 4th Movement (named after the date that four students were murdered by National Guardsmen at Kent State University) called for the liberation of the festival. They picketed the headquarters of Eaton-Walker at Dupont and Davenport and they distributed leaflets throughout the city and its suburbs urging young people to crash the festival. They felt that the $16 price tag was exploiting young people at a time when unemployment was high, and they did not like the fact that Thor and George Eaton were part of the Eaton's department store, which they accused of being anti-union, anti-women, and anti-young people. In a June 16 letter to Eaton-Walker, they referred to the promoters as "Capitalist Ripoff Pigs" and demanded that the festival be completely free or that 20 percent of ticket revenue be returned to the community for the purpose of, among other things, paying for "bail funds to fight Toronto pig repression."

While between 15,000 and 20,000 fans bought tickets for each day, at least 2,500 fans successfully broke in to the CNE Grandstand for the Saturday show, throwing stones, bottles, and cans at police in the process. Nine cops were injured and, in an effort to stem the violence, the Grateful Dead, Ian and Sylvia, and James and the Good Brothers agreed to play a free second festival outside Exhibition Stadium in Coronation Park. In the meantime, the Dead, New Riders of the Purple Sage, the Band, Ten Years After, Delaney and

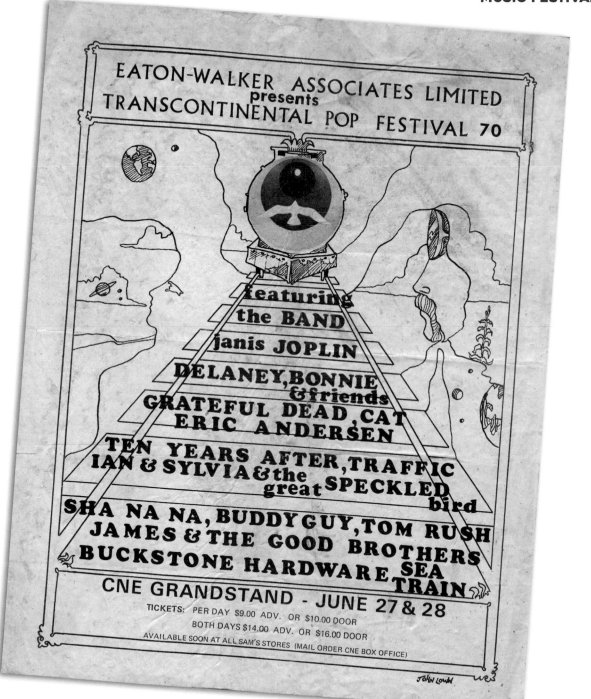

June 27–28, 1970, CNE Grandstand

Bonnie and Friends, Traffic, and Janis Joplin played extraordinary sets for those inside the stadium. Joplin would die three months later, and this would be Traffic's only appearance in Toronto in their original incarnation. The reviews in both the *Globe* and the *Star* mention Miles Davis as a no show, as he was listed in some of the festival's newspaper ads. Oddly enough, he does not appear to have ever been on the posters for the show.

Six weeks after Festival Express, John Brower, no longer a partner with Ken Walker, staged the Strawberry Fields Festival August 7–9 at Mosport Speedway, two hours east of Toronto. The festival grew out of a plan that John Lennon and Brower had for a Peace Festival that originally was announced by Lennon at a press conference in Toronto in December 1969. Lennon told the assembled throng of media that the stage would be like one giant bed covered by a massive mattress. The organizers hoped to get Elvis Presley and the other three Beatles to perform. Lennon ended up backing out, partially because by early 1970 the Beatles were in the throes of disintegrating and also he and Brower had disagreements as to whether or not the festival should be free. On February 25, 1970,

an official announcement was made that the festival was cancelled.

While the Peace Festival was dead, Brower decided to go ahead with what he now called the Strawberry Fields Festival. He had planned to stage the event in Shediac, near Moncton, New Brunswick. When local officials in New Brunswick refused to grant the necessary permits, Brower moved the festival to Mosport. To avoid permit issues in Ontario, Brower played down the music aspect of the festival, advertising the weekend as "The First Annual Strawberry Cup Trophy Race," featuring a championship motorcycle race and "some contemporary entertainment."

In the United States, Brower took a different tack, promoting the lineup heavily under the slogan "Love, Sun and Sound." While the festival posters listed Led Zeppelin and Leonard Cohen as scheduled to perform, the eventual lineup was headlined by Sly and the Family Stone, Grand Funk Railroad, and Ten Years After. Also appearing were Jethro Tull, Mountain, José Feliciano, Richie Havens, Melanie, Procol Harum, Alice Cooper, the Youngbloods, Syrinx, and a host of other local bands.

August 7–9, 1970, Mosport Park

Despite an attempt by local authorities to stop the festival the day before, their request for an injunction was denied. It is estimated that between 75,000 and 100,000 people came, the majority from the United States. On the Facebook page dedicated to the festival, it is amazing how many Americans have posted stories about hitchhiking to the festival with no money or tickets, meeting people along the way, and having three of the greatest days of their life.

On the day of the event, after several motorcycle crashes occurred due to drivers riding in both directions at once, and a woman rode around the track on a motorcycle completely nude, it was announced that the motorcycle races were cancelled and the concert proper began. Apparently the medical tent dealt with an unbelievable number of overdoses. The festival finished with a very high Sly Stone coming on at 4:30 a.m. and finishing his set as the sun came up.

In 1971, Cymba mounted three one-day mini-festivals at the Borough of York Stadium, each of which was called Beggar's Banquet. On June 26, Lighthouse, Chilliwack, Bread, the Beach Boys, Bloodrock, Alice Cooper, and Steppenwolf performed. Sly and the Family Stone were scheduled but cancelled. On July 18, Steel River, the Grease Band (without Joe Cocker), Humble Pie, Black Sabbath (in their first Toronto appearance), and Three Dog Night provided the day's entertainment. The Humble Pie set mirrored their *Performance Rockin' the Fillmore* album from the same tour, and was mesmerizing. The final Beggar's Banquet festival that summer was held August 21, and featured Sundance, Edgar Winter and White Trash, Lee Michaels, Sha Na Na, Seatrain, and Toronto's beloved the Band.

June 26, 1971,
Borough of York Stadium

Several years after the Strawberry Fields Festival, Mosport would be used for two other large-scale rock festivals: Canada Jam (August 25, 1978) and the Heatwave Festival (August 23, 1980).

The latter was an extraordinary event, promoted by John Brower of Toronto Rock and Roll Revival and Strawberry Fields fame, featuring the first performance by the newly expanded nine-piece Talking Heads, who debuted their funk-imbued *Remain in Light* material. This was followed by a blistering set by Elvis Costello and the Attractions, who closed the festival with five energy-fuelled encores. Also entertaining the audience of 45,000 that day were Rockpile, the Pretenders, and the B-52's. The Clash had been originally scheduled, but did not show up. The event lost a reported one million dollars.

There would be many subsequent festivals in the Toronto area over the years, including a one-off jazz festival at Varsity Stadium in the early 1970s and a great one-off two-day blues festival on the Toronto Islands in 1974, featuring Son House and Bobby "Blue" Bland. In the punk era, in addition to Heatwave, the Garys put

July 13–14, 1974,
Toronto Island

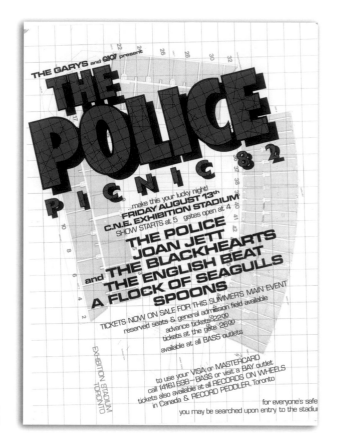

August 13, 1982,
CNE

the Specials, Iggy Pop, and the Police. The Garys apparently tried to get a very young Prince booked for the festival, but came up empty handed. In 1982 and 1983, they moved the event to CNE Stadium. Both years were stellar, but 1983 especially stands out for killer sets by Nigerian King Sunny Ade, James Brown (although he endured a rough reception from the audience), and Peter Tosh.

The Toronto Jazz Festival became an annual event starting in 1987, followed two years later by the Beaches Jazz Festival. CFNY mounted Edgefest in 1987, which continued for three decades. From 1988 through 1992, the WOMAD (World of Music, Arts, and Dance) festival brought an astonishing array of world music artists to Toronto, including Sufi Qawwali singer Nusrat Fateh Ali Khan, Zimbabwean chimurenga musician Thomas Mapfumo, Malian blues god Ali Farka Touré, Tuscarora native Pura Fé, and a stunning acoustic concert by Ry Cooder and David Lindley. The latter ended with an insane version of "Wooly Bully." The Nusrat and Cooder shows remain among the greatest concerts of my life.

on the Police Picnic for three consecutive years. On August 23, 1981, the event was held in Oakville's Kiev Park (which for some reason was called the Grove in both the ads and reviews of the festival). Thirty thousand fans showed up to hear John Otway, Killing Joke, Nash the Slash, Oingo Boingo, the Payola$, the Go-Go's,

From 1991 through 1997, Jane's Addiction lead singer Perry Farrell's Lollapalooza Festival came to the Toronto area, the first year at CNE Stadium (August 7), with subsequent years (except 1997) being held at Molson Park near Barrie. The annual event presented outstanding lineups featuring the finest alternative rock and hip hop acts, including Nine Inch Nails, Butthole Surfers, Ice Cube, Red Hot Chili Peppers, Pearl Jam, Rage Against the Machine, Fishbone, Beastie Boys, Nick Cave, George Clinton, A Tribe Called Quest, the Smashing Pumpkins, Hole, Sonic Youth, Beck, Metallica, the Ramones, and Snoop Doggy Dogg. Looking at the Lollapalooza lineups year by year, the quality of the musical talent is stunning, and reminds one of the great festivals of the late 1960s and early 1970s.

In 1993, the Tragically Hip mounted the two-night travelling "Another Roadside Attraction" festival. The first year featured the Hip, Hothouse Flowers, Midnight Oil, Daniel Lanois, and Headstones. The festival was held again in 1995 and 1997.

That same year, Molly Johnson, former lead singer of Alta Moda, put together the

September 2, 1984, Lamport Stadium

first Kumbaya Festival. Held every year at Molson Amphitheatre, and broadcast nationally by MuchMusic, proceeds from the festival were given to Canadian organizations doing work on HIV and AIDS. The festival was held between 1993 and 1996, and over those four years, between ticket sales,

July 5, 1996,
Molson Park

broadcast advertising, and donations through a toll-free number, more than a million dollars was raised. In addition to rock music performers such as Blue Rodeo, Cowboy Junkies, the Tragically Hip, Mary Margaret O'Hara, Lorraine Segato, Barenaked Ladies, Junkhouse, Blackie and the Rodeo Kings, Alex Lifeson, and Jeff Healey, the festival featured dub poets Lillian Allen and Clifton Joseph, Indigenous artists Shingoose and Derek Miller, rappers Michie Mee and Dream Warriors, and readings by authors, and speeches by AIDS activists.

In 1995 the Warped Festival debuted. Advertised as an "Extreme Sport and Music Festival," the event featured demonstrations of skateboarding, wall climbing, surfing, and snowboarding plus punk/hardcore bands such as L7, Quicksand, SNFU, Skankin' Pickle, Orange, Seaweed, No Use for a Name, and Swingin' Utters. In 1996 the shoe manufacturer Vans took over sponsorship of the tour and the name was changed to the Vans Warped Tour. The July 1996 Toronto stop was held at the Docks and featured Fishbone, Beck, Blink-182, 311, Dick Dale, and NOFX. In 1997 the festival skipped Toronto, stopping in London, Ontario,

"This was my second Lollapalooza. Rage opened the show and slayed. They blew my mind. In the greatest moment of irony I ever witnessed, 35,000 people screaming 'Fuck you, I won't do what you tell me!' after being told to."

— Bill Aitkins
(Lollapalooza, Molson Park, 1993)

instead. In 1998 the festival returned to the Docks and included performances by Bad Religion, Fu Manchu, Incubus, Kid Rock, NOFX, Rancid, Reverend Horton Heat, and the Specials.

The year 1995 also marked the start of the successful Sno-Jam Festival. Featuring punk bands from both the United States and Canada, the festival crossed the country and was the first to integrate punk bands with the emerging X Games culture. An impressive list of bands played Sno-Jam in

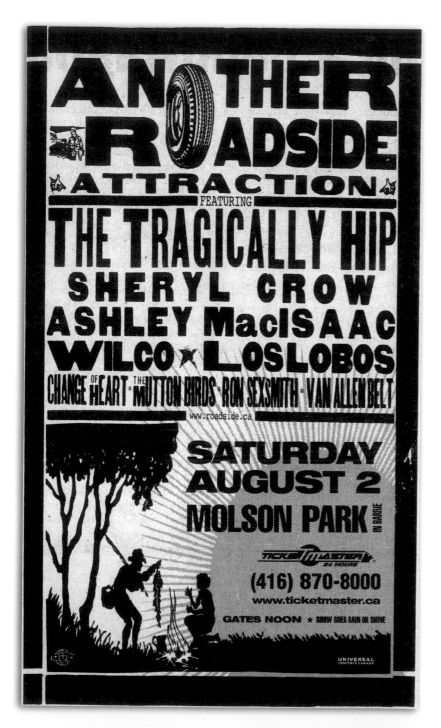

the late '90s, including Guttermouth, AFI, Blink-182, SNFU, and Anti-Flag.

The last great festival of the 20th century in Toronto was Sarah McLachlan's Lilith Fair, held each year over two nights from 1997 through 1999 at the Molson Amphitheatre. The concept of the festival partially arose when McLachlan was told it would be bad for the box office if she had a female artist open up for her. Her response was to mount a travelling all female artist tour. The Lilith Fair festivals made McLachlan's point loud and clear and were unqualified successes. The first year included Shawn Colvin, Jewel, and Indigo Girls; the second, Natalie Merchant, Liz Phair, Emmylou Harris, and Diana Krall; while the last featured the Dixie Chicks, Deborah Cox, and Sheryl Crow. McLachlan closed out the festival every night each year and a number of lesser-known artists were featured on a second stage.

August 2, 1997, Molson Park

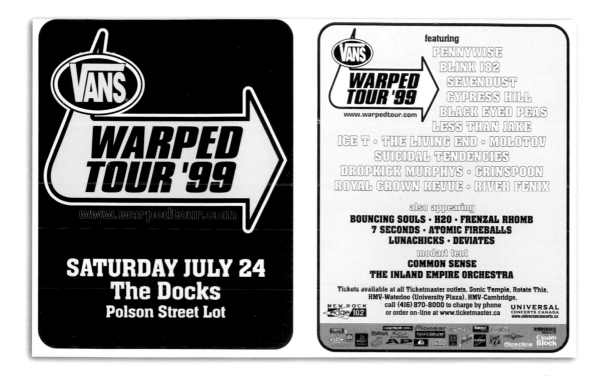

July 24, 1999,
the Docks

"As two people left, I saw the backstage sticker/passes on them, so I said, 'Yo, can I have one of those?' and the girl was like, 'Yeah, sure,' and then I went back, and it was sorta like that *Wayne's World* moment when I just danced past security and ended up on stage during Suicidal Tendencies ... It was def an epic moment for me."

— Philip Rayos (Vans Warped Tour, 1999)

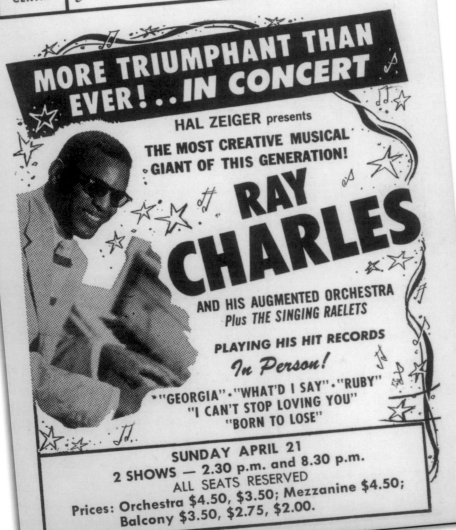

April 21, 1963, O'Keefe Centre

10

SOUL AND R&B

Prior to the opening up of Canada's immigration laws in 1962 and 1967, Toronto was a very WASP-dominated city. Despite the demographic composition, in the 1960s "Toronto the good" was a staunch R&B town. Local heroes the Hawks (later the Band), Jon and Lee and the Checkmates, Dianne Brooks and Eric Mercury and the Soul Searchers, the Rogues, Kay Taylor and the Regents, Bobby Dean and the Gems, Shawne and Jay Jackson and the Majestics, and Jackie Shane were playing R&B- and soul-influenced music nightly at Club Bluenote, the Brass Rail, and Le Coq d'Or on Yonge Street; the Saphire Tavern on Richmond; the Holiday on Queen; and the Concord Tavern on Bloor near Ossington. Many of

April 27, 1963, Maple Leaf Gardens

the city's rock bands of the period, including the Domenic Troiano–led bands Mandala and Bush, George Olliver, Robbie Lane and the Disciples, and Luke and the Apostles, also played music heavily influenced by black musicians. Many of the musicians and a number of fans would drive to Buffalo to buy soul records that were not available locally. There was also a store at 59 Avenue Road near Yorkville called the Village Record Shop (later the Record Villa) that made a point of importing lots of great American R&B and gospel records.

The first appearance by a soul artist in Toronto was arguably Sam Cooke, who headlined a rock and roll package tour at Maple Leaf Gardens on April 27, 1958. Two years later, Ray Charles rolled into town for the first time, playing two shows at Massey Hall on June 8, 1960. The Charles show was billed "Hit-Makers of 1960!" and included Ruth Brown, the Drifters, Marv Johnson, Redd Foxx, the Ray Bryant Trio, Ron Holden, Billy Bland, Preston Epps, and the Doc Bagby Band. At the time, Charles was unbelievably hot, having taken the pop charts by storm the previous summer with "What'd I Say." Since then

MASSEY HALL
WED., JUNE 8
2 SHOWS — 7.30 p.m., 10 p.m.

HIT-MAKERS OF 1960

Starring **IN PERSON!**

The Most Creative
Musical Giant
of this Generation!

RAY CHARLES
HIS ORCHESTRA
AND THE RAELETS
Playing His Hit Records
"WHAT'D I SAY"
"ROCK HOUSE"
"COME RAIN OR COME SHINE"
"JUST FOR A THRILL"
"LET THE GOOD TIMES ROLL"
"GENIUS OF RAY CHARLES"

RUTH BROWN
"Don't Deceive Me"
"Teardrops From My Eyes"

DRIFTERS
"This Magic Moment"
"There Goes My Baby"

MARV JOHNSON
"You Got What It Takes"
"I Love The Way You Love"

REDD FOXX
"Laugh Of The Party"
"The Best Laff"

Extra Added! **RAY BRYANT TRIO**
"Madison Time"

RON HOLDEN
"Love You So"

BILLY BLAND
"Let The Little Girl Dance"

PRESTON EPPS
"Bongo, Bongo, Bongo"

DOC BAGBY BAND

Tickets Now on Sale
Box Office, Massey Hall
A. & A. Book Store
Promenade Music Centre
All Seats Reserved
$2.00, $2.50, $3.00, $3.50

June 8, 1960,
Massey Hall

he had repeatedly hit the charts with his cover of Hank Snow's "I'm Movin' On," the ballad "Don't Let the Sun Catch You Crying," and, right as the show pulled into town, Titus Turner's "Sticks and Stones." Unfortunately, neither the *Globe and Mail* nor the *Star* chose to review the show. If I ever get a time machine, this will be one of the first shows I go back to!

Starting in 1962, the Masonic Temple hosted dances run by Norm Muir, who named the venue Club 888 after its Yonge Street address. Typically two bands would play at Muir's dances with a rotating stage

"I went on the first night of her six-night run, then went back every single night after. I would arrive early to get the best seat in the house. Ruth was the personification of class and soul, with emotional experience and depth in her sound."

— Aaron Keele, The Record Guys
(Ruth Brown, Bermuda Onion, 1990)

enabling one band to set up while the other was playing their set. On more than one occasion, as the stage began to turn, the band that had just set up would start playing a previously agreed upon song along with the band that was finishing up, enabling a seamless transition between sets.

Weekly ads appeared in the newspapers advertising dancing at the club every Friday and Saturday. Unfortunately, the ads were generic and never mentioned which acts were actually playing at the dances, instead listing a phone number one could call to find out what artist would be at the club that week. Fortunately, one of the columnists in the *Toronto Star* would sometimes list shows he thought would be worth checking out. On these occasions he often mentioned soul artists who were playing Club 888. The Supremes played there on Friday, March 13, 1964. This is the first time a gig by a Motown artist in Toronto was mentioned in a newspaper, although Ray Harrison recalls his band, Anthony and the Apollos, opening up for the Supremes at the Brave New World teen club on Davenport in 1962 or 1963. (This could have actually been after the gig at Club 888, but for the record, Duff Roman, who owned Brave New World, says the Supremes did not play there.) Other internet posters have mentioned that both Doris Troy and Little Eva played Brave New World after sets at Club 888. I would love to know more about that club and those gigs.

The night after the Supremes' Club 888 show, the group appeared with Matt Lucas and Kelly Jay and the Jamies at the Masaryk Hall at 220 Cowan Avenue near Queen and Lansdowne. After the Masaryk gig they went by Club Bluenote to sit in. Bringing their weekend to a close, on Sunday, March 15, the Supremes played a Catholic Youth Organization gig at the St. Rose of Lima Catholic Church at 3260 Lawrence East! This was typical of promoter Howie Moore's modus operandi. Whenever he brought an artist to town to play the Masaryk, he would also book one or two other local gigs for the artist. After the Saturday night Masaryk show, he would take the artists to the Bluenote on Yonge Street to sit in with the house band. One of his favourite nights was when Tommy Hunt closed down the Bluenote at 4:00 a.m. singing "Old Man River." "He was bending down on his knees and really tearing the shit out of everybody that was in the audience," says Moore, smiling.

Soul music at the Masaryk Hall has an interesting history. For a period of about six months, Howie Moore and Ron Scribner ran the first rock agency in the city, booking bands such as Little Caesar and the Consuls and Robbie Lane and the Disciples. Moore next started promoting dances at the Masaryk Hall every Saturday. Most Saturdays it was just Moore spinning soul records that he picked up on his once-a-week trips to Buffalo, but whenever possible, he would bring in R&B acts from the States. Motown founder Berry Gordy had convinced him to bring in the Supremes for the three shows March 13–15, 1964. He recalls very clearly the moment the Supremes first pulled into town: "They showed up with their mother driving the station wagon!"

His first show at the Masaryk featured Maxine Brown and Chuck Jackson. Between late 1962 and 1966, in addition to the Supremes, Tommy Hunt, and Maxine Brown and Chuck Jackson, Moore brought to town Junior Walker, Barbara George, the Vibrations, and Timi Yuro, among others. None of these shows were advertised in the newspapers. Instead, Moore made his own posters, having agents send him eight-by-ten promotional pictures of the artists, putting them on card stock, and hanging them up around local high schools. In between the live sets, Moore would DJ at the club, in his own words "spinning records that Al Slaight [program director of CHUM radio] said were too racial for CHUM." In 1966, when the Toronto Musicians' Union told Moore he had to use local bands to back up the visiting artists or the union would shut him down, he decided to pack up his tent and head down to New Orleans. That was Toronto's loss.

Doris Troy, alongside a host of local artists, appeared at Club 888 on April 2, 1964, in a benefit concert for the Easter Seals campaign. Jimmy Ruffin played there in 1966 backed by Richie Knight and the Mid-Knights (when the Mid-Knights still included King Biscuit Boy). Apparently, Club 888 also booked the finest blue-eyed soul groups of the day, bringing in the Righteous Brothers (most likely in 1965) and the Spencer Davis Group with Stevie Winwood in 1965 or 1966. According to internet comments, Clarence "Frogman" Henry, Little

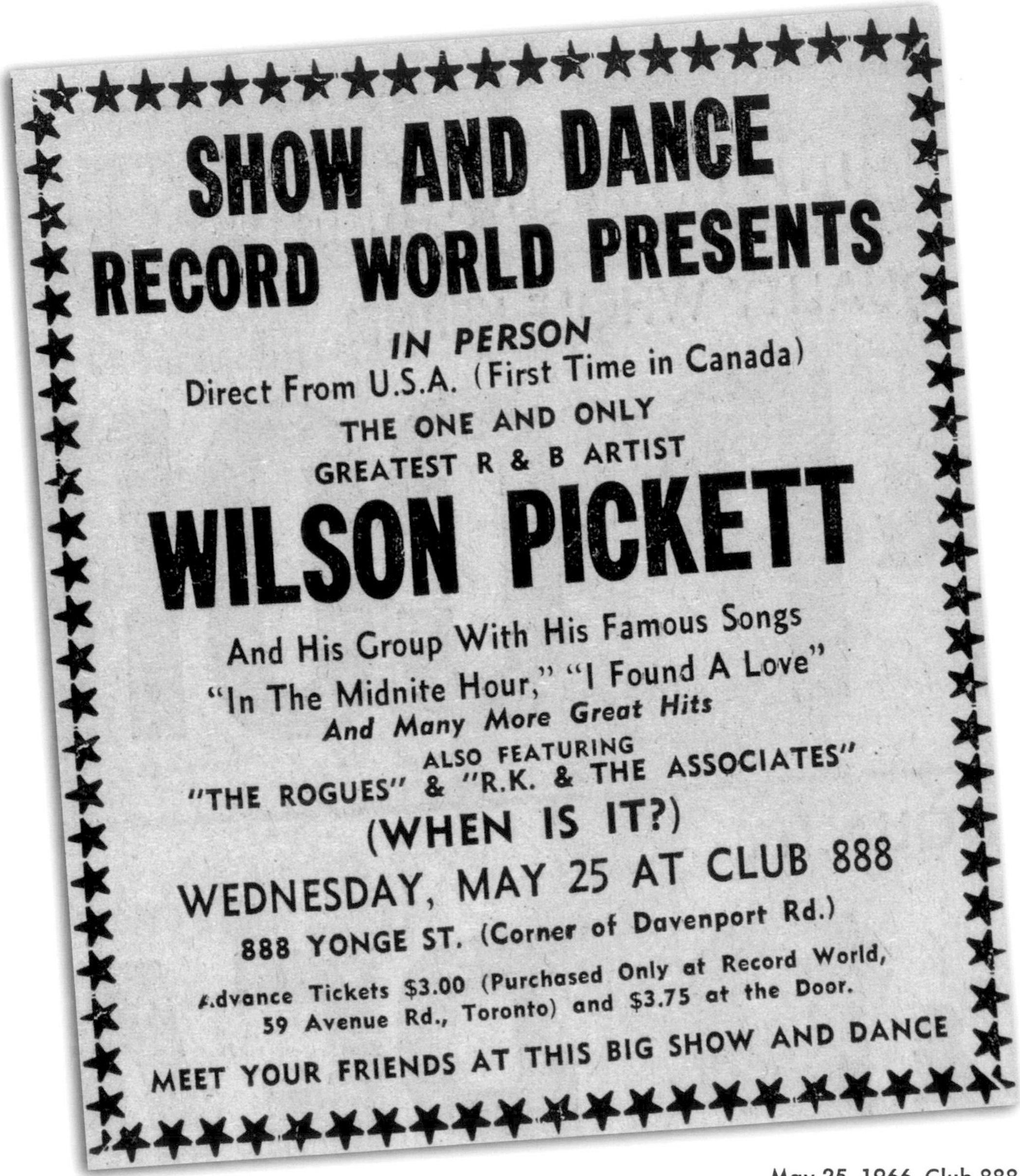

SHOW AND DANCE
RECORD WORLD PRESENTS

IN PERSON
Direct From U.S.A. (First Time in Canada)
THE ONE AND ONLY
GREATEST R & B ARTIST

WILSON PICKETT

And His Group With His Famous Songs
"In The Midnite Hour," "I Found A Love"
And Many More Great Hits
ALSO FEATURING
"THE ROGUES" & "R.K. & THE ASSOCIATES"

(WHEN IS IT?)
WEDNESDAY, MAY 25 AT CLUB 888
888 YONGE ST. (Corner of Davenport Rd.)
Advance Tickets $3.00 (Purchased Only at Record World,
59 Avenue Rd., Toronto) and $3.75 at the Door.
MEET YOUR FRIENDS AT THIS BIG SHOW AND DANCE

May 25, 1966, Club 888

Eva, and Bobby Goldsboro also appeared at Club 888 sometime during this period and the local dynamic duo, Jon and Lee and the Checkmates, were regulars at the club.

In May 1966, Wilson Pickett appeared at Club 888. This was his first Toronto appearance. The Rogues, R.K. and the Associates, and Bobby Kris and the Imperials provided support. With "In the Midnight Hour" tearing up the charts, the "Wicked" Pickett must have burned the place down! In Pickett's band that night were Buddy Miles on drums and a then unknown guitarist named Jimi Hendrix.

The latter fact is apparently not generally known in the world of Hendrix biographers and collectors. I stumbled on this while reading an online interview with the late Marty Fisher, who was the keyboard player with Bobby Kris and the Imperials. The group's drummer, Gordon MacBain, confirmed in a phone interview with me that Hendrix was indeed with Pickett that night. He distinctly remembers that Pickett's guitarist played with his teeth and that all the Toronto musicians were raving about this guitarist for several weeks following the show (of course, no one at that point knew what his name was or that he would be famous within a year!).

Mike McKenna, lead guitarist of Luke and the Apostles and later McKenna Mendelson Mainline, was in the audience that night and was stunned to see Pickett's guitarist playing left-handed with an upside-down right-handed guitar. When Hendrix became famous a year later, the local musicians who were at the Pickett gig realized that Jimi Hendrix was the gunslinger they had seen with Pickett. By all accounts Hendrix literally stole the show! Pickett was back just over four months later, playing a show with the Paupers opening up at Club Kingsway.

On November 23, 1966, Ike and Tina Turner made their first appearance in Toronto, not surprisingly at Club 888. The *Toronto Star* reviewer was clearly taken with Tina, writing, "I can't remember seeing anything quite like her before. And judging from last night's crowd, no one else had either.... The girl moves, ripples, writhes, throbs — she's so supple, so lithe you'd swear there wasn't a bone in her body."

Unfortunately, besides saying in general terms that the show was fantastic, as

7.00 p.m. — **TONIGHT** — 9.30 p.m.

DYNAMIC JAZZ SHOW

LITTLE STEVIE WONDER SHOW

13 year old blind genius of the drums, organ, piano, bongos & harmonica—Hit records: Finger-tips 1 & 2, Castle in the Sand & Jazz Soul of Stevie.

. . . PLUS . . .

FABULOUS BABE WAYNE SHOW
MONTICELLOS VOCAL GROUP
CANADA'S OWN "SPELLBINDER GIRL" JUDI JANSEN
ROBBIE LANE AND THE DISCIPLES
BIG NORM SHEPPARD "The Comical" M.C.

2 SHOWS — FRIDAY, APRIL 10, 7 P.M., 9.30 P.M.

MASSEY HALL

Tickets: $2.00 — $2.75 — $3.50 — Box Office
SAM THE RECORD MAN, 347 YONGE STREET

April 10, 1964, Massey Hall

per usual very little was written about the actual music. Approximately 1,200 people attended the 1966 show, but only 400 showed up when Ike and Tina returned on September 27, 1967. My guess is that the low turnout in 1967 was due to Club 888's policy of not advertising specific shows. Arthur Conley's gig on May 31, 1967, is the last soul listing that we could find for Club 888. We will probably never know what other cool soul artists came to the club between 1962 and 1967 before it was turned into the Rock Pile in late 1968, bringing in the hippest rock groups of the day.

The Supremes may have been the first Motown act to play in Toronto, but 13-year-old Little Stevie Wonder was the first Motown artist to play a major venue when he performed two shows at Massey Hall on April 10, 1964. Unfortunately there were no reviews of Wonder's show, but many musicians remember that he dropped by Club Bluenote after the Massey Hall gig and jammed. He would be back in July 1972, opening up for the Rolling Stones for two concerts at Maple Leaf Gardens that people still talk about nearly a half-century later!

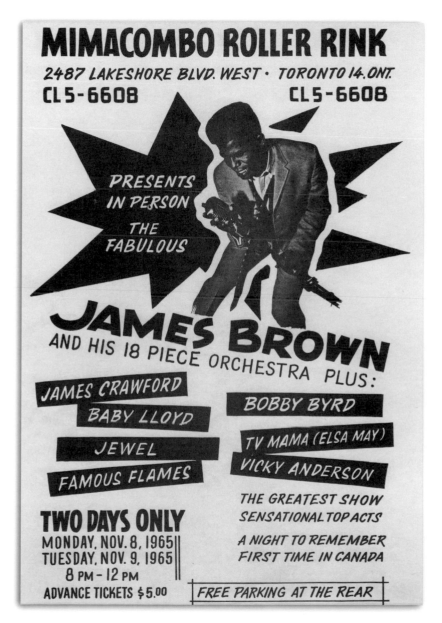

November 8–9, 1965, Mimicombo Roller Rink

The most exciting early soul show in Toronto has to be James Brown and the Famous Flames' appearance November 9, 1965, at the Mimicombo Roller Rink at 2487 Lakeshore Boulevard West. As fate would have it, that was the night of the famous blackout on the eastern seaboard that shut down New York, Boston, Toronto, and a host of other cities. In what might be a testimony to the power of soul, the only electricity still on in all of Toronto was for some unknown reason in the small segment of Mimico where the show took place. I have read an account of four teenagers leaving for the show from Scarborough when the power suddenly shut down, rendering all traffic lights null and void. These fans were undeterred, headed for the show anyway, and were delighted upon arriving to find the lights on at the Mimicombo. When the show was over and they headed back to Scarborough, totally transfixed by what they had encountered that night, they were stunned to find the whole city was still blacked out. Their parents were apparently frantic when they finally got home, as people all over the city were trapped in elevators, many couldn't make it home for the night, and there was a much higher level of crime than usual due to the blackout. James Brown was clearly unstoppable. Brown played Maple Leaf Gardens in 1967, twice in 1968 (April and November), and again in 1969. Brown's next stop in Toronto was at Massey Hall in the early 1970s.

The Supremes, now superstars, played the O'Keefe Centre for a week in 1966 and again for a week in 1968. The Staple Singers, repositioned from their role as gospel stars in the 1950s to soul-folk musicians, played the Mariposa Folk Festival in both 1966 and 1967. In October 1967 they came back to the Toronto area to play the Riverboat for a week. It would not be until 1987, when Derek Andrews booked them at Harbourfront, that the group would return to Toronto once again.

On October 15, 1967, Otis Redding was scheduled to play the CNE Coliseum. Unfortunately, in September he had an operation to remove nodules from his vocal chords and cancelled all dates for a couple of months. Tragically, he would die in a plane crash December 10, on the way to a gig in Madison, Wisconsin, and never did play Toronto. Four days after the cancelled

Redding date, Ray Charles played two shows at Massey Hall, once again tearing the roof off the building while permanently changing the lives of all who were there.

By 1968, a number of clubs, including the Colonial, the Embassy, and Friar's Tavern, began to book soul artists for a week at a time. The Colonial brought in the Hesitations, the Embassy booked Gladys Knight and the Pips, and Friar's brought in Jimmy Ruffin, all in the first six months of that year. Patti LaBelle and the Blue Belles played two weeks at the Hook and Ladder Club in the Beverly Hills Motor Hotel as part of Chubby Checker's Freak Out Revue in May 1968. They had first appeared in Toronto opening up for the Rolling Stones in 1965.

Aretha Franklin was scheduled to make her Toronto debut at Maple Leaf Gardens August 18, 1968. Six thousand fans had bought tickets, but three hours before showtime, the concert was cancelled and then rescheduled for September 29. The official reason was that Aretha had a virus, but according to Ian Harrison of opening group the Mission, that wasn't what really happened. At the sound check, members of Aretha's band told Ian that the night before, after a show in Cleveland, Aretha's husband and manager, the notorious Ted White, had knocked her down backstage and broke her arm. While both groups played the requisite sound checks, Aretha's band told the Mission that they doubted that Aretha would be coming. The rescheduled gig, set for September 29, was also cancelled, supposedly due to scheduling conflicts due to recording obligations. It's curious that these recording sessions didn't interfere with a gig in Pittsburgh four days later. Aretha would not actually play her first Toronto concert until September 12, 1981, at the Ontario Place Forum.

Joe Tex came to Massey Hall September 15, 1968, with the incomparable Jackie Shane opening up. That November, Wilson Pickett, with country singer Jeannie C. Riley and soul artists the Fantastic Johnny C and the Masqueraders, played the O'Keefe Centre.

In early 1969, George Clinton's Parliament began to play the Hawk's Nest and Le Coq d'Or. Soon they were managed by Ron Scribner, who booked the two clubs, and several members of the group, including George, Bootsy Collins, and Bernie Worrell,

Club Bluenote
372½ YONGE ST. — 368-0410
(Just South of Gerrard)

The Parliaments
— plus —
THE STATLERS
Fri.-Sat.-Sun.—8.30 p.m.-4 a.m.

June 13–15, 1969,
Club Bluenote

up the charts with "Tear the Roof Off the Sucker (Give Up the Funk)," "Flash Light," and "One Nation Under a Groove."

In the late 1960s and the first half of the 1970s, Le Coq d'Or presented King Curtis and the Kingpins, the Commodores, Billy Stewart, Ben E. King, the Jimmy Castor Bunch, The Bar-Kays, Carolyn Franklin, Little Charles and the Sidewinders, the Undisputed Truth, Tavares, Quiet Elegance, Solomon Burke, the Sweet Inspirations, and Carla Thomas. Jay Douglas's group, the Cougars, were also a regular at Le Coq d'Or during this period. While not as active in terms of bringing in soul artists as Le Coq d'Or, the Colonial did book Young-Holt Unlimited, Maxine Brown, Chuck Jackson, Sam and Dave, and Martha Reeves and the Vandellas.

In August 1969, Al Steiner opened Soul City at 167 Church Street (later known as Club Trinidad and even later as the Party Centre). A former real estate agent, during the 1950s Steiner and his wife regularly vacationed in Florida. While down south, Steiner listened non-stop to black appeal radio stations. Suitably inspired, he decided to give up the real estate business and

moved to Toronto. Their shows at the Hawk's Nest were allegedly wilder than anything the city had ever seen and have become the stuff of legend. Oddly, they never played Toronto in their prime when both Parliament and their alter ego, Funkadelic, were tearing founded Club Bluenote on Yonge Street just north of Gerrard. From 1960 to 1969, the Bluenote was one of the first after-hours clubs in Toronto, staying open until 3:00 or 4:00 a.m. on weekends.

The house band at the Bluenote changed over the years. Bobby Dean and the Gems were there from 1959 through October 1960. They were followed by Kay Taylor and the Regents, who held down the job until August 1962, at which point the Silhouettes, featuring organist Doug Riley and saxophonist Steve Kennedy, took over. In early autumn 1964, Domenic Troiano's group the Rogues became the house band, staying on until early 1965. The last two house bands were the lesser-known Peepers and the Statlers. The featured singers were the cream of what Toronto had to offer, including Shawne and Jay Jackson, Jay Smith, Dianne Brooks, and Eric Mercury.

The downside of the Bluenote was that it only could hold 150 people, which meant it was not a viable option as a place to book big names. Hence, Steiner's decision to open Soul City. A former labour hall, and before that an athletic club for gentlemen, Soul City could hold 2,500 people. Steiner

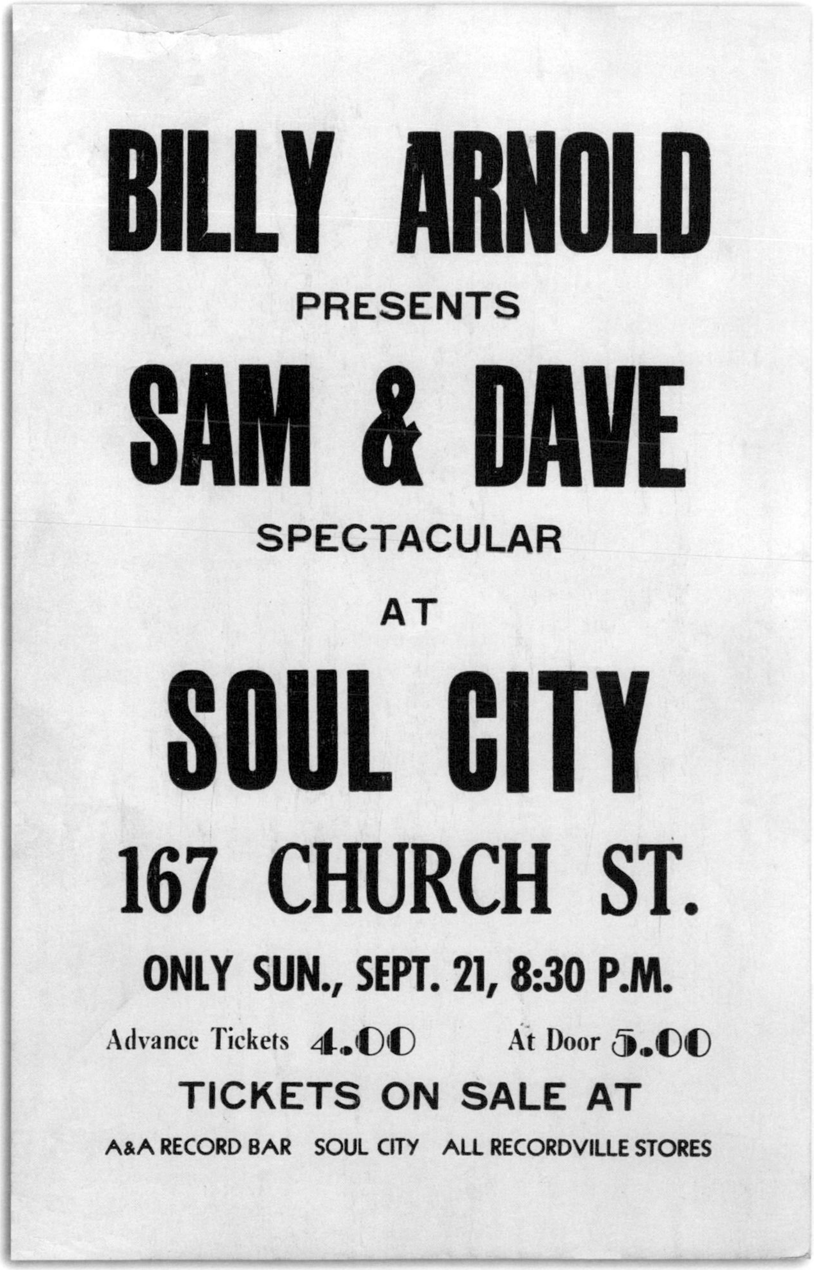

BILLY ARNOLD

PRESENTS

SAM & DAVE

SPECTACULAR

AT

SOUL CITY

167 CHURCH ST.

ONLY SUN., SEPT. 21, 8:30 P.M.

Advance Tickets 4.00   At Door 5.00

TICKETS ON SALE AT

A&A RECORD BAR   SOUL CITY   ALL RECORDVILLE STORES

September 21, 1969, Soul City

April 3, 1970, Maple Leaf Gardens
(Sly & the Family Stone cancelled and were
replaced by Delaney and Bonnie and Friends)

opened the club August 22, 1969, with Motown star Jimmy Ruffin. Over the next several weekends he booked in Little Carl Carlton, the Vibrations, the Precisions, Sam and Dave, and, September 26–28, the Esquires. Amazingly enough, there is no other mention of Soul City after the end of September. Whether there were additional shows and when and why it closed down, there is simply no information available.

Sly Stone was notorious for cancelling local appearances, but he did play festivals in the area in 1969 and 1970 and an infamous indoor show at the Wentworth Curling Club in Hamilton with Bush and Crowbar opening up on August 2, 1970. The Wentworth Curling Club show was so oversold that the temperature inside must have reached 110 degrees Fahrenheit. Numerous concertgoers fainted and had to be carried out. As per usual, Sly came on extremely late, and after about 30 minutes asked for the stage lights to be turned off due to the heat. Halfway through the next song, the band stopped. Sly said his drummer had fainted, and the show was over. A year later, Sly finally managed to make it to Maple Leaf Gardens. In 1982, he played

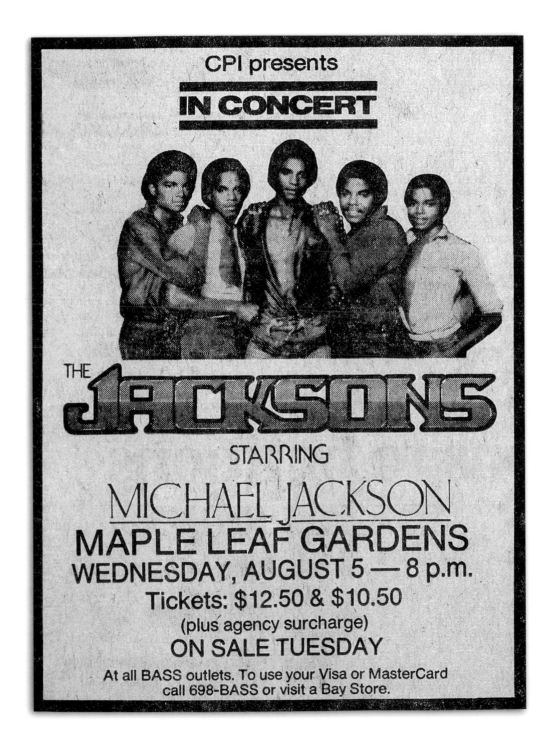

August 5, 1981,
Maple Leaf Gardens

ONE WEEK ONLY! MAY 21-26

THE ISAAC HAYES MOVEMENT
starring
ISAAC HAYES
special guest stars **HOT, BUTTERED AND SOUL**

MON.-THURS. 8:30 P.M.	$7.00	$5.50	$4.50	$3.50
FRIDAY 8:30 P.M.	$8.00	$6.50	$5.00	$3.50
SAT. 7:00 & 10:00 P.M.	$8.00	$6.50	$5.00	$3.50

MAIL ORDERS NOW!
BEFORE BOX OFFICE OPENS MAY 8
WHEN ORDERING BY MAIL
SHELL, CHARGEX & AMERICAN EXPRESS CARDS ACCEPTED
To help us process your order please send us a cheque (or signed Shell invoice, Chargex or American Express card number) with the amount left blank but marked ON THE BOTTOM OF YOUR CHEQUE "not to exceed . . ." Make your cheque or money order payable to O'Keefe Centre and mail to O'KEEFE CENTRE, Front and Yonge, Toronto M5E 1B2. Please include stamped self-addressed envelope.
TICKETS MAY ALSO BE ORDERED AT EATON'S ATTRACTIONS TICKET OFFICE OR PHONE 364-6487 AND CHARGE TO YOUR EATON'S AC-COUNT.
TICKET AGENCIES: TORONTO — Salsberg's, Moodeys, OAKVILLE — John Black, HAMILTON — Connaught, Maple Leaf, COOKSVILLE — Marmac, BURLINGTON — Brant.
SPECIAL GROUP RATES — 366-8484

DINNER — In the Theatre before evening performances For reservations phone 366-8484
DANCING — In the main lounge after opening nights and Friday and Saturday evening performances No minimum or cover charge.

May 21–26, 1973, O'Keefe Centre

two shows for the Garys at the Nickelodeon on Yonge Street. Sly was in pretty bad shape at that point, and the shows lasted 12 and 18 minutes respectively!

Dionne Warwick played the O'Keefe Centre in both 1970 and 1971 (she had first played Toronto as a relative unknown on a bill with Sam Cooke at Maple Leaf Gardens in 1963). At the first O'Keefe show she was backed up by Moe Koffman's band. By 1970, the CNE had started booking a number of soul stars as part of the annual grandstand shows during the Canadian National Exhibition. The Temptations, with Yvonne Fair as the opening act, played the Grandstand in 1970, as did Ray Charles. The Jackson 5 played the Grandstand the following year. The Jacksons would return in the early 1980s to Maple Leaf Gardens and to the CNE Stadium on their final tour with Michael Jackson in 1984.

Booker T. and the M.G.'s made their only Toronto appearance with original drummer Al Jackson when they opened up for CCR at Maple Leaf Gardens September 19, 1970. Ike and Tina Turner followed them into the Gardens a year later on December 3, 1971.

Perhaps the greatest soul show in the city's history took place on September 12, 1971.

American saxophonist King Curtis had been tragically stabbed to death by a pair of drug dealers that he encountered on the front steps of his home on August 13 of that year. A month later a tribute concert was mounted in Toronto at the Canadian Room at the Royal York Hotel. The majority of acts, including the Bar-Kays, Rufus Thomas, the Soul Children, the Dramatics, and the Emotions all recorded for Stax Records. In addition, Al Green made his first Toronto appearance along with Laura Lee, his girlfriend at the time. Rounding out the bill were Sam and Dave, and Wilson Pickett. What an insane night that must have been! Green wouldn't be back to Toronto until he played Massey Hall in June 1981.

With the album *Hot Buttered Soul*, Isaac Hayes pioneered a whole new approach to R&B, and, in the process, completely transformed the political economy of the black music industry. He first came to Toronto to play a week at the O'Keefe Centre May 21–26, 1973. He returned for five more nights August 13–17, 1974, and then came back again to play Maple Leaf Gardens Concert Bowl on November 19, 1975. Only 3,500 people turned out to the Gardens show, and

November 18, 1973, Massey Hall

it would not be until the 1990s that Hayes would return to Toronto, playing both Massey Hall and Roy Thomson Hall a number of times before his death in 2008. Barry White

COOKIE GILCHRIST and
CONCERT PRODUCTION INTERNATIONAL
presents

MARVIN GAYE

**IN HIS FIRST-EVER CANADIAN APPEARANCE
TOGETHER WITH**

IKE and TINA TURNER
and TAVARES

MAPLE LEAF GARDENS
FEBRUARY 6, 7:30 P.M.

**MAPLE LEAF GARDENS INTRODUCES
SPECIAL SOUND FOR THIS EVENT**

**BENEFIT CONCERT FOR THE UNITED ATHLETES COALITION OF CANADA,
A NON-PROFIT, CHARITABLE ORGANIZATION**

If you cannot attend the concert, please send your donation to:
U.A.C.C., P.O. BOX 490, POSTAL STATION "Z" TORONTO, ONTARIO, M5N 1A0.
Receipts will be sent for income tax purposes.
Cheque or Money Order should be made payable to United Athletes Coalition of Canada.

$6.60, $7.70, $8.80

Tickets available at Maple Leaf Gardens, Simpsons, A&A Records, Salsberg's,
and Eaton's Ticket Agency — Simpsons Phone In Charge 861-2333

1. JOHN AGRO	5. KID GAVILAN	9. JOE LOUIS	13. ALEX PONTON
2. MUHAMMAD ALI	6. ROSEY GRIER	10. JOHN MUNRO	14. PETE ROZELLE
3. HOWARD COSELL	7. SAM HUFF	11. JOE NAMATH	15. O. J. SIMPSON
4. JAKE GAUDAUR	8. JACK KEMP	12. MARCEL PRONOVOST	16. BOB JOHNSON

followed Hayes's first Toronto show, playing Massey Hall with local reggae legend Jackie Mittoo supporting on November 18, 1973.

On February 6, 1975, Marvin Gaye, Ike and Tina Turner, and Tavares were slotted to play Maple Leaf Gardens in a benefit concert for the United Athletes Coalition of Canada. Unfortunately, at the last moment, Tina Turner came down with a stomach ailment and cancelled. About 1,000 of the 13,000 fans in attendance asked for their money back, but the remaining fans witnessed Marvin Gaye deliver a stunning performance. Gaye would come back and do it again in the summer of 1983 at the CNE Bandshell while riding high with his hit "Sexual Healing."

While soul began to fade as a dominant genre of music in the second half of the 1970s, various legacy artists still came to town. One of the more interesting gigs took place in May 1978 when New Orleans piano player Professor Longhair was booked to play several nights at the El Mocambo. Longhair proved so strange to the management of the club that they paid him off and asked him not to finish out his run. Longhair would come back one more time in 1979 to play the Edge for the Garys. Chicago-born soul

February 6, 1975, Maple Leaf Gardens

singer and poet Gil Scott-Heron, famous for "The Revolution Will Not Be Televised" and "Johannesburg," made his Toronto debut at the El Mocambo May 27–29, 1976.

Between 1982 and 1992, George Olliver opened a new Club Bluenote on Pears Avenue. During the venue's 10-year run, Olliver booked a slew of great R&B artists, including the Dramatics, Solomon Burke, Sam and Dave, Wilson Pickett, Etta James, Hank Ballard and the Midnighters, Martha Reeves, and Mary Wells.

The last great soul/R&B performer of the 20th century was undoubtedly Prince. The Garys had tried to book Prince for the first Police Picnic in 1981, but unfortunately were unsuccessful. He finally played Toronto on December 2 and 3, 1984, filling Maple Leaf Gardens to capacity both nights, selling out with a single radio announcement and no print ad or poster. The rush for tickets was so intense that it crashed the then state-of-the-art BASS ticket system.

"It was an awesome show. He played a cover of 'Whole Lotta Love,' and he ordered pizza to give the audience. He opened with 'Musicology' from the new album at the time, and then he played 'Let's Go Crazy' and a suite of songs from *Purple Rain,* and even after all that, the set just kept getting better and better!"

— Rik Maclean (Prince, Air Canada Centre, June 2004)

October 5, 1988, Maple Leaf Gardens

October 1–3 1987, BamBoo

11 CALYPSO, REGGAE, AND DANCEHALL

In 2019, Toronto is one of the most multicultural cities in the world. But that was not always the case. Until Canada's laws were changed in 1962 and 1967 to make immigration based on merit rather than on where one was emigrating from, the city was pretty white. Nonetheless, in the 1950s, there were a few calypso shows going on in the city. On February 4, 1950, for example, the mysterious Don Jose and His Caribbean Calypso Boys held forth at the El Mocambo Tavern. Five years later, the Esso Tropitone Steelband, direct from Trinidad, played the CNE. This was the first time a steel band had come to Toronto. The Esso Tropitone Steelband came back to the CNE in 1957. This time one of their members, Selwyn "Sello" Gomes, elected to stay in Toronto.

Gomes went on to play an important role in the city's developing steel band culture.

In 1955, the Canadian Negro Women's Association (CNWA), which had formed a few years earlier with the goal of increasing the black community's visibility, staged a celebration of Caribbean music and culture called the Calypso Carnival. Eric Vernon "Tiger" Armstrong, whose stage name was Lord Power, organized the music for the event. The Calypso Carnival was held every year through 1964.

At the end of September 1957, a "Carib-Creole Carnival" featuring Haitian choreographer Jean-Léon Destiné and his Company of 20 from the Caribbean, including a steel band and the calypsonian Duke of Iron, played the Eaton Auditorium for two nights. A native of Trinidad, the Duke of Iron had moved to New York City as a teenager and for many years made his living as a star in New York clubs. He would be a regular visitor to Toronto, playing many times at the Frontenac Arms Hotel (306 Jarvis Street) and the Columbus Hotel (382 Sherbourne Street). In August 1957, another group, the Strangers, was playing the Barclay Hotel at Front and Simcoe Streets, mixing calypso and Canadian folk songs.

Although Toronto's black population was only 3,153 in 1961, in the late 1950s and early 1960s there were five different clubs owned and operated by Caribbean immigrants being run as private members clubs, which meant that they couldn't serve liquor but could stay open until four in the morning. The first such venue was Club One Two at 12 Adelaide Street East. In the late 1950s Club One Two featured Ray Carroll and his Jamaicans.

In June 1960, Harold Wintraub and Tiger Armstrong, a.k.a. Lord Power, opened the Calypso Club at 248 Yonge Street on the second floor above a men's clothing shop. A *Toronto Star* writer dryly commented on the club's opening, "Toronto's first calypso club opened over the weekend with more than 150 devotees of Caribbean music squeezed into a tiny room. Scantily clad waitresses attired in tropic costumes, eased among the patrons, carrying out soft drinks.… Like the jazz clubs which have sprung up throughout Toronto, it operates weekends, doesn't close until 4 a.m. and attracts the unusual as clients."

November 18, 1960, Caribbean Club

With a capacity of only 150 and a membership after their first year of 8,000, the Calypso Club moved to a larger location at 32 Front Street West in June 1961. The Tropitones, Toronto's only steel band, now lead by Selwyn Gomes, served as the house band. The Calypso Club closed in 1964. The Yonge Street location would reopen as the Club Jamaica a few years later, co-owned by manager and promoter Karl Mullings.

The Caribbean Club opened at 314 Yonge Street in the fall of 1960. It would soon relocate to larger premises at 51 Dundas Street West. The Little Trinidad Club was founded by a number of Trinidadian students at the University of Toronto. The club opened in the summer of 1961 with a steel band from Port of Spain, Trinidad, Los Trinidados, serving as the house band. Selwyn Gomes would eventually take over as leader of the house band while future activist lawyer Charles Roach led the Tropic Knights, who also regularly played at the club. The Mighty Sparrow played the club for two weeks in late 1964, and at various times Little Trinidad held benefits for hurricane relief efforts in the Caribbean. The club also once held a benefit for Malcolm X's widow. Little Trinidad closed its doors in either 1967 or 1968.

The Port of Spain, at 47 Laplante Avenue (near Bay and College), was in business by late 1961. The club was owned by a musician by the name of Eddy Edgehill, and the house band for a period was the ubiquitous Tropitones.

Calypso went mainstream in November 1966 when a "Calypso Festival" featuring "30 Authentic performers" was staged at Massey Hall. The two headliners were Lord Kitchener and Lord Brynner, and the rather salacious ad read "See the authentic rituals of the islands: the Devil Dance; Dance of Fire; the Exotic Rites — never before seen, performed by the beautiful Nevelle Shepard Dancers." Perhaps not surprisingly, the review in the *Toronto Star* was incredibly condescending and ethnocentric.

The Mighty Sparrow returned to Toronto to play the Ryerson Theatre May 27, 1967. A month later, the first Jamaican touring artist of note, Byron Lee and the Dragonaires, played the "Centennial Fashion Show & Ball" at the Automotive Building at the CNE. Lee returned to Toronto on a yearly basis well into the 1970s, playing the Club Kingsway, the Royal York, and the Hook and Ladder Club in the Beverly Hills Hotel at 1677 Wilson, just west of Jane Street.

On April 19, 1968, Maple Leaf Gardens hosted an event billed as "Club Calypso Festival '68." CHUM-AM DJ Bob McAdorey was the MC with a bill featuring the Expo Steel Band, the Tradewinds, Jeff Cumberbatch, limbo dancers, folk dancers, folk singers, and carnival queens of the Caribbean with Shakira Baksh, Miss Guyana! The Mighty Sparrow played the Ryerson Theatre for two nights in May 1970. He and other calypsonians, and eventually soca artists, from Trinidad would be regular visitors to Toronto for the next several decades.

In 1971, Byron Lee and the Dragonaires headlined the first really significant Jamaican music concert in Toronto. On August 21, Lee, along with Millie Small, who had the first international ska hit with "My Boy Lollipop" back in 1964, and Desmond Dekker, who hit the international charts in 1968 with "Israelites," all performed at the Royal York as part of what was billed as a "Caribbean Extravaganza." This would be the only time that Small or Dekker would perform in Toronto. What an extraordinary night, and yet there were no reviews in either the *Globe* or the *Star*.

Two years earlier Karl Mullings, who had convinced Jamaica's the Sheiks to move to Toronto, persuaded Studio One legend Jackie Mittoo to relocate to the city. Mittoo would play a significant role in Toronto's reggae scene for many years, recording a number of albums and gigging all over town. In 1973, Mittoo opened up for Barry White at Massey Hall.

The watershed reggae concert in Toronto, though, was the appearance of Bob Marley and the Wailers at Massey Hall June 8, 1975. Peter Tosh and Bunny Wailer had both left the Wailers the year before. With the I-Threes now handling background vocals, Marley put on one of the greatest performances I have seen in a half-century of concert attendance. The audience was mostly Jamaican, as only a small number of non-Jamaicans at this point knew who Bob Marley was. From my perspective, the concert was akin to entering a different world that would change me forever.

The reviewers for both the *Globe* and the *Star* were equally impressed. Peter Goddard wrote in the latter, "Listening to reggae singer Bob Marley last night at his sold-out Massey Hall concert was like discovering John Coltrane, Ray Charles, [a] Brahms lieder, or the Beatles for the first time…. In his first Canadian appearance, Marley was truly a remarkable artist. He commandeered the stage the way few artists in pop music can these days."

Marley would return to Toronto three more times, in May 1976 for two shows at Convocation Hall, and in 1978 and 1979 at Maple Leaf Gardens. The first Convocation show started late and consequently was cut short, leading many in the audience to refuse to leave. After interminable efforts to clear the hall, the promoters finally agreed to let the first audience stay as the second audience filed in. Convocation Hall has probably never been so overcrowded before or since.

September 29, 1988, BamBoo

BOB MARLEY & THE WAILERS!

Massey Hall Sun. June 8 7 pm

June 8, 1975, Massey Hall

"Probably the two shows that stand out as a fan were Bob Marley at MLG, and Miles Davis at Massey Hall. What ... these artists have in common is they are/were great live performers — ultimately performing live, and the art of the show presentation is its own art form. And that is what has impacted me as a fan, and throughout my career as a promoter."

— Arthur Fogel, president, Global Touring, Live Nation

The first Toronto appearance by Toots and the Maytals occurred just over a month after Marley's debut at Massey Hall. The Maytals played the Concert Hall on July 20, 1975. They came back in December, opening up for the Who at Maple Leaf Gardens, then a few months later, they played their most electrifying Toronto show ever at Moss Park Arena on July 31, 1976.

Burning Spear followed Toots a few weeks after his 1976 show, playing three incendiary nights at the El Mocambo August 19–21, 1976. This was during Spear's first tour ever and he seemed awed by the reception he received. Spear would return many times over the years, quickly evolving into a mystical reggae elder. Jimmy Cliff, the star of *The Harder They Come*, first played Toronto on October 14, 1975, when he headlined Massey Hall.

In the 1970s, the Heptones' Leroy Sibbles moved to Toronto, and by April of 1977 he was playing the El Mocambo. For years after, he was a regular at various clubs in Toronto, most specifically the BamBoo on Queen Street. It would be hard to exaggerate the influence Sibbles had on local musicians.

While reggae was breaking big time in North America and Europe in the mid-1970s, by the end of the decade, Britain was experiencing the Two-tone ska revival led by the Specials, Madness, the Selecter, and the English Beat. All four bands would play Toronto in 1980, driving local audiences into a frenzy. In November 1980, local promoters the Garys brought the first important all-English reggae band, Steel Pulse, into the Edge for two ear-bending evenings. The promoters brought Steel Pulse back in

May 8, 1986, Copa

August 21–24,
1978, Horseshoe

over the BamBoo on Queen Street. In addition to Steel Pulse, Britain produced another major reggae band of the era, UB40. UB40 would play Toronto for the first time performing two shows at the Concert Hall on June 29, 1983.

The year 1981 saw Peter Tosh play his first Toronto concert, hitting the Ontario Place Forum July 22 for a hard and edgy performance. In October he was back, playing three nights at O'Keefe Centre with Jimmy Cliff. October 1981 also saw Black Uhuru tearing it up at the Concert Hall. A year later, Uhuru, with Sly and Robbie holding down the rhythm section, played a devastating set opening up for the Clash at the CNE Grandstand September 5. Third World made their debut Toronto appearance a few months earlier on June 30, 1982, at Massey Hall.

Dub poetry became part of Toronto's music life in 1983. Lillian Allen, from Jamaica, and Clifton Joseph, from Antigua, headed up the local scene. The most renowned dub poet based in Jamaica, Mutabaruka, would finally play Toronto August 17, 1990, on a bill with "The Children of Bob Marley," Judy Mowatt, Freddie McGregor, Cat Coore (formerly of Third World), Arnold Bertram,

the summer of 1981 with the roots-oriented trio Culture slated to open. Unfortunately, Culture didn't make it across the border because of visa problems. Culture would finally play Toronto two years later, taking

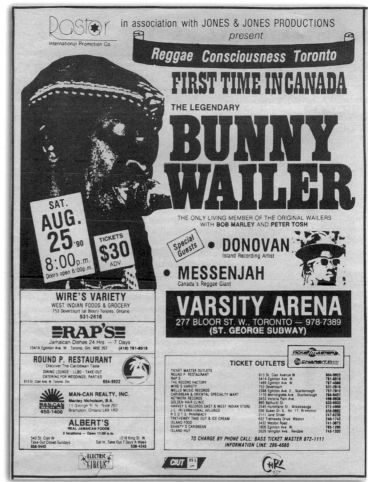

and Lloyd Parks, at the Jamaican Canadian Association at 1621 Dupont Street. Eight days later, local promoters Jones and Jones would present the first Toronto performance ever by Bunny Wailer at the cavernous Varsity Arena. British dub poet Linton Kwesi Johnson would first play Toronto May 7 and 8, 1984, at Larry's Hideaway.

In the 1980s and 1990s, roots reggae gave way to dancehall. The first dancehall performance in Toronto appears to have been when Yellowman and Brigadier Jerry appeared at the St. Lawrence Market on July 10, 1982, as part of a bill advertised as "Jack Ruby High Powered Sound." Jack Ruby was the Jamaican producer best known for his early work with Burning Spear.

(left) July 10, 1982, St. Lawrence Market

(right) August 25, 1990, Varsity Arena

September 15, 1989, Concert Hall

Youth, Mikey General, and Dean Fraser to the Island Club at Ontario Place.

Known as a focal point for hip hop shows in the 1980s, the Concert Hall was also a major hub for reggae and dancehall. For the majority of the decade, a consistent run of shows put on by independent promoters such as True Tone, Bluenotes, and Reggae International brought in a cavalcade of star deejays and singers such as Tenor Saw, Pluggy Satchmo, Frankie Paul, Horace Andy, Chaka Demus, Sister Nancy, and Toronto fan-favourite Super Cat. The burgeoning dancehall scene at the time was supported by the Concert Hall's diverse policy on concert programming, and helped build dancehall culture in the city.

A number of dancehall shows were actually part of mini-festivals featuring several of the biggest names in the dancehall world. Every year during the Caribana celebrations, a "Reggae Superfest" show would be put on at Lamport Stadium. In 1993, Buju Banton, Michael Rose, and Garnett Silk headlined. In 1995, Dennis Brown, Beenie Man, Apache Indian, Snagga Puss, Dance Hall Divas, Tanto Metro, Little Kirk, and Silver Cat entertained revellers.

For the next 20 years, two promoters, Jones and Jones and Lance Ingleton, would bring in the majority of reggae and dancehall shows to the city. Among the dozens of shows they presented, Jones and Jones booked a lot of artists into the Opera House, including Marcia Griffiths, Culture, Half Pint, Buju Banton, Luciano, and Tony Rebel. They also brought Beenie Man, Big

A particularly active year for dancehall package shows was 1995. On January 21, Shabba Ranks, Buju Banton, Third World, Lady Saw, and the Jah Postles Band performed for 6,000 spectators at Maple Leaf Gardens. This was the first reggae show to be held at the Gardens since Bob Marley last played there in November 1979. The day after Canada Day, Reggae Sunsplash was held at the Molson Amphitheatre, with Buju Banton and Freddie McGregor headlining a show that included the Wailing Souls, Sister Carol, Worl-a-Girl, Junior Tucker, Christafari, and Skool MC.

April 27, 1997, Scooter's Roller World

November 13, 1994, RPM

12 PUNK, HARDCORE, AND GRUNGE

Over the course of popular music history there have been a handful of seminal movements that proved to be game-changing. The first series of black jazz recordings in 1923 by King Oliver's Creole Jazz Band featuring Louis Armstrong was one of the those moments. The birth of 1950s rock out of late 1940s R&B was another. The radically different, yet complementary, sounds of the Beatles and the Stones transforming American music and then taking it back to the States was one more. But equally impactful was the incredible moment in the second half of the 1970s when punk rock emerged, first in NYC with bands such as the Ramones and Television and then in London with the Sex Pistols, the Clash, Buzzcocks, and so many others.

Toronto was a great punk city, perhaps only superseded by New York and London. The roots of punk stemmed from the radical sounds, lyrics, and performance practices of the Velvet Underground, the MC5, Iggy and the Stooges, and perhaps the New York Dolls. All four of these bands came through Toronto in the late 1960s and early 1970s. The Velvets played Toronto only once, at the June 1969 Toronto Pop Festival. Being based in Detroit, the MC5 came to Toronto a number of times; their debut performance was opening for the Who in 1968 at CNE Coliseum. Sadly, it wasn't until January 25, 1974, that Iggy and the Stooges finally came to town during their *Raw Power* tour. Appropriately enough, they played the rather seedy Victory Burlesque, a former strip club on the east side of Spadina just north of Dundas.

I was at that Stooges show, and it was a lesson in performance art and, at the time, one of the most extreme shows in Toronto's history. The reviewer for the *Globe and Mail* commented, "The Stooges' music tends to blend together into an indistinguishable mass because of the band's unremitting efforts to stab ice picks into your ears." He clearly didn't get it, but that was his loss. Iggy Pop as a solo artist would return to Toronto many times over the years, including at a riveting show at the Seneca College Field House in March 1977 with David Bowie accompanying him on piano and Blondie opening up.

The New York Dolls played Toronto twice in their original incarnation, debuting at the Victory Burlesque in October 1973, three months before the Stooges gig. Rush was the opening act.

March 14, 1977, Seneca Field House

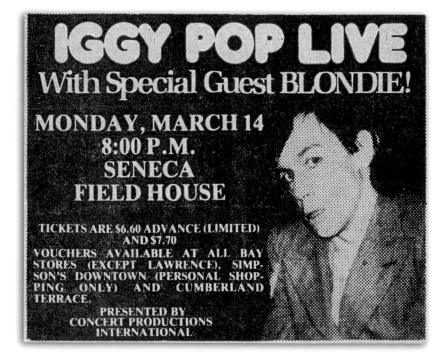

Some might argue that punk poetess Patti Smith's debut performance at Massey Hall April 15, 1976, was the first punk show proper in Toronto. Smith had emerged out of the CBGB scene in New York City alongside the Ramones, Television, and Talking Heads. The Massey Hall show was a special one for her band, as it was the first time they had played an actual theatre as opposed to a club. The show came close to selling out, and while Smith was a master at long, improvised poetic treatises such as "Land" (a.k.a. "Horses") that were far from most people's idea of classic punk, her snarling, anarchic, manic versions of Them's "Gloria" and the Who's "My Generation" were as straight-out punk as anything the Ramones or the Sex Pistols ever played. Smith would return to Toronto that December to play the Seneca College Field House. Her next Toronto performance would be at the Phoenix, launching her comeback in 1995.

For many Toronto punk fans, the Ramones' three shows at the New Yorker Theatre September 24 and 25, 1976, were landmark moments in Toronto history, inspiring the formation of a number of local bands. The first night they played at 7:30 and 10:30.

The second night there was a single show at midnight. The midnight show sold out all 500 tickets. The first two shows each drew about 250 nascent punk fans.

Gary Topp booked the group after reading about their CBGB performances in New York. The band members appeared dressed in their standard black leather jackets, white T-shirts, and jeans, with Dee Dee Ramone screaming "1, 2, 3, 4" to introduce every song. Blasting their way through close to 20 songs in a space of 30-plus minutes, the Ramones redefined the very notion of what modern rock music could be. While the music seems tame by 2019 standards, in 1976 the sonic onslaught, frenzied adrenaline rush, irreverence for anything and everything, and the aura of NYC-style danger that the group embodied was either the antithesis of what rock should be or everything the music always promised. It was a transformative moment that anyone who was there will never forget.

The first wave of so-called punk was a fascinating, if disparate, mash up of bands such as the Dead Boys and the Ramones, who played simplistic two-minute songs featuring

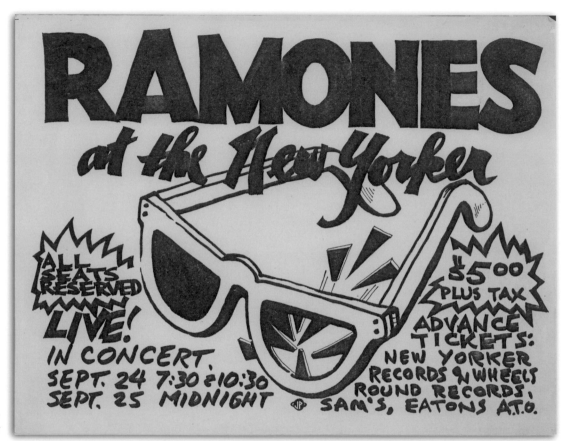

September 24–25, 1976,
New Yorker

buzz-saw guitars at a feverish speed that more often than not celebrated an ironic combination of humour and nihilism in songs such as "Gimme Gimme Shock Treatment." At the same time, and in direct contrast, bands such as Talking Heads and Television came from an artistic, intellectual bohemian tradition drawing on the sensibilities of beat authors such as William Burroughs, and, even though they downplayed it initially, these bands had artistic ambitions in the old-school sense of the word.

Television's Tom Verlaine was a virtuosic guitarist, but the kind of improvisations he

June 17–18, 1977, New Yorker

engaged in during songs such as "Little Johnny Jewel" had little to do with the playing of rock gods such as Eric Clapton or Jimmy Page. His compadres, Talking Heads, were also about growth and expansion. Their songs and performances, from the very beginning, betrayed a sense of intellectualism, and within three albums they were creating an astonishing fusion of world beat, funk, and primal rock that went far beyond the initial impulses of punk.

Television broke up in July 1978, which meant that their one and only scheduled Toronto show at the El Mocambo in early fall of that year was cancelled. Talking Heads first played Toronto as a three-piece, performing at the tiny second floor room dubbed A Space on Nicholas Street on January 27, 1977. The next night they played at the Ontario College of Art with the Diodes opening. In March of the same year, the group expanded to a four-piece with the addition of keyboardist Jerry Harrison, formerly of Jonathan Richman's Modern Lovers. Local promoters the Garys booked this version of the band into the New Yorker Theatre on September 16 with local heroes the Scenics opening up.

Three months earlier, the Garys had brought the Ramones back to the New Yorker with Cleveland's legendary Dead Boys opening up, and in November they booked U.K. punk band the Vibrators. By the end of 1977, with local bands such as the Viletones, the Diodes, and the Nerves, punk had truly arrived in the city. On May 17, 1977, the Diodes opened up Toronto's first DIY club, the appropriately named Crash 'n' Burn at 15 Duncan Street, just south of Queen. Located in a converted warehouse with cement floors and no ventilation, every Friday and Saturday the club was filled with sweat-drenched fans who had stumbled into a scene filled with an anything-goes atmosphere that was much more vital and exciting than almost anything else happening in the city. Although the Crash 'n' Burn lasted a mere two and a half months, its impact on the local punk scene was monumental. Fittingly enough, the Diodes and the Dead Boys played the last shows at the club the weekend of August 5–6.

With the Crash 'n' Burn closed, local punk bands such as the Viletones, the Ugly, the Curse, the B-Girls, the Cardboard Brains, the Androids, the Diodes, and Hamilton's Teenage Head began to play Club David's at 16 Phipps Street, near Yonge and St. Joseph. David's had opened in 1975 as a gay disco with an adjacent billiard room, a 16+ policy, and no liquor licence. By late summer 1977, the club was in decline and owner Sandy LeBlanc happily made it available for punk shows on the weekends. But in the early morning hours of January 1, 1978, after a New Year's Eve show featuring the Cardboard Brains, the Ugly, and the Viletones, Club David's was destroyed by a mysterious fire.

For a brief period in late 1977 and early 1978, a handful of punk shows, including the release party for the Diodes' first album on December 16, 1977, and a Misfits gig a week or so later, were held at the 400-seat Shock Theatre at 565 College Street.

In March 1978, the Horseshoe on Queen Street changed its music policy, making a deal with Discreet Music to book its shows. Discreet was a partnership between Gary Topp, Jerry Silverman, and Gary Cormier. The shows they promoted were always advertised under the simple but catchy moniker the Garys. Gary Topp had dabbled in

July 22–23, 1977, Crash 'n' Burn

concert promotion for a few years, booking Nash the Slash and Rough Trade during his four-year tenure programming movies at the Original 99 Cent Roxy Theatre on the Danforth, as well as bringing Captain Beefheart to Convocation Hall in April 1974. Gary Cormier became a partner when Topp hired him to build a stage at the New Yorker Theatre in the fall of 1976. With the New Yorker becoming too expensive, the Garys began to look around for a club that they could book on an ongoing basis.

As they were preparing to take over the booking at the Horseshoe, Topp, in a typically understated way, told the *Globe and Mail*, "We're probably not going to do strictly new wave, although it is probably the most significant music expression today. I don't think it should be overlooked." He would later estimate that about 40 percent of their bookings there were either punk or new wave.

At the Horseshoe, the Garys built a new stage and improved the P.A. and lighting systems in order to provide concert quality in a club environment. With alcohol ostensibly taking care of the Horseshoe's owners' needs, the Garys increased the number of shows they presented, booking bands most nights of the week while showing free movies Saturday afternoons. Included among their stellar bills at the Horseshoe that year were such seminal punk shows as Pere Ubu

in March and October, the Stranglers in April, Richard Hell and the Voidoids in May, Destroy All Monsters in June, the Cramps in July, the Dead Boys in August, the then-unknown Police in November (with fewer than 30 people attending each night!), and a staging of the Sam Sheppard and Patti Smith play *Cowboy Mouth* featuring the Foolish Virgins in November.

When the Horseshoe's owner, Jack Starr, decided he wasn't making enough money with the punk shows, he gave the Garys notice. On December 1, they staged their penultimate show at the Horseshoe, the appropriately titled and infamous Last Pogo. The name The Last Pogo was taken from the Band's 1976 farewell show entitled The Last Waltz, which had featured a star-studded lineup that included Bob Dylan, Van Morrison, Neil Young, Joni Mitchell, Eric Clapton, Dr. John, and Muddy Waters. The Last Pogo showcased a whole other breed of great acts, including some of the finest Toronto punk bands of the era: the Secrets, the Cardboard Brains, the Mods, the Ugly, the Viletones, local reggae heroes Ishan People, and Hamilton's immortal Teenage Head.

The evening ended in a riot when plain-clothes cops decided to shut the show down just as Teenage Head was about to take the stage, claiming that the club was over-crowded. Eventually the cops agreed to let Teenage Head play one song, and then Gary Topp got on the microphone from the soundboard, explained that the cops were shutting the show down, and put on the Sex Pistols song "Anarchy in the U.K." Predictably, all hell broke loose. Topp re-members: "People were slamming the wooden chairs into tables. It sounded like 10,000 lumber jacks clearing Algonquin Park." Others recall flying glass, flying bod-ies, people getting hurt, and the whole bar being turned upside down.

Colin Brunton caught much of the even-ing on film, although he had stopped shoot-ing before the riot happened. He eventually assembled his footage into a 25-minute docu-mentary simply titled *The Last Pogo*. Brunton would later expand the film with numerous interviews and other footage and release it as *The Last Pogo Jumps Again* in 2013.

After The Last Pogo, the next night couldn't help but be somewhat anticlimac-tic. Dubbed The Last Bound Up, the name

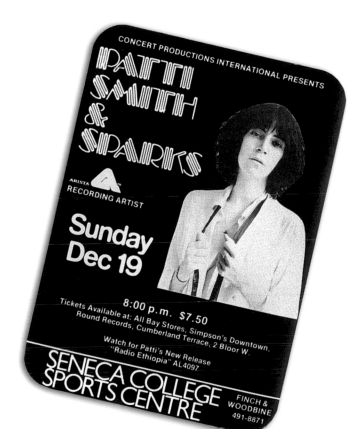

December 19, 1976,
Seneca College
Field House

came from Toronto heroes Rough Trade, whose lyrics and persona traded heavily on what for more conservative types were taboo notions of sex and sexuality. Gary Topp re-calls walking into the club that night and going into the kitchen where he saw broken chairs and tables from the night before stacked everywhere.

While the Garys were certainly the pioneers and the prime movers when it came to bringing punk to Toronto, for a variety of reasons, mostly due to management, agent, or record company politics, they were not able to book every punk and new wave act that they would have liked to. The El Mocambo was the venue for debut Toronto appearances by Elvis Costello, Devo, and Stiff Little Fingers. The Costello shows were held March 6 and 7, 1978, and were among the hardest tickets to acquire in Toronto history. Fans lined up for hours before the show, dozens being turned away after two hours or more when they were told that there was no more room in the club.

One of Costello's sets from the El Mo was broadcast on radio and then subsequently pressed as a promotional album by Columbia Records. It was soon thereafter heavily bootlegged, making it a legendary show not just in Toronto but among Costello fans worldwide. Costello came back to Toronto just over a month later to play two incredible shows at Massey Hall on April 29 with Rockpile and Mink DeVille opening. He would come to Toronto yet again later that year, hitting the boards for two shows at the O'Keefe Centre

November 3. The night before his O'Keefe performances, he played a surprise show at the El Mo as a thank-you gesture to Toronto for helping him gain a foothold in North America. Only 320 tickets for the gig were available at the club, with sales starting at noon the day of the show!

The Garys made a pitch for the Sex Pistols when the British group was planning their solitary North American tour in early 1978, but unfortunately their rather short eight-gig tour was routed across the southern United States, ending in California. Apparently, they had no interest in coming north.

On February 20, 1979, the Clash made their Toronto debut, playing the Danforth Music Hall in a stunning display of proto first-wave punk at its best. The Clash returned in November to play the O'Keefe Centre in what was an even harder-hitting show. According to Paul McGrath in the *Globe*, "The band was monstrously loud, quick, angry, feverishly energetic and totally committed to moving the crowd to another plane of consciousness." For once, the paper got it right. The show ended with two rows of seats being ripped up by the frenzied crowd.

The Buzzcocks and the B-52's would both play the Music Hall that fall (the B-52's had played the Edge earlier that summer), and the following year Siouxsie and the Banshees played their first Toronto show at the Music Hall. Their second appearance in Toronto was three months later at the El Mocambo.

By the end of December 1978, the Garys had moved once again, this time to a folk club called Edgerton's at 70 Gerrard Street East, which had the capacity for only 200 customers. Edgerton's had a restaurant licence, so anyone of whatever age could come to the shows. Under a more appropriate name, the Edge, the Garys christened their new venue with a New Year's Eve bash featuring Martha and the Muffins.

Martha and the Muffins played the Edge a number of times over the next few years. At one of those dates, the night manager of the Edge, Arthur Fogel, met the group and found out they needed a tour manager. Fogel recalls: "I left the Edge and became their tour manager. Being on that side and touring gave me an entirely new perspective." Through touring with the Muffins, Fogel met Norman Perry of Perryscope Productions. Norman Perry moved to Toronto to join CPI and soon thereafter hired Fogel to work at CPI. Today Fogel is the president of Global Touring at Live Nation Entertainment. As he wrote to us in an email, "Thank you to Martha and Mark," referring to the two leaders of Martha and the Muffins.

While the Garys presented wonderful shows at the New Yorker and the Horseshoe Tavern, the two and a half years they booked the Edge were without precedent. Although the place was small, the dynamic duo tended to book bigger name artists for two or more shows. When the shows sold out, they put speakers out front and on the patio at the back so people who couldn't get tickets could still hear the music. Amazingly, they kept the venue open in the afternoon so fans could drop by and hear the sound checks and meet the bands. It is also important to note how supportive the Garys were of local bands, regularly booking the B-Girls, the Mods, the Viletones, the Ugly, the Curse, the Government, and virtually every other notable Toronto punk or new wave band as openers or headliners when they weren't presenting touring acts.

October–November 1979,
Music Hall

It is impossible to adequately summarize just how many great shows the Garys presented at the Edge. Highlights included Pere Ubu (with lead singer David Thomas smashing a hammer on an anvil during "Non-Alignment Pact"), the Police, the Cramps (lead singer Lux Interior ending up completely nude hanging from the pipes above the stage), XTC, Ultravox (when John Foxx was still in the band), the Slits (one of the greatest shows ever!), Richard Lloyd (heroically playing with gloves on during one night in February when the furnace broke down), 8-Eyed Spy, Magazine, and Gang of Four.

They also regularly booked solo shows by former Velvet Underground members John Cale (whom they had first brought to the New Yorker Theatre in February 1977) and Nico. As well, they booked beat legend William Burroughs with John Giorno for two days in spring 1981 and closed the venue with three mesmerizing shows by Kevin Coyne ending June 6, 1981. The posters for the Coyne shows include a June 7 performance, but on that final night the club was closed and Dick Duck and the Dorks played for friends and family of

March 23–24, 1979, the Edge

the Garys, with Coyne, still in town, joining them for a few songs (when he wasn't throwing empty beer bottles at the chandeliers!).

The Edge was incredibly special and the time it was open marked a magic period in Toronto concert life. "The scene was so small back then," recalled Gary Topp, "that it was actually like a club — like the Mickey Mouse Club. We were all punkateers."

By mid-1981 the Garys parted ways with the Edge and began booking shows all over the city, at venues that included Larry's Hideaway, the Nickelodeon, the Music Hall, the Concert Hall, the Voodoo Lounge, the Palais Royale, RPM, the Diamond, and, on occasion, Massey Hall and CNE Stadium.

It is not an overstatement to suggest that their influence on Toronto's music and film culture is immeasurable. While best remembered for their punk and new wave promotions, they did so much more, bringing in some of the most exciting and radical avant-garde jazz imaginable, staging multiple shows by Sun Ra, Cecil Taylor, Carla Bley, Anthony Braxton, Julius Hemphill, and others; bringing in blues artists such as Lightnin' Hopkins (his only Toronto appearance), Son Seals, Taj Mahal, Professor Longhair, and Etta James; world music artists including Nigeria's King Sunny Ade and the virtuosic sarod player Ali Akbar Khan; as well as shows by iconoclastic, for lack of a better word, "rock" artists such as Tom Waits, John Martyn, and Kevin Coyne. For good measure, they also brought to Toronto British folk guitar virtuosos Bert Jansch, Ralph McTell, and John Renbourn; and, to cap things off, George Clinton and the P-Funk All-Stars, as well as reggae stalwarts Black Uhuru with Sly and Robbie! This city owes them an awful lot.

From 1977 through 1992, when they staged their final show featuring the band X at Lee's Palace, the Garys literally transformed Toronto concert life. They deserve a book unto themselves.

In the early 1980s, Elliott Lefko began to book punk bands that for one reason or another the Garys decided not to bother with. Lefko's first show presented punk poet Jim Carroll at the Ontario College of Art. Carroll had initially come to Toronto December 10, 1980, to play the El Mocambo. In 1984, Lefko would bring him back again, paired with Lou Reed, at the Danforth Music Hall, both of them reading poetry and lyrics rather than performing music. This was a very unique gig in Lou Reed's history and was quite a coup for Lefko at that point in his career. In 1984 he also brought New York City No Wave queen Lydia Lunch, formerly of 8-Eyed Spy, to Toronto to read from *The Intimate Diaries of the Sexually Insane* at Hotel Isabella.

One of the most notorious shows in Toronto during the first wave of punk was Teenage Head and Bob Segarini's appearance at the Ontario Place Forum June 2, 1980. When the Forum reached its capacity of 12,500 people, there were still around 1,000 fans outside trying to get in. As things began to get rowdy, Toronto police closed the gates. Enraged, fans began throwing rocks and beer bottles at the cops. When the drawbridge over the water that led to the Forum was lifted, a number of fans jumped off of it, trying to swim to the concert, with one fan nearly drowning. The melee lasted for four hours and resulted in 37 arrests. Ontario Place decided to cancel all remaining concerts that summer that they deemed to be "rock," including shows by Rough Trade,

May 11, 1984,
Music Hall

FM, Jefferson Starship, Devo, Kool & the Gang, Dr. Hook, and Peter Tosh.

By the time the Garys wrapped up their tenure at the Edge in June 1981, many people felt that the original wave of punk from both the United Kingdom and the United States had grown stale. A new generation of kids had begun playing guitars, bass, and drums, and many of them saw the original punks as passé. This attitude

July 28, 1982,
Concert Hall

is clearly expressed by Buzz of the Toronto hardcore band Direct Action. He is quoted in the superb chronicle of the Toronto hardcore scene *Tomorrow Is Too Late* stating, "We're gonna be louder, faster, harder, meaner, thrashier and punkier than what you've turned into."

Local bands such as Young Lions and Youth Youth Youth manifested that attitude in spades. Although the music wasn't called hardcore yet, there were bands sprouting up in Los Angeles (Black Flag, the Germs, Circle Jerks), San Francisco (Dead Kennedys), and Washington, D.C.

June 16, 1982,
Klub Domino

(Bad Brains, Minor Threat) that exuded an air of danger, aggression, and alienation from the norms of mainstream society and produced extraordinary, exciting, dynamic, and creative music scenes in each of those cities. As with all new marginal and/or extreme music cultures, there were numerous aspects to the scene that divided those on the inside from those on the outside. Stage-diving, mosh pits, and circle pits all helped to keep the timid away while providing a keen sense of identity and "insiderness" for those who chose to be part of the scene.

Although the Garys promoted a handful of hardcore shows, it was never their favourite music. Instead, a new generation of promoters emerged. The first was Jamil Meer, who operated under the name Jam Jam Productions. Jamil arguably promoted the first hardcore show in Toronto when he brought Dead Kennedys to the Concert Hall (formerly Club 888 and the Rock Pile) September 25, 1981. Ten months later, on July 28, 1982, he brought Dead Kennedys back to the Concert Hall with Young Lions and Youth Youth Youth (minus their lead singer, Brian Taylor, who was stuck out west) opening up. For some concertgoers, Dead Kennedys' lead singer Jello Biafra was scary. For others he was mesmerizing and inspired them to start bands. This was one of the first, if not *the* first, shows where members of the audience were stage-diving off the balconies.

In between the two Dead Kennedys shows, L.A.'s Black Flag, featuring Henry Rollins, played their first Toronto show at the rarely used Domino Klub, just off Yonge Street at 1 Isabella. Opening up was Saccharine Trust. In September, the Garys brought Washington, D.C.'s Bad Brains to Larry's Hideaway. Unfortunately, only a

November 26, 1982, Edgewater

handful of people showed up. Two months later, Bad Brains were back, playing the basement of the Edgewater Hotel at 14 Roncesvalles. This time, the audience size had increased significantly.

A new promoter, Jill Heath, operating as Jill Jill Productions (sometimes spelled JilJil), brought Circle Jerks from Los Angeles into the Edgewater April 22, 1983. Local hardcore heroes Zeroption opened up. The country fans upstairs at the Edgewater were probably none too

June–July 1986, the Bridge

April 4, 1985, Larry's

excited by the racket coming from the basement. Neither were the cops who took one look at flailing young people moshing around the room and decided a riot was about to ensue and that the show needed to be stopped. After a fair bit of negotiating between Heath and the cops, it was agreed the show could continue if the audience sat down. Circle Jerks decided that if the audience was going to sit down, they would, too. With chairs brought up onstage, the show began and the cops left. Within a song or two everyone was back up moshing, sweating, and feeling they were indeed part of a new musical movement. Circle Jerks was in town for the week and played the Beverley Hotel (under the alias Spanking Monkeys as the owners of the Edgewater had put word out that their place had been destroyed at the band's show) and the River Street booze can.

Hardcore shows were numerous throughout the 1980s and into the 1990s. Among the most memorable were Black Flag, Meat Puppets, and Nig-Heist at the Party Centre at 167 Church Street April 19, 1984, promoted by JilJil. The Garys, a year later, on April 4, 1985, brought the hyper-charged Suicidal Tendencies to Larry's Hideaway with Sudden Impact and Terminal Rage as openers. This was just Terminal Rage's third ever show in a club, and they were over the moon to be opening for Suicidal Tendencies.

At the Battalion of Saints, Chronic Submission, and Terminal Rage show May 25, 1985, promoted by JilJil at the DMZ at 337 Spadina Avenue, full nudity broke out on the dance floor. At the same club in August of that year, at a show headlined by 7 Seconds, legend has it that the first circle pit spontaneously occurred that involved audience members thrashing in a circle counterclockwise as opposed to the typical mosh pit where fans on the dance floor slammed into each other, many getting bruised and occasionally cut in the excitement. The circle pit had the advantage that women and men could both participate with less fear of getting hurt.

One of the most infamous circle pits in Toronto occurred when Edmonton hardcore band SNFU played the Desh Bhagat Temple at 62 Claremont Street on September 6, 1985. The opening band, Asexuals, played a complete set, but by the time SNFU took the stage, neighbours

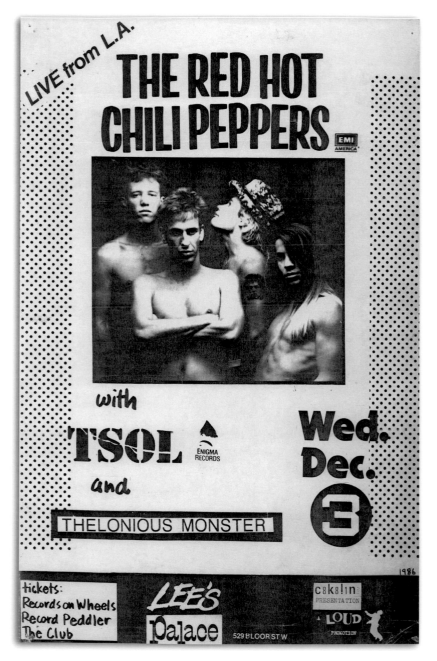

December 3, 1986, Lee's Palace

"The place was packed and jumping for the 2.5-hour set. I counted nine ambulances outside after the show. My life was changed; my identity found. The yearning in my soul met."

— Oliver Rendace
(Red Hot Chili Peppers, Concert Hall, October 30, 1991)

October 28, 1993, Concert Hall

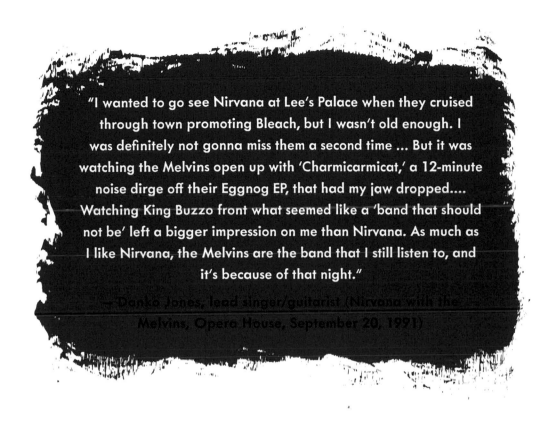

"I wanted to go see Nirvana at Lee's Palace when they cruised through town promoting Bleach, but I wasn't old enough. I was definitely not gonna miss them a second time ... But it was watching the Melvins open up with 'Charmicarmicat,' a 12-minute noise dirge off their Eggnog EP, that had my jaw dropped.... Watching King Buzzo front what seemed like a 'band that should not be' left a bigger impression on me than Nirvana. As much as I like Nirvana, the Melvins are the band that I still listen to, and it's because of that night."

— Danko Jones, lead singer/guitarist (Nirvana with the Melvins, Opera House, September 20, 1991)

were complaining about the noise and the cops arrived to shut down the show. When they cut the power to the P.A. system, the band played at least a couple of songs without vocals. According to Derek Emerson, co-author of *Tomorrow Is Too Late*, "A massive circle pit erupted when SNFU kept playing. That was my first memory of punks resisting a bunch of cops." A year later, on May 17, 1986, the Crucifucks, Vancouver's

Dayglo Abortions, and Toronto's legendary Bunchofuckingoofs played the Bridge (later Ildiko's at 507 Bloor Street West). Toronto's so-called "alternative" weekly newspaper *NOW* refused to print the band's names and instead used abbreviations. The promoters consequently refused to pay for the ad.

The same year as the Crucifucks concert, Fishbone and Red Hot Chili Peppers finally made it to Toronto. Both bands were from L.A., had emerged out of that city's punk scene, and were early progenitors of a punk/funk crossover. With only their eponymously titled EP out, Fishbone played the BamBoo April 30 and May 1, with locals L'Étranger opening up. Loud Promotions brought Red Hot Chili Peppers to Lee's Palace later that year, on December 3, 1986. The Peppers were touring their second full-length album, *Freaky Styley*, produced by P-Funk's George Clinton. Thelonious Monster and Long Beach hardcore darlings TSOL opened up the show.

Rage Against the Machine emerged from the same Los Angeles funk/punk/rap scene and embraced a similar cross-pollinating aesthetic, which they combined with a highly refined sense of political outrage. Elliott Lefko was the first local promoter to realize their potential. On January 17, 1993, he booked them into the Opera House, charging only five dollars admission — as he put it, "to raise the hype, and it worked." The band's first album had been out for less than a year. Six months later they would be back in the Toronto area playing the Lollapalooza festival.

In the mid- to late 1980s, in the northwest corner of the United States, a fusion of punk and metal developed that quickly took on the moniker *grunge*. The three biggest bands to emerge out of Seattle's grunge scene were Nirvana, Soundgarden, and Pearl Jam. Soundgarden was the first to arrive in Toronto, playing the Apocalypse Club on November 4, 1989. Five months later, Elliott Lefko brought Nirvana to Lee's Palace, paying them $1,000 for their efforts. Their debut album, *Bleach*, had come out the previous summer on the Sub Pop label. Still being relatively unknown, only 100-plus people showed up for the gig. The band was two hours late, Kurt Cobain was worn out from the road, and neither he nor bassist Krist Novoselic were happy with their drummer. The show became infamous when Cobain, out of frustration with the overly-reserved Monday crowd and impatience with his drummer, Chad Channing, decided to launch beer bottles into the air near the close of their set. The crowd reciprocated. When a well-thrown bottle barely missed drummer Chad Channing's head and landed in the drywall behind the stage, the show was over. For years after there was

"There weren't a lot of people there. At one point, Kurt put a table on stage and sat down. Said something like, 'If you're just going to sit there, so am I.' Halfway through the song, he kicked it over and rocked out. Yes, a few beer bottles were thrown — audience/band alike. It was more funny than ugly though.... Generally, people thought they were pretty cool, but like a Toronto crowd, they stare at you and watch the band, which can make you think *WTF, are they not into us?* ... 'Nah, just a Toronto crowd,' I told them — 'they liked you guys.'"

— Joel Wasson (Nirvana, Lee's Palace, 1990)

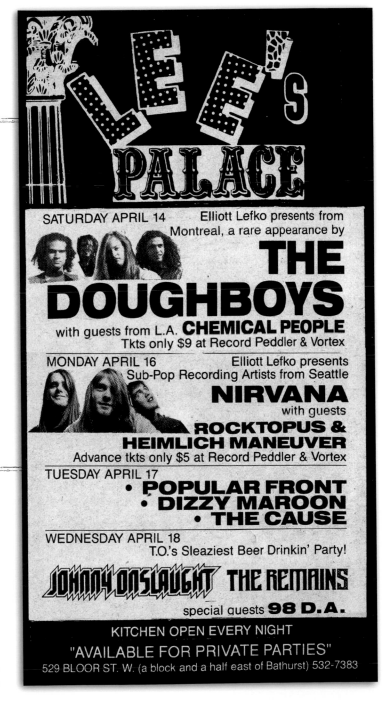

April 1990,
Lee's Palace

November 1, 1991, Rivoli

"As an emerging high school music dork ... this show had everything in terms of real noise and fake danger that the suburbs lacked. It offered moshing, the guy from Nirvana on guitar, the guy from Pearl Jam under a wig.... Fun night!"

— Cam Gordon (Foo Fighters, Opera House, 1995)

August 18, 1993, Exhibition Stadium

a prominent hole in the Lee's logo where the beer bottle had landed.

Nirvana returned to Toronto twice before leader Kurt Cobain committed suicide. They played their best show in Toronto on September 20, 1991, at the Opera House with the Melvins opening up. After they became superstars with the success of "Smells Like Teen Spirit" they returned to Toronto, this time selling out Maple Leaf Gardens. In typical Cobain fashion, the show was a hit-and-miss affair, and they refused to play "Teen Spirit."

Cobain's girlfriend Courtney Love and her band Hole played Toronto for the first time November 1, 1991, at small Queen Street club the Rivoli.

Pearl Jam's debut show in the city was a few days earlier, on October 29, when they played the Concert Hall, opening up for Red Hot Chili Peppers and the Smashing Pumpkins. The band was originally scheduled to play the Rivoli, but when they were asked to join the Chili Peppers for their whole North American tour, the Rivoli show went up in smoke. When Pearl Jam returned to headline the Concert Hall on April 10, 1992, lead singer Eddie Vedder put on quite a show, climbing up a bank of speakers, precariously moving along the outside of the balcony rail until he reached the other side of the hall, whereupon he jumped off the balcony, plunging approximately 20 feet into the outstretched arms of fans on the floor! The reviewer in the *Globe and Mail* opined, "Rock fans haven't seen such a close-to-the-edge display since the days Iggy Stooge/Pop was in his prime."

The most commercial version of punk emerged in the early 1990s with bands such as the Offspring and Green Day. Both bands played their debut Toronto shows within a month of each other, the Offspring tearing up the Opera House September 8, 1993, and Green Day following them October 6 at the Concert Hall. Green Day's breakthrough record *Dookie* wouldn't be released until February of the following year. By October 25, 1995, Green Day would be headlining Maple Leaf Gardens.

March 24, 1994,
Opera House

February, 1969,
Rock Pile

13

HARD ROCK AND METAL

The speed with which rock music developed in the 1960s was astonishing, with new bands, new sounds, and new styles seeming to appear every couple of months. The earliest bands coming out of the London R&B scene, such as the Rolling Stones and the Yardbirds, tended to exploit electronic effects and played at louder volumes than most of their forebears. In 1966, former Yardbird and member of John Mayall's Blues Breakers, Eric Clapton, formed Cream with Jack Bruce and Ginger Baker from the Graham Bond Organisation. While much of Cream's repertoire was simply electric blues, the band played through multiple stacks of Marshall speakers at a volume and with a level of aggression that simply had no precedent.

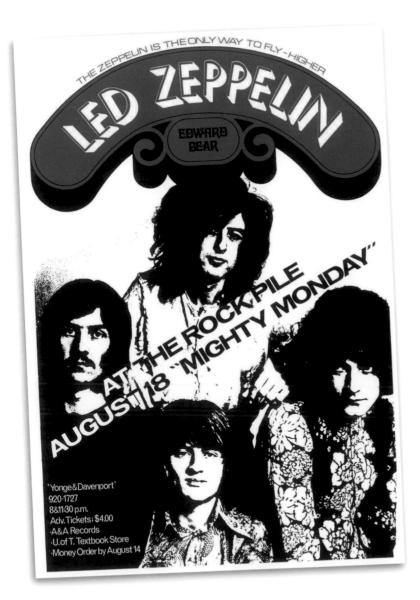

August 18, 1969, Rock Pile

Cream's debut album would be released in December 1966, the same month that the equally intense, blues-based Jimi Hendrix Experience released their first single. Both Cream and Hendrix would visit Toronto in 1968. That same year a number of newly formed bands had started playing what can be considered hard rock. San Francisco's Blue Cheer was without a doubt the loudest and heaviest of them. Unfortunately, the original incarnation of the band never made it to Toronto. Two of the less interesting heavier bands of the day, Vanilla Fudge and Iron Butterfly, did play Toronto in May and November of 1968 at the CNE Coliseum and the Rock Pile respectively. Both bands were riding the tails of their one and only hit singles: in Vanilla Fudge's case it was their cover of the Supremes' "You Keep Me Hangin' On," in Iron Butterfly's case their big hit was the interminable "In-A-Gadda-Da-Vida."

In 1969 two more ex-members of the Yardbirds, Jimmy Page and Jeff Beck, brought their new bands to Toronto. Page's band, Led Zeppelin, pulled in to the city to play the Rock Pile February 2, 1969, while the Jeff Beck Group, featuring Rod

Stewart on vocals and future Rolling Stone Ron Wood on bass, played the same venue on October 27. When Zeppelin took the stage at the Rock Pile, their first album had yet to be released. Twelve hundred people came to each of the two shows on the basis of Jimmy Page's reputation with the Yardbirds. Ritchie Yorke, in the *Globe and Mail*, praised the group to the hilt and suggested that lead singer Robert Plant "could well develop into one of the big name group singers of the year." For once, one of the newspaper critics had it right.

Led Zeppelin would be back at the Rock Pile in August, and in November they played the much bigger O'Keefe Centre, putting on a very short show. Steppenwolf, whose hit single "Born to Be Wild" contained the lyric "heavy metal thunder," which eventually gave the genre its name, grew out of a Toronto group called the Sparrow. Their first Toronto show as Steppenwolf was as the headliners of the June 1969 Toronto Pop Festival.

Two other hard rock groups made their debut in Toronto in 1969. Humble Pie opened up for the Moody Blues at Massey Hall on November 29, 1969. Jack Batten,

in the *Toronto Star*, referred to Humble Pie as a "tough, relentless bunch." Deep Purple headlined at the Rock Pile a month later, on December 22. At the time the group was somewhat in transition, still playing their early hit singles "Hush" and "Kentucky Woman," while showcasing Jon Lord's heavy-handed organ and Ritchie Blackmore's razor-sharp guitar lines alongside new singer Ian Gillan and new bassist Roger Glover.

Grand Funk Railroad from Flint, Michigan, would be one of the biggest hard rock bands in the first half of the 1970s. Their first appearance in Toronto was second on the bill to Delaney and Bonnie and Friends at Maple Leaf Gardens April 3, 1970. This was the first show promoted by Eaton-Walker, who in a few months would stage the Festival Express shows. The *Toronto Star* reviewer loved Delaney and Bonnie but referred to Grand Funk as "mindless, dumb, unmusical stuff." Grand Funk would play the Strawberry Fields Festival in August 1970 and headline at Maple Leaf Gardens October 9, 1972.

Mountain, whose "Mississippi Queen" is surely one of the heaviest songs to ever get

July 31, 1972, Varsity Stadium

Top 40 airplay, played the Electric Circus at 99 Queen Street East in May 1970, and a month later were featured on the second night of Festival Express. Two other hard rock groups of the time, Cactus and James Gang, made their Toronto debuts in 1971; Cactus opening up for Free at the short-lived Fillmore North (located across the street from St. Lawrence Market), while James Gang played Maple Leaf Gardens on a multi-act bill headed by Sly and the Family Stone, which also included Buddy Miles and Taj Mahal.

Black Sabbath, the first heavy metal band according to many aficionados, played their debut Toronto show on July 18, 1971, second billed to Three Dog Night at the second Beggar's Banquet festival at the Borough of York Stadium. While guitarist Tony Iommi and bassist Geezer Butler pounded out the group's leaden but powerful riffs, Ozzy Osbourne spent most of the show jumping up and down flashing peace signs. So much for doom and gloom and satanic worship.

Alice Cooper was seminal in initiating what critics of the day called "shock rock." Based in Detroit in 1969 and 1970, Cooper regularly visited Toronto, on occasion playing at local high schools. While he had played the Toronto Rock and Roll Revival in 1969, New Year's Eve 1969 at the Rock Pile, and the Strawberry Fields Festival in August 1970, his first Toronto gig as a star after "I'm Eighteen" became a megahit was at the first Beggar's Banquet in June 1971. By December 1973, Alice Cooper would be headlining Maple Leaf Gardens with Texas riff-rockers ZZ Top opening up. ZZ Top had been scheduled to headline at the Victory Burlesque earlier that year, but cancelled according to the *Globe and Mail* "because the local promoter [presumably SRO] refused to allow [the band] to use equipment powerful enough to demolish the poor old Victory Theatre." When ZZ Top eventually headlined Maple Leaf Gardens on January 9, 1976, they were referred to as a "dumb boogie band" by yet another idiotic reviewer.

With his extensive makeup, it could also be argued that Cooper played a role in the onset of glam. Be that as it may, Marc Bolan's group, T. Rex, epitomized glam. Their one and only Toronto appearance was at Massey Hall September 9, 1972. The

December 14, 1973, Maple Leaf Gardens

then unknown Doobie Brothers opened up. The heaviest glam rock band of the era, Slade, came to Toronto once only, and that was to open for Johnny Winter at Maple Leaf Gardens on April 25, 1973. The *Globe and Mail*'s rock critic Robert Martin, while praising the group for getting the audience on its feet and earning an encore, summed up his thoughts about the band, stating, "It's a mindless sort of rock with a tub-thumping beat." As I am sure is becoming evident, hard rock was rarely appreciated by mainstream music critics.

Mott the Hoople is often lumped into the glam and/or hard rock camp. On October 14, 1973, they played Massey Hall with two other hard rock bands making their Toronto debuts, Blue Oyster Cult and Aerosmith. Aerosmith would headline Massey Hall September 2, 1975, but were not yet popular enough to sell it out. Mott the Hoople returned to Massey Hall May 27, 1974, with Queen as the scheduled opening band. Queen, unfortunately, cancelled most of their tour when Brian May came down with hepatitis. They would finally play Toronto as headliners at Maple Leaf Gardens November 21, 1977.

Kiss made their Toronto debut June 15, 1974, opening up for the New York Dolls at Massey Hall. Not surprisingly, the Dolls made Kiss look silly. Robert Martin commented in the *Globe and Mail*, "Kiss, on the other hand, is a totally plastic band. The group is a tribute to the imaginative powers and organizational ability of Neil Bogart [president of Casablanca Records]. It doesn't matter that the players' makeup hides their faces because they are only marionettes anyway. Every step Kiss made on the stage has been heavily choreographed. It was all part of the package deal."

While Martin was dead right, the cynical construction of Kiss was unbelievably commercially successful. By April 1976 they were headlining Maple Leaf Gardens. In September of that year they headlined Varsity Stadium.

That June, local heroes Rush played a triumphant three shows at Massey Hall, recording their *All the World's a Stage* album at the glorious Shuter Street venue. Growing up in the Willowdale area of Toronto, Rush had been playing high schools and then Yonge Street bars such as the Gasworks and the Colonial since 1968. They had also opened up for various bands, including the New York Dolls at the Victory Burlesque in 1973 and Manfred Mann's Earth Band at Convocation Hall in the same period. Their three nights in 1976 at Massey followed their breakthrough record *2112* and, for both their fans and the band itself, represents a significant moment of arrival in their career. Rush's gigs at Massey Hall are among the most iconic performances in the Hall's 125-plus-year history.

Australia's impish over-the-top kickass entry into the hard rock sweepstakes, AC/DC, first played Massey Hall as the opening act for UFO in June 1979. That same night Cheap Trick played Maple Leaf Gardens. Alan Niester spent most of his review focusing on AC/DC, stating that their set "may well have been one of the most furious extended evenings of sonic overkill the bedraggled old edifice [Massey Hall] has ever seen. If audience reaction is any indicator, it certainly won't be too long before Australia's AC/DC are headlining the largest venues in town." Angus Young, using an early wireless guitar, rode on top of one of his roadie's backs, traversing the floor and both balconies of the theatre, electrifying

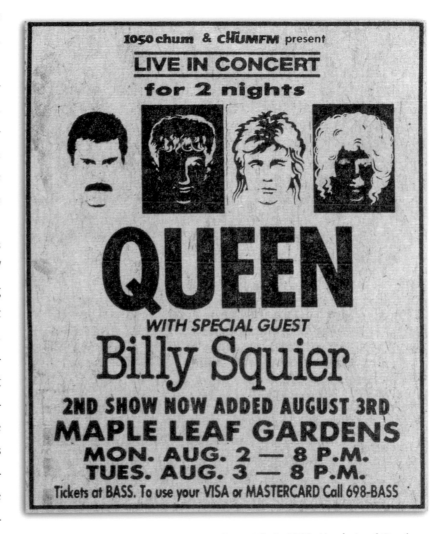

August 2–3, 1982, Maple Leaf Gardens

(left) July 2, 1973, Colonial
(right) October 27, 1973, Victory Burlesque

> "Ah ... 1982. I was into many things metal. Priest was one of them, and this was a show not to be missed. All I remember was Halford making his entrance riding a big Harley.... I kid you not when I say that MLG was filled with 18,000 males that evening, all clad in black leather jackets. A classic Spinal Tap moment. Hello, Toronto!"
>
> — Pat Valente (Judas Priest, Maple Leaf Gardens, 1982)

April 18, 1979,
El Mocambo

the crowd in the process. This would be AC/DC's only Toronto appearance with original lead singer Bon Scott, who passed away in February 1980. In July 1980 they returned to headline Maple Leaf Gardens before 9,000 rabid fans with their new lead singer Brian Johnson.

By 1979 Van Halen had emerged out of Los Angeles to become the most popular hard rock band of the era. They never played a small gig in Toronto, debuting April 16, 1979, as headliners at Maple Leaf Gardens. Rock critic Alan Niester suggested they were a "macho joke" who wouldn't last more than a year. Yet, just over two years later, on August 4, 1981, they were once again headlining the Gardens.

The New Wave of British Heavy Metal (NWOBHM) hit Toronto hard in the late 1970s and early 1980s. Judas Priest, supporting their *Hell Bent for Leather* album, was the first NWOBHM band to hit our shores, storming into the El Mocambo Wednesday, April 18, 1979. Lead singer Rob Halford actually made his entrance riding a motorcycle onto the stage. Considering how small the El Mo was, that must have been quite the trick. By October 1982, Priest would be headlining at Maple Leaf Gardens.

Motörhead, led by the great Lemmy Kilmister, came next, performing at the Danforth Music Hall on May 7, 1981. Writing for the *Globe and Mail,* Paul McGrath referred to them as "the loudest, most feverish blast of noise currently available on record." He wasn't wrong. McGrath went on to write that their "show is more threatening and repulsive than anything the old masters have created here in the past couple of years. In a word: success."

Iron Maiden made their Toronto debut six weeks later, rocking the Masonic Temple June 21, 1981. Def Leppard skipped the usual routine of playing an opening slot or headlining at a small club or theatre. After their *Pyromania* album came out, they headlined at Maple Leaf Gardens on a triple bill with Krokus and Gary Moore.

Quiet Riot were one of the first glam metal or hair metal bands to come out of the same Los Angeles hard rock/heavy metal scene as Van Halen. Oddly enough, their first two Toronto appearances were within two months of each other. On September 11, 1983, they opened up for ZZ Top at the Kingswood Amphitheatre at Canada's Wonderland. Six weeks later, on October 25, they were opening for Black Sabbath at Maple Leaf Gardens. At the time Sabbath was led by their new lead singer, former Deep Purple member Ian Gillan. Other L.A. glam metal bands to visit Toronto for the first time in the 1980s were Motley Crüe, who played for 3,000 fans headlining at the CNE Coliseum June 10, 1984, and Poison, who managed to come into the city on their debut trip on the top of the bill at Maple Leaf Gardens April 13, 1988.

The biggest band to emerge out of the Los Angeles hard rock scene was undoubtedly the largely dysfunctional Guns N' Roses. They first played Toronto as the opening act

"When GNR was performing, no one really knew them. After a few songs, someone yelled out, 'You suck!' Axl Rose turned and said, 'Suck my dick' into the mic, and the crowd roared. After that, people starting to give them a good listen for the rest of their opening act. Respect earned that moment."

— Ramy Sellouk (The Cult, with Guns N' Roses, Exhibition Stadium, 1987)

for the Cult at CNE Stadium on August 19, 1987. They didn't seem to make much of an impression with critics, as they weren't mentioned in the reviews in the *Globe and Mail* or the *Star*. Nine months later, on May 20, 1988, they opened up for Iron Maiden at the same stadium before finally headlining CNE Stadium June 7 and 8, 1991, with Skid Row in support. Perhaps the best Guns N' Roses show in Toronto was their double bill with Metallica on September 13, 1992, also at the CNE. That night, Axl Rose, putting his ongoing beef with Nirvana front and centre, ripped up a Kurt Cobain shirt onstage. While Axl clearly felt it was a revolutionary gesture, the odds are Nirvana hardly gave a damn.

In the early to mid-1980s a number of California bands began to mix heavy metal with hardcore punk. The result was what was typically referred to as thrash or speed metal. Slayer was the first such band to play Toronto, performing at Larry's Hideaway October 27, 1984. Four months later the Garys would book them on a bill headlined by Venom at the Concert Hall.

Metallica, without a doubt, was the most successful and most important of these bands. The group initially played Toronto, opening up for WASP, at the Concert Hall

THE GARY'S & CKLN...881
LIVE!
venom
Slayer
and
RAZOR
SATURDAY FEBRUARY 16
AT THE CONCERT HALL
TICKETS AT:
PEDDLER, WHEELS, BASS

February 16, 1985, Concert Hall

on January 19, 1985. According to at least some fans who were at the show, most of the audience left before WASP took the stage, indicating that Metallica was who the audience had come to see. By the end of 1986, Metallica was playing Maple Leaf Gardens with Metal Church opening. While only 5,000 fans showed up, leaving the seats 75 percent empty, Metallica would play both Maple Leaf Gardens and CNE Stadium several times over the years to capacity houses.

In 1983, long before they became famous, Metallica kicked guitarist Dave Mustaine out of the group. He quickly formed Megadeth, who would open for Alice Cooper at Maple Leaf Gardens February 26, 1987. A year later the band would open for Dio at the same venue.

New York City's contribution to thrash metal was Anthrax. They debuted at the El Mocambo July 30, 1987.

In the 1980s, in various parts of Europe, more extreme sub-genres of heavy metal began to emerge under names such as black metal and death metal. The first black metal band to play Toronto was the Danish group Mercyful Fate who came to Larry's Hideaway

November 4, 1984. Venom, whose second album gave the sub-genre one of its names, followed with a show at the Concert Hall on February 16, 1985, arranged by the Garys. Just over a year later, in July 1986, Celtic Frost also played the Concert Hall.

Not a lot of death metal made it to Toronto, as the majority of groundbreaking bands in that genre, such as Bathory, Burzum, and Emperor, were based in Europe and didn't tour. Buffalo's Cannibal Corpse was an exception. They played the Apocalypse Club on December 14, 1990. L.A.'s Fear Factory came through a few years later, playing the Opera House on April 19, 1993.

In the early 1990s a number of metal bands added elements of hip hop and funk to their sound. Dubbed nu metal, the two biggest bands of the sub-genre, Korn and Limp Bizkit, both played Toronto in the last few years of the 1990s. Korn opened up for Megadeth at Molson Amphitheatre July 14, 1995. Limp Bizkit would open for Korn March 25, 1997, at the Warehouse. Two years later, Limp Bizkit headlined the SkyDome on November 18, 1999. Two months earlier, Slipknot played their first Toronto show at the Warehouse. Slipknot

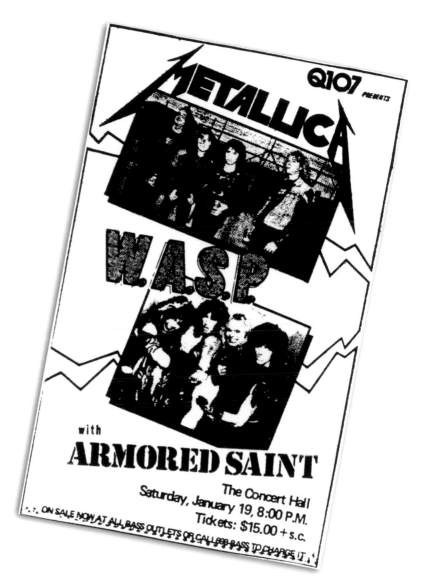

January 19, 1985, Concert Hall

would remain an important part of heavy metal well into the 21st century. Both Korn and Limp Bizkit were influenced by Los Angeles band Tool. Heavy metal to the core and yet influenced by prog band King Crimson, Tool first headlined in Toronto on February 23, 1994, at the Concert Hall. Three months later they were back playing the much bigger Varsity Arena.

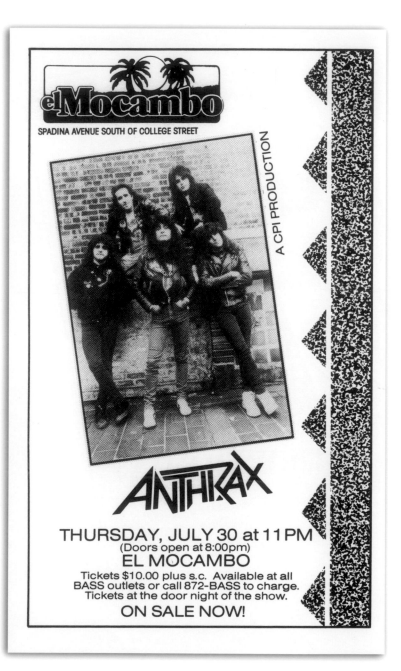

July 30, 1987, El Mocambo

> "I body surfed for the first three songs of this set, from the front to the very back of the room. The whole floor was moving.... I went to school the next day with a Doc Martens–shaped bruise on my forearm."
>
> — Andrea Watson
> (Tool, February 23, 1994, Concert Hall)

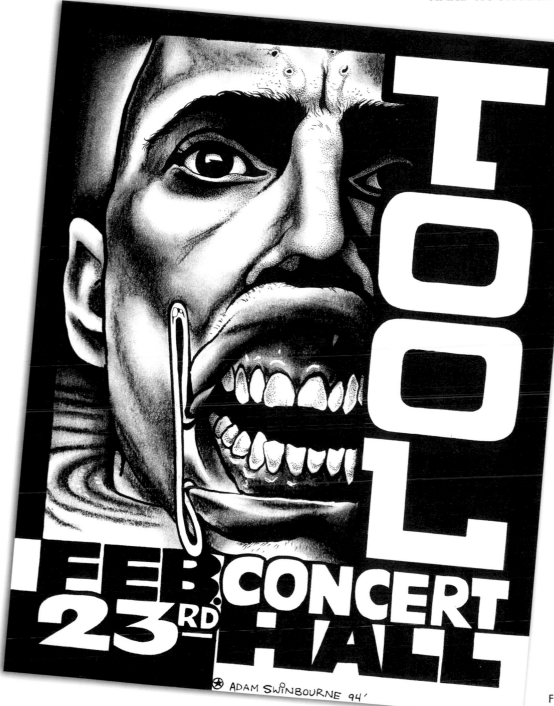

February 23,
1994, Concert Hall

March 1990,
BamBoo

THE QUEEN STREET SCENE

14

In the 1960s and the early 1970s Toronto had two thriving local scenes.

Yorkville Avenue between Bay Street and Avenue Road was the home to numerous coffee houses that featured both local and touring folk and blues artists. A few of the Yorkville clubs also served as the home for some of the city's finest rock bands of the era, such as the Paupers, the Ugly Ducklings, Jack London & the Sparrows, the Mynah Byrds, and Luke and the Apostles. By the early 1970s, Yorkville was in the process of being transformed into a yuppie enclave dominated by high-end retail stores and restaurants. When the Riverboat finally closed its doors in June 1978, Yorkville lost the last venue that had once made it special.

Yonge Street had a similar trajectory. In the 1960s, jazz, blues, and R&B reigned supreme from Davenport down to Queen

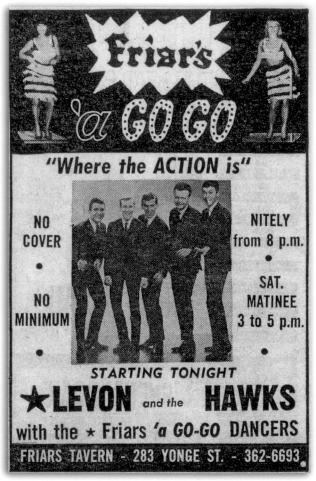

(left) August 26, 1963, Le Coq d'Or
(right) September 13, 1965, Friar's

Street, with clubs such as the Town Tavern, the Colonial Tavern, Friar's Tavern, Le Coq d'Or, the Hawk's Nest, the Bluenote, the Brass Rail, and Club 888/Rock Pile showcasing a surfeit of great touring artists as well as hosting residencies for Ronnie Hawkins, the Regents, the Rogues, Shawne and Jay Jackson, Levon and the Hawks, and Dianne Brooks and Eric Mercury's Soul Searchers. Just off Yonge, at the Saphire Tavern, soul chanteuse Jackie Shane was turning heads, and, of course, Massey Hall was just a few doors east of Yonge on Shuter.

In the mid-1970s, Queen Street West, between University and Spadina, began to show signs of musical life. At the time the area largely consisted of greasy spoons, low-cost housing, a meat-packing plant, an assortment of low-end stores, and an immigrant community in transition. Just off the main street were a number of warehouses and factories. The only music venue of any importance in the area was the Horseshoe Tavern, which had been a bastion of country music during the 1950s and '60s. In the 1970s, the only restaurant of note was Peter Pan. Amazingly, it had originally opened in the late 1890s as the Savoy, being renamed the Peter Pan Lunch at the end of the 1920s. In the late 1970s, Peter Pan changed hands and became one of the first cool places to eat in the area. Le Select Bistro opened up around the same time, providing a second quality restaurant.

Things began to change in the second half of the 1970s. For some years the Beverley Tavern, located at 240 Queen Street West between John and McCaul,

had by default served as the watering hole for Ontario College of Art (OCA) students simply because it was the nearest bar to the college and it served cheap beer. Until early 1976 the second floor of the bar, more often than not, featured mundane local country bands serving up a sonic backdrop for the odd mix of working-class locals and art students, both camps alternating drowning their sorrows and/or planning their futures.

In March 1976, OCA student Steven Davey convinced the Beverley's management to let his band, the Dishes, play a series of weekends in the upstairs room. While not really a punk band, the Dishes played original material, had a DIY approach (which included designing and putting up their own handbills), and drew enough of their OCA colleagues to make the venue a going concern. Over the next couple of years, the Cads, Johnny and the G-Rays, the Country Lads, the Biffs, the Government, the Cardboard Brains, Mary Margaret O'Hara, and Martha and the Muffins regularly graced the Beverley stage.

Many patrons of those early Beverley shows make the argument that Toronto's

DIRECT FROM NEW YORK CITY !!!!!!!!!!!

The Talking Heads plus The Diodes

Ontario College of Art   100 McCaul St.

Friday Jan. .28   8 p.m. $3.00

January 28, 1977,
Ontario College of Art

punk scene started there. Others insist the scene began when the Ramones played the New Yorker Theatre in September 1976, but that was six months after the Dishes started their run at the Beverley. Whatever people want to believe, there is no argument that the DIY independent band scene in Toronto that helped kick-start many of the city's punk bands started at the Beverley. When CITY-TV moved in across the street in the mid-1980s and Queen West began to gentrify, the Beverley stopped booking bands and was transformed into a sports bar.

Between the Dishes and the shock and awe of the Ramones at the New Yorker, by late 1976 a number of OCA students and a few denizens of the east end began forming bands. The Diodes, formed in October 1976, would become one of the more famous of the OCA bands. When New York City's Talking Heads were booked to play A Space January 27, 1977, the Diodes convinced OCA to book Talking Heads for a second show at OCA on the 28th, with the Diodes holding down the opening slot. This would be the band's debut gig. A few weeks later the Diodes, the Dishes, and the Doncasters played what they dubbed the 3D Show (as

the names of all three bands started with the letter D) at OCA and the scene officially started. Martha and the Muffins would play their debut gig at OCA October 31, 1977.

For a brief moment, the Colonial Tavern on Yonge Street booked some of the city's nascent punk bands into the club's basement room, which had been renamed the Colonial Underground. The Viletones played their debut gig there in March 1977. Hamilton's Teenage Head, featuring the charismatic Frankie Venom, followed suit the weekend of April 28–30.

As detailed in this book's punk chapter, in May 1977 the Diodes opened the Crash 'n' Burn at 15 Duncan Street just south of Queen. Although it would close in early August, the Crash 'n' Burn helped set the stage for the Garys' incredible run of shows at the Horseshoe Tavern from March through December 1978. In 1976 and 1977 the Horseshoe had been booking roots-oriented artists such as the Original Sloth Band, David Wilcox, and Colin Linden. The former country bar was utterly transformed when the Garys took over for nine months in 1978, turning the Horseshoe into the epicentre of the punk scene in Toronto.

GALA GRAND OPENING
Tonite!
Monday March 6
And Tonite önly!
Tuesday March 7
CBGB Reggae from NYC
FULL HAND
featuring Al Anderson ex-Wailers
and THE DISHES
Toronto's #1 New Wave Power Polka!
HORSESHOE!
QUEEN & SPADINA
FROM THE GUYS THAT GAVE YOU THE ROXY AND THE NEW YORKER

March 6–7, 1978,
Horseshoe

At the same time as they were booking virtually every touring and local punk band, the Garys also booked an astonishing array of avant-garde jazz (Sun Ra, Carla Bley, Anthony Braxton), reggae (the I-Threes, Ishan People, Leroy Sibbles), country rock (the Dillards), folk (Ramblin' Jack Elliott, Jesse Winchester), soul (Etta James), British folk and rock (John Martyn, Bert Jansch, Ralph McTell, John Renbourn), blues (Koko Taylor, Son Seals, Ellen McIlwaine), and Celtic Rock (Figgy Duff).

When the Horseshoe's owner, Jack Starr, decided he was tired of punk rock kids patronizing his club, he gave the Garys their walking papers and the club went through a rough few years. Between 1979 and December 1982, with the stage shifted to the west side of the room, there were only a handful of gigs at the Horseshoe that sparked interest, including visits by legendary zydeco accordion wizard Clifton Chenier, a cappella R&B masters the Persuasions, Scottish funksters the Average White Band, a surreal gig in which Richard and Linda Thompson broke up onstage, Sleepy LaBeef, Texas roots icon Doug Sahm, and local singer-songwriters Jane Siberry and Meryn Cadell. It is also

> "This was a magical night; I still get goosebumps thinking about it. They were still babies, but also larger than life ... perfect for the little stage at the Horseshoe.... Jules crowd-surfed, and we all got a handful (and some got a kiss). A new phase of my life commenced that night!"
>
> — Karen Keller (The Strokes, Horseshoe Tavern, 2001)

May 1978, Horseshoe

worth noting that future Blue Rodeo front men Jim Cuddy and Greg Keelor's first band, the Hi-Fi's, played the club alongside the Black Slacks on January 15, 1980. They would also play the Horseshoe March 1, 1980, as part of the Pogo Resurrection Party. In December 1982, the Horseshoe sign came down and the club changed its name to Stagger Lee's, operating for a brief period as a '50s-themed bar.

In February 1984, the club was renovated and the stage returned to the north end of the room. Once again the building proudly donned the moniker the Horseshoe Tavern.

In its new incarnation, run by the consortium of Richard Kruk, X-Ray Macrae, and Kenny Sprackman, the Horseshoe quickly became an integral part of the Queen

Street West scene, booking artists such as Alta Moda, the Shuffle Demons, the Parachute Club, Prairie Oyster, Blue Rodeo (numerous times), the Watchmen, and the Tragically Hip. The latter referenced the Horseshoe's checkered floor in their 1998 hit "Bobcaygeon."

Ironically, the most famous show the club ever hosted was when the Rolling Stones played a warm-up gig there September 4, 1997. Including rarely played oldies such as "The Last Time," "19th Nervous Breakdown," and Chuck Berry's "Little Queenie" in their set, the Stones were transcendent. It was the third of five club shows the Rolling Stones blessed Toronto with over the years.

As the original explosion of late seventies Toronto punk began to fade away, in 1981 and 1982, three new venues on Queen Street West began booking local and touring bands. The Cameron House, the Rivoli, and the BamBoo would all play central roles during the second wave of Queen Street West's glory years. The Cameron House, at 408 Queen Street West, started booking music acts in October 1981 when Anne Marie Ferraro, her brother Paul Sannella,

and their friend Herb Tookey took over what was then a nearly 100-year-old hotel. The distinctive bugs crawling up the east side of the building made the club hard to miss. Inside, there was a front and back room, each of which held about 60 patrons.

On January 9, 1982, Handsome Ned (real name Robin David Masyk) was hired to play Saturday matinees at the Cameron. Ned would continue playing Saturdays at the Cameron until his tragic death in January 1987. The iconoclastic musician single-handedly introduced the 1980s Queen Street West scene to the deep-seated authenticity of 1940s and 1950s country music. As was the case with Stompin' Tom Connors' days at the Horseshoe in the late 1960s and early 1970s, Ned's five-year run at the Cameron had an inordinate influence on many local musicians. When Greg Keelor and Jim Cuddy returned to Toronto after a three-year stint in New York City, seeing Ned in the back room of the Cameron played a decisive role in influencing the direction they would take with their new band, Blue Rodeo. For most of his all-too-short career, Ned played the Cameron exclusively. The exceptions were

Valentine's Day 1985 and 1986, when he staged special shows at the Rivoli and the Horseshoe respectively.

The Rivoli show featured Blue Rodeo as the opening act, playing just their second gig ever! (In David McPherson's book *The Legendary Horseshoe Tavern* and in a number of articles, it has been written that this gig occurred at the Horseshoe Tavern. According to a *Globe and Mail* article printed the day before the show and original Blue Rodeo keyboardist Bob Wiseman, the show was definitely at the Rivoli.)

To make the evening special, Ned had the Rivoli decked out as a country saloon. The walls were papered over to look like wood; bales of straw were brought in; swinging saloon doors were installed at the entrance. Ned also had the red barn backdrop and the sign that read "The Grand Ole Cameron" that hung behind him at his Cameron shows set up at the back of the Rivoli stage. To round out the festivities, the evening began with square dance instruction and a quick draw contest with someone named Black Bart! Ned's Valentine's Day 1986 show was at the Horseshoe, where he invited Johnny and the G-Rays front man Johnny MacLeod

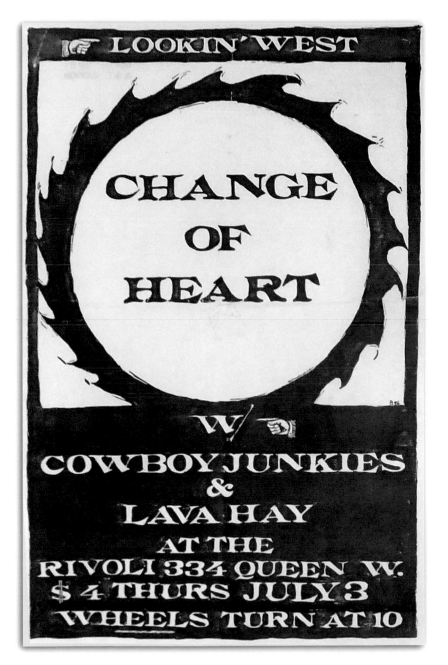

July 3, 1986, Rivoli

and singer-songwriter Murray McLauchlan to join him as part of what he dubbed "The Ned Big Band."

Over the years, in addition to Handsome Ned, the Cameron hosted a who's who of Queen Street artists, including Blue Rodeo, Jane Siberry, Ron Sexsmith, Molly Johnson, Holly Cole, Barenaked Ladies, Lorraine Segato of the Parachute Club, the Government, Fifth Column, and Mary Margaret O'Hara.

The Rivoli, located at 334 Queen Street West, opened in 1982 with a restaurant up front, a pool hall upstairs, and a performance space in the back. The logo and signage in the club consisted of illustrations that Mary Margaret O'Hara had drawn when she was still a student at the Ontario College of Art. The Parachute Club played one of its earliest gigs at the Rivoli in 1982. Blue Rodeo played their debut gig in the back room February 8, 1985 (Greg Keelor has stated the date was February 7, but the ads in the newspapers list the gig as February 8; Shadowy Men on a Shadowy Planet are listed as playing February 7). In the 1990s, the Rivoli occasionally hosted performances by touring bands, such as Bad Religion, Stone Temple Pilots, and L7.

Iggy Pop debuted three songs from his *Brick by Brick* album there in June 1990, and New York punk poetess Patti Smith played a surprise acoustic gig at the club in March 1997 following a talk she gave as part of Canadian Music Week.

From 1983 until 2002, the BamBoo was the most important club on Queen. Dubbed in the *Toronto Star*'s weekly listings as "the pride of Queen West," the BamBoo was unlike any club that Toronto had seen before or since. Owners Richard O'Brien and Patti Habib had both worked at the CBC before opening the MBC booze can in 1980 in Habib's third-floor loft at Liberty and Jefferson. The MBC was open on Mondays and Thursdays only, and the Parachute Club (partially arising out of the ashes of the legendary feminist band Mama Quilla II) played their first gig there — with an invite designed by eclectic local artist Barbara Klunder. Other notable bands booked by O'Brien into the MBC were Rough Trade and Junior Walker. In early 1981, O'Brien leased a building that had most recently housed a furniture store called Wicker World at 312 Queen Street West. With Habib helping to finance and

(left) May 1999, BamBoo
(right) August 1, 1993, Cameron House

organize the operation, nearly 18 months were spent renovating the near-derelict building. When they were ready to open, they called the new club the BamBoo due to the massive amount of wicker that they had to clear out of the place. With neither a liquor permit nor running water in place, the first event at the BamBoo nevertheless went ahead in July 1983: a record release party for Parachute Club's debut album.

The BamBoo officially opened August 26, 1983, with Philadelphia funk legends Prince Charles and the City Beat Band. For the next 20 years, O'Brien booked an amazing mélange of ska, reggae, funk, soul, R&B, hip hop, jazz, and African bands into the BamBoo. With a few exceptions, such as during a week in January 1986 when the club hosted a run of nights that they billed as "neo-psychedelia," featuring Rochester's the Chesterfield Kings, Boston's the Lyres, and Toronto's own Cowboy Junkies, the club avoided booking artists that might be thought of as playing one or another form of mainstream rock music.

In addition to its incredibly progressive and diverse music policy, the BamBoo had a unique look, an innovative menu, and a vibe wholly unto its own that captured the diversity that makes Toronto such an incredible city. The club's logo, menus, ads, posters, T-shirts, and wall murals were all designed by O'Brien's then girlfriend Barbara Klunder.

"Since the music (reggae, jazz, funk, blues) was black, I turned to my art books on Africa for inspiration and information," Klunder wrote in the BamBoo cookbook. "A lot of African art is simple, bold, often black-on-white, with zigzags and patterns, fabulously powerful in its simplicity." Klunder's "funky, vibrant and playful style" also became associated with the visual identity of progressive community radio station CKLN-FM in the 1980s and 1990s.

The building that housed the club was slightly recessed from the street. To access it, patrons passed though large green iron gates that Habib and O'Brien had salvaged from the original Drake Hotel, and then walked down a tropical garden pathway/alley that opened up onto an outdoor patio with bamboo, tropical plants, and outdoor tables. Double doors that provided the entranceway to the club itself were marked by a blue mosaic on the floor, again designed by Klunder. The mosaic featured a very animated yellow moon.

Inside was the main room with the stage straight ahead and a restaurant on the right side. Upstairs was the Treetop Lounge, an outside bar on the club's roof that Habib and O'Brien opened in the summer of 1984.

The BamBoo's menu was as unique for Toronto at the time as its decor and artwork.

A fusion of Caribbean and Thai cuisine, for many Torontonians the club's menu was their introduction to callaloo soup, pad Thai, and gado-gado. Within a few years, as Toronto blossomed into one of the most cosmopolitan cities in the world, such food offerings were to be found all over the city, but in 1983 the BamBoo was a trendsetter. Unbelievably, the menu never changed over the club's 20-year history, and according to Habib, they were the only club in Toronto to make more money serving food than liquor.

The musical offerings at the BamBoo were as unique as the decor and menu. Highlights abound, including appearances by Hugh Masekela, Erykah Badu, the Last Poets, Papa Wemba, Cecil Taylor, Boukman Eksperyans, the World Saxophone Quartet, Baaba Maal, Fishbone, Slim Gaillard, the Art Ensemble of Chicago, the Mighty Sparrow, and Screamin' Jay Hawkins.

In 1989, Sam Mensah and Thaddy Ulzen, through their company Highlife World, convinced Richard O'Brien to host the first Afrofest May 4 through June 3. Among the incredible artists that played the festival that first year were Sonny Okosun from Nigeria, Kanda Bongo Man from the

April 18, 1997, Rivoli

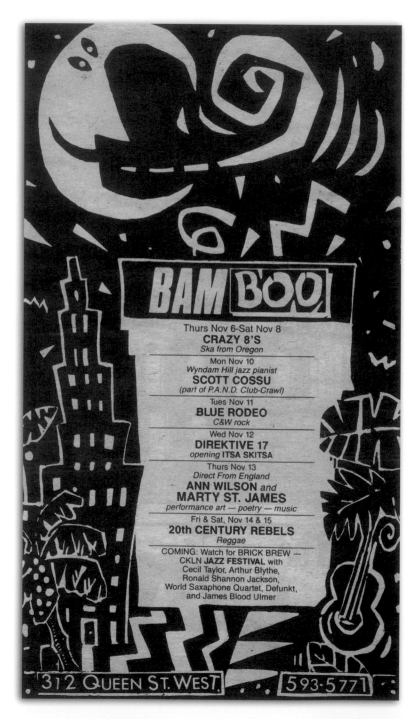

BAM BOO

Thurs Nov 6-Sat Nov 8
CRAZY 8'S
Ska from Oregon

Mon Nov 10
Wyndam Hill jazz pianist
SCOTT COSSU
(part of P.A.N.D. Club-Crawl)

Tues Nov 11
BLUE RODEO
C&W rock

Wed Nov 12
DIREKTIVE 17
opening ITSA SKITSA

Thurs Nov 13
Direct From England
ANN WILSON *and*
MARTY ST. JAMES
performance art — poetry — music

Fri & Sat, Nov 14 & 15
20th CENTURY REBELS
Reggae

COMING: Watch for BRICK BREW —
CKLN **JAZZ FESTIVAL** with
Cecil Taylor, Arthur Blythe,
Ronald Shannon Jackson,
World Saxaphone Quartet, Defunkt,
and James Blood Ulmer

312 QUEEN ST. WEST. ... **593·5771**

Congo, and Sankofa, Native Spirit, and Okyerema Asante from Ghana.

In addition to the international artists coming through, the BamBoo constantly programmed local reggae acts such as Leroy Sibbles, the Sattalites (who recorded a live album at the club in 1987), Messenjah, Tabarruk, and dub poets Lillian Allen and Clifton Joseph, as well as Queen Street habitués such as the Parachute Club, Blue Rodeo, Molly Johnson, and the Shuffle Demons.

The BamBoo finally closed its gates Halloween night 2002 with performances by Parachute Club's Billy Bryans and the Sattalites. Queen Street had become the home to chain retailers such as Gap and Anthropologie and had lost much of what had made it so special.

There are two other clubs that should be mentioned as being integral to the Queen Street scene: the Cabana Room and the Holiday Tavern. The Cabana was actually located south of Queen on the northwest corner of King Street and Spadina Avenue. The building was originally constructed in 1875 as the Richardson House Hotel. Renamed the Spadina Hotel, the

November 1986, BamBoo

art deco Cabana Room was located on the second floor. In the 1980s and early 1990s, post-punk bands such as Fifth Column, the Party's Over, the Woods Are Full of Cuckoos, Rheostatics, and Skydiggers regularly played the upstairs venue.

The Holiday Tavern, located at 651 Queen Street West on the southeast corner of Queen and Bathurst, was constructed in 1876 for the Toronto Masons. In the late 1950s and early 1960s it hosted a number of touring R&B bands, largely catering to members of Toronto's then small but fervent black community, who were mostly nestled a few blocks north and east of the building. Frank Motley's band were regulars at the club and soul star Jackie Shane's first Toronto gig was at the Holiday in September 1961.

On July 11, 1985, the Holiday once again began hosting bands with Traffic Jam and Alta Moda featuring Molly Johnson playing the opening-night party. Through the rest of 1985 and into early 1986, the club brought to town the Fabulous Thunderbirds, John Mayall, the Beau Brummels, Dr. John, the Neville Brothers, and West Coast blues legend Lowell Fulson, as well as booking local artists Blue Rodeo, V, and expatriate Jamaican reggae star Willi Williams. Unfortunately, listings for the club stopped in early 1986 amidst rumours of financial troubles. By June the venue had reopened as the Big Bop, but live bands were not part of the new owner's business model. For the next 10 years the Big Bop was a dance club spinning rock and roll on the first floor and disco and house on the second floor, while the third floor served as a small chill room.

While the Horseshoe Tavern and the Rivoli remain, by the early 2000s there was little about Queen Street West to remind one of the halcyon days of the 1980s when the street and the area surrounding it served as the germinating point for Toronto's burgeoning popular music scene featuring local bands and touring acts alike.

Saturday, September 17th, '88
The Concert Hall   888 Yonge
8:00 PM – 5:00 AM
(10:00 pm showtime)
$19.50 Advance /
$22.50 at Door

Ron Nelson Productions
Presents

THE BADDEST BACK-TO-SCHOOL
CONCERT & DANCE FOR '88!!!

Starring:

from N.Y.C.

Ain't No Half Steppin
Raw

from Philadelphia

Danger Zone

from N.Y.C.

Strong Island
Stylin' Lyrics

My Part Of Town

TUFF CREW

JVC FORCE

BIG DADDY KANE
& the I.O.U. Dancers & Crew

from Toronto
D-SHAN
(Alive With Pleasure)

...Music by CKLN's RON
NELSON, the very best in
mastermixed   Hip-Hop,
Reggae, House & Slow.

...10,000 Watts of Sound
by CHIC DYNASTY
...& the spectacular light
show returns...

ADVANCE TICKETS AVAILABLE AT:

CARNIVAL RECORDS – 596-0561
361 Yonge (Downtown)

STARSOUND RECORDS – 977-0525
427 Yonge (Downtown)

MELLO MUSIC – 757-7812
2388 Eglinton E. (Scarborough)

WORLD OF MUSIC – 635-7119
(Jane & Finch Mall)

NORTHERN LIGHTS – 673-8944
7205 Goreway Dr. (Malton)

MONICAS – 789-5722
1553 Eglinton W. (York)

NETWORK RECORDS – 498-0938
3453 Victoria Park (N. of Finch)

Call the JAM LINE, 291-4338 for 24-hr concert & dance information. Stay tuned to CKLN 88.1 FM's
Fantastic Voyage Program (Saturdays, 1 - 4 pm) and WBLK for ticket giveaways and more information.

September 17, 1988,
Concert Hall

15

HIP HOP

On November 3, 1979, in a nondescript nightclub behind Toronto City Hall, Rapper Billy G got on a microphone and delivered ad libbed rhymes over disco grooves and breakbeats. Local disc jockey Maceo was on the decks. Sugarhill Gang's "Rapper's Delight" had been released two months prior, so it's likely he rhymed over the instrumental — a bass-heavy rendition of Chic's disco smash "Good Times."

Through the smoke and sweat, one thing was clear: hip hop had arrived in Toronto. We know this because the first mention of *hip hop* in a Toronto print publication was in the October 30, 1979, issue of community newspaper *Share*.

But let's go farther back.

One of the most basic elements of hip hop was on full display in May 1972 when the Last Poets brought their streetwise poetry to the Masonic Temple at Yonge and Davenport. Or perhaps we can go even farther back, to James Brown's debut show in 1965 at an Etobicoke roller rink, where precursors of breakdancing and a funk-infused dialect were on offer.

So, how did modern hip hop migrate from the streets of the Bronx to Toronto? Most likely the same way it travelled from the Bronx to Manhattan: through word of mouth and the humble mix tape. Many Torontonians (especially of African and Caribbean ancestry) travelled to New York City to see family and friends, and returned with tapes of parties by the likes of DJ Kool Herc, Grandmaster Flash, and Busy Bee Starski. Perhaps you had a cousin who lived in the South Bronx, and you went there every summer. Then you came back telling everyone you were "rocking and shocking the microphone, and telling all sucka emcees to go home." The ethnic, social, and cultural connections between immigrant communities in Toronto and New York most certainly played a pivotal role in the import of early hip hop.

By late 1979, everything had changed. "Rapper's Delight" (the first recorded rap single) had entered the *Billboard* Hot 100 chart, and was receiving regular radio play. However, Toronto radio stations were still catering to predominantly white audiences and rarely played the song. Thanks to WBLK, a small radio station transmitting out of Buffalo, Torontonians for the first time could hear the following words on their FM dial: "I said a hip hop …"

Back to the nondescript club behind City Hall: 14 Hagerman Street, was, by all accounts, Toronto's first club to play rap music. It featured a rotating cast of the city's top selectors: Mr. Magic, Rose Royce, Maceo, Sunshine, and many others who played a regular mix of funk and disco, interspersed with rhymes from a local MC, whether it was Billy G, Butch Lee, Oral D, or other toasters of the time.

In late December 1979, Mellow Man productions presented Soul at the Centre, a five-day festival at the O'Keefe Centre, headlined by the Godfather of Soul, James Brown. However, it was the Fatback Band's show on the second day (January 1, 1980) that stands out as possibly the *first* rap performance on a Toronto stage. We say *possibly* because we can't say for certain that King Tim III (Timothy Washington) toured with the band. If he did, he certainly would have performed his rap from the song "Personality Jock," notable as the first recorded rap verse in history.

Two weeks later, a watershed moment occurred. On January 12, 1980, the Sugarhill Gang played the Concert Hall inside the Masonic Temple. Writer Peter Goddard of the *Toronto Star* said in his review, "'Rapper's Delight' is pure jive. It's an all-night deejay playing with words over some slick rhythm with a heavy backbeat." He would go on to describe the music as "punk funk." Not bad for a review of a completely new art form by a rock critic. The *Toronto Sun*'s Jonathan Gross was less enthralled, saying "poor lighting and tacky staging gave the show an amateur-hour look, and the Gang depended heavily on their funky band to pad a one-song repertoire." No flyer or poster was ever made, as according to Gross, "a rookie promoter sold almost a thousand tickets on word of mouth in disco record stores." A fascinating look back at the first hip hop show in Toronto.

September 10, 1980, Ontario Place Forum

In September, the Sugarhill Gang would return to play in front of 2,500 at the much larger Ontario Place Forum, and Kurtis Blow would make his debut, performing his only record at the time, the dance-floor hit "The Breaks," at the aptly named SuperJamm 80 party at 14 Hagerman. Hip hop was in its infancy, and would be closely associated with disco for at least a couple more years.

"T.O. Raps It Up" was the headline for the February 18, 1982, cover story of local Toronto weekly *NOW*. Whereas 14 Hagerman was still a full-fledged disco and funk club, the article points to the Dub Club (115 McCaul) as Toronto's first establishment with dedicated rap programming. The cover story profiled some of the city's earliest rappers, including T.O. Express, Hugo Samuels, and Tony Langley. "At the Dub Club, the rapping starts at 8 p.m. and runs until 1 a.m. How can somebody talk basically non-stop for all that time? 'Once I start rapping, I can hit a groove and rap all night, the music carries me,' says Langley. 'If the people in the crowd are giving me something back, I could rap for days.'"

In 1982, hip hop was becoming a force to be reckoned with. The Roland TR-808 drum machine was revolutionizing music, and dancehall (with its gritty take on Jamaican toasting) was packing Toronto venues. On August 18, perennial punk and new wave favourites Blondie rolled into Exhibition Stadium for their second last show before eventually disbanding. Debbie Harry's performance of "Rapture," with her weird and twisted raps about eating cars, would become the first rap performance by a female artist in Toronto. Sadly, the performance of the band was panned by critics, with positive reviews reserved for their opening act, a new band out of Birmingham called Duran Duran.

Rapping or "punk-funk" or disco-rap (hip hop had not yet gathered traction as the culture's namesake) continued to gather steam. However, up to that point the vast majority of records were intended for the dance floor. That all changed in July 1982 when Grandmaster Flash and the Furious Five released "The Message." In an instant, the raw and gritty reality of New York City street life was broadcast to the world. The Black CNN was born, and rap music became the mouthpiece of disenfranchised American black youth.

That brings us to January 7, 1983, when local promoting duo the Garys presented the group in their debut Toronto show at the Concert Hall. "We were really excited about hip hop. We read about it in the *Village Voice*, and it was interesting and avant-garde. And the way Flash could work the turntable, to us, he was the new Hendrix," recalls Topp. The show attracted 700 people, and the crowd was eclectic and racially diverse. However, it was a financial flop. "The band's guarantee was $7,000. And with the venue fee, marketing, production and other costs, we lost money," recalls Topp.

In 1983, emerging artists were innovating and putting new spins on what hip hop could be. Afrika Bambaataa released "Planet Rock," which infused rap with the sonic influences of German electro and P-Funk. And a new outfit from Queens, Run-DMC, released the groundbreaking single "Sucka MCs." Hip hop was taking off.

Many would argue that 1984 was a milestone year for hip hop, and this was certainly evident in Toronto. Ron Nelson was regularly broadcasting rap tunes on his hugely influential community radio program *Fantastic Voyage*, and movies like *Wild Style* and *Beat Street* were bringing the culture of hip hop to the masses. It was these films in particular that showcased the four elements of hip hop culture, and, in particular, graffiti and breakdancing. Breaking became all the rage in '84 and many high schools in Toronto held breakdance events. In January 1984, Toronto after-hours club the Twilight Zone booked NYC's Dynamic Breakers for a dance showcase, making it one of the first (if not *the* first) international b-boy/b-girl events in the city.

Around this time, Jonathan Gross was a Toronto native living in New York City, writing for *Rolling Stone*. "I was at a club, and I bumped into Nile Rodgers, and I remember him telling me that rock was dead, and hip hop was all that mattered," recalls Gross. "So I decided to try my hand at promoting shows."

A few months later, on April 18, 1984, Jonathan brought the Godfather of Hip Hop, Afrika Bambaataa, and his Zulu Nation cohort DJ Jazzy Jay to Club Heaven under the promotion banner Gross National Product.

"That show was significant. It had breakdancers, graffiti writers, DJs, and MCs. It was the first show of its kind in Toronto — one which featured the key elements of hip hop culture," remembers Gross.

By mid-1984 Herbie Hancock's song "Rockit" had become a huge hit and de

January 7, 1983,
Concert Hall

facto hip hop anthem. It was notably groundbreaking for its use of scratching and cutting courtesy of Grand Mixer DXT who was a member of Hancock's Rockit band. Hancock's embrace of DXT's wax manipulations brought the art of turntablism to the global stage. On September 11, 1984, they arrived to play in front of 800 fans at the Copa in Yorkville. The show received positive reviews, with a *Globe and Mail* reviewer writing, "Scratcher DXT had an individual showcase that turned Hancock's rituals into an Apollo-like revue." By all accounts, this was the first turntablist routine performed on a Toronto stage.

A few days later, on September 21, Gross presented "America's Number One Rap Group," Run-DMC, for their first show outside the United States. It was also at Heaven (located in what is now the shopping concourse at Bloor-Yonge station), and tickets were just seven dollars. "We paid them their guarantee of $1,500 USD plus airfare to Buffalo. So I went to Buffalo in my GMC Blazer to pick them up and bring them into Canada. I packed Darryl, Joe, Jay, and their manager Jeff into the car. Four black guys in leather jackets and fedoras, and me at the wheel. When the [border] guard saw us pull up, he was so scared he just waved us through." Gross would also bring Whodini to Regent Park's Dance Theatre before the close of the year. By the end of 1984, live hip hop was coming of age in Toronto.

The year 1985 would continue to see milestone moments in Toronto's hip hop concert history. On May 23, Madonna brought her Virgin Tour to Maple Leaf Gardens. She invited NYC trio Beastie Boys to open the show. Undoubtedly, this was the first time a mainly white, suburban (and predominantly female) audience were treated to live hip hop in the city. By most accounts, the crowd of 18,000 teen queens rolled their eyes at the loud and obnoxious Beasties. However, later that night the group was scheduled to perform at the Twilight Zone for a midnight performance (also promoted by Gross). "I remember calling Mike D. at his parents' condo in Florida, asking if they'd do the after-party, and he said they would for a case of Molson!" remembers Gross. In their first Toronto solo gig, the pre–*Licensed to Ill* trio would go on to perform songs from their punk catalogue and tear up the walls with graffiti. "We walked in on the Beasties tagging the walls, and they were apologetic. But we said no, it looks great! Keep going. That's how the words *Busting Loose* and *Twerk* made it onto our walls," recalls Twilight Zone owner Albert Assoon.

It's important to note that despite having a short run as a concert promoter, Jonathan Gross was the first person to take substantial risks in order to bring world-class hip hop talent to Toronto. In 1984 and '85 he successfully introduced Toronto audiences to the magic of Run-DMC, Beastie Boys, Whodini, UTFO, and others. He certainly set the stage for others to pick up where he left off. "Jonathan was this white, Jewish guy who absolutely loved hip hop. He promoted to suburban black neighbourhoods. He took risks, and I learned a lot from him," recalls Ron Nelson.

As hip hop grew in popularity, more promoters and artists got involved in concert production. One well-renowned crew, Sunshine Sound, put on an impressive string of groundbreaking shows that year. In April 1985 they introduced Toronto audiences to the Juice Crew's Marley Marl and his 15-year-old protege Roxanne Shante at the Concert Hall. A few months later they rebooked Shante for a solo appearance at the same venue (most likely accompanied by her tour DJ at the time, Biz Markie). That year Sunshine also orchestrated the return of Run-DMC for their second show on March 10, 1985. "We cold-called William Morris Agency in New York and said hey we're from Toronto, how much to book Run-DMC? And they said $5,000," recalled Tony D. of Sunshine on the Views Before The 6 podcast. "We put 3,000 people in the Concert Hall. You couldn't move." Although the passage of time lends itself to embellishment, no doubt the place was packed to the rafters. According to the *Globe and Mail* review, "The show began with Jam Master Jay … dressed in a black fedora, black leather jacket … taking over the turntables for a dazzling display of scratching, creating a rhythmic pattern of scratches and jumps accompanied by a pulverizing beat box that shook the room." Writer Liam Lacey continued, "The routine between the three is complex and extensive."

What made the show particularly unique was how it was promoted. The Sunshine Crew drove to different (mainly black) suburban neighbourhoods all over the city

May 23, 1985,
Twilight Zone

LIVE IN CONCERT

RUN - D.M.C.

AMERICA'S NUMBER 1 RAP GROUP!

SUNDAY MARCH 10th 1985
AT THE CONCERT HALL
888 YONGE STREET
(CORNER OF DAVENPORT)

MARCH
BREAK EVENT

DOORS OPEN 6 P.M.
SHOW TIME 9 P.M.
PARTY UNTIL 5 A.M.

ALSO APPEARING

TORONTO'S VANITY 6 GIRLS (LIPSING)
AND TORONTO'S HOTTEST BREAK DANCERS

ADMISSION: $10.00 WITH FLYER

MUSIC BY

Sunshine SOUND
& CREW

FOR INFORMATION CALL:
292-9413
656-1848

SONGS INCLUDE:
ROCK BOX
IT'S LIKE THAT
30 DAYS
HARD TIMES
KING OF THE ROCK
YOU TALK TOO MUCH
ROOTS, RAP, REGGAE
AND MORE. . . .

TO AVOID DISAPPOINTMENT BE EARLY

"I remember going to this show when I was 14yrs old … My brother took me on a school night and it was amazing!!! I bumped into @unclerush and he took me backstage to meet my childhood heroes … cut to 30yrs later and I can say that I am friends with #RussellSimmons and @dmcmakescomics my life has become something that a little brown boy from Brampton could never have even imagined … I've never stopped being a fan of my childhood heroes … Don't ever get too caught up to enjoy the greatness that life provides!!!"

— Russell Peters, comedian and actor (Run-D.M.C., Concert Hall, March 10, 1985

March 10, 1985, Concert Hall

and littered them with flyers. The concept of the street team was essentially born with this show. It was also one of the first hip hop concerts to be promoted by black entrepreneurs, to a predominantly Jamaican Canadian audience. The *Globe* review of the show prophetically concluded that it was "completely packed. It shouldn't be long before experienced professional promoters start making money from this burgeoning musical market."

The Garys, Jonathan Gross, and Sunshine Sound may have been the first wave of hip hop promoters in the city; however, it was the efforts of a young Jamaican Canadian named Ron Nelson that took the business of hip hop to unprecedented new heights. In 1985, Ron had been DJing parties and running his popular *Fantastic Voyage* program on Ryerson's radio station. Then he decided to take a run at promoting shows. "We were seeing all these big shows, such as Fresh Fest, come as close as Buffalo, but they never came to Toronto. It was almost like we didn't exist," recalls Ron about those early days. "It was like we were being teased. It was all happening over there. But we had a scene. We loved the music.

The Americans just didn't know it." Ron's radio show would become the impetus for his concert career. "Listeners were calling in and asking where they could see these artists? And then asking me, 'can you bring them to town?' Nobody else had the will to reach out and do the dirty work, and get these artists to come to town. I was not qualified, but I said 'let me look into it.' It was intimidating calling these agents. But I was trying to break down these walls. To let them know that it was worth coming to Canada. I was essentially providing a community service."

Ron's first show was bringing DJ Jazzy Jay to the Dance Theatre in Regent Park in January 1985.

The deep Caribbean influences that existed in Toronto, coupled with the advent of dancehall, enabled the development of sound clash culture in the city. Armed with their proprietary speaker systems, several sound crews would criss-cross the city to represent their hood as they battled one another. "It wasn't uncommon to go to a party and witness one crew playing on their system, and then another crew playing on theirs — in the same room!" recalls MC

Thrust on Views Before The 6. Names like Maceo, Sunshine, TKO, Kilowatt, and Chic Dynasty were playing dances all over the city, including inner-city neighbourhoods such as Jane and Finch, the Jungle (Lawrence and Dufferin), Flemingdon Park, Rexdale, and Regent Park. This vibrant culture set the stage for July 6, 1985, when Ron Nelson produced the first of several legendary Monster Jams, showcasing DJ crews from all over southern Ontario and New York State. These dances would provide a forum to see which crew would be the "champion sound." This spark would help ignite Toronto's hip hop scene.

The golden age of hip hop in Toronto began in 1986. Ron's success with Monster Jam opened the door to a very prosperous multi-year run as the pre-eminent hip hop promoter in the city. On March 15, 1986, an epic battle of beat-boxers, female MCs, and DJs was on full display when he produced the first of several "Ultimate Hip Hop Battles." The show pitted the best and brightest from New York City in a battle with the best and brightest from Toronto. At a time when New York was considered the mecca of hip hop, it was truly unthinkable to see artists travelling to Toronto to battle us on our home turf. Biz Markie battled Kid Icy Beats and Mighty Mouse Rock for beat box supremacy, and Roxanne Shante would make her third appearance in as many months to battle Fly K and Mischievous C. "The Battle was one of my favourite and [most] important concerts. At that time, nobody gave Canadian hip hop respect. We were very misunderstood. They didn't think we could rap. To see New York artists such as Big Daddy Kane, Biz Markie, and Roxanne Shante come up and compete with the likes of Michie Mee, Rumble and Strong … that's when I got the most chills up my spine. That's when I knew Canadian hip hop had arrived," remembers Nelson.

The second week of April 1986 would also be historic, as the Beastie Boys played the Copa in Yorkville, followed by LL Cool J at the Concert Hall three days later. The era of Def Jam had officially arrived in Toronto. According to a *Toronto Star* review, "The Beastie Boys bounced onto the stage yelling obscenities and spitting beer at the crowd. The first few minutes were brash and exciting, as the three deejays leapt about throwing down streams of rhymes." The reviewer went on to call the Beasties "a novelty act."

By the latter half of the 1980s, live hip hop in Toronto was synonymous with two things: Ron Nelson and the Concert Hall.

The Concert Hall's embrace of hip hop and reggae, and their willingness to host all-ages events made it the de facto home of rap shows in the 1980s. Thrust would go so far as to call it "The Apollo" of Toronto's hip hop scene. "The Concert Hall was owned by the Stonemasons, and their goal was to serve the community non-prejudicially. Other venues would turn us away because we didn't have that suit-and-tie look. But the Concert Hall gave us a chance," recalls Nelson. The venue's open policy toward hip hop and communities of colour was not the only redeeming quality. "The room could comfortably accommodate 2,000 people, had a central location (meaning it was neutral territory for rival crews), and the masonry of the room lent itself to incredible acoustics. The place unified the scene," says Nelson.

By 1987, with his radio show, street team (of which DJ X and Mastermind are alumni),

and production studio, Ron Nelson *was* the infrastructure for hip hop in Toronto. From 1987 to 1993, he produced a spectacular run of very important, milestone shows. On March 14, 1987, he hosted the second annual Ultimate Battle, which featured a then 16-year-old Michie Mee battling Sugar Love of New York. Mee's use of patois-slang riled the crowd, ensuring victory over her adversary and guaranteeing respect for Canada's hip hop scene from our friends south of the border. That same show would feature the return of beat box legend Biz Markie with his then unknown hype man Big Daddy Kane.

The next few years would see a remarkable run of shows from hip hop's new school: In 1987, Salt-N-Pepa and Heavy D & the Boyz on August 22; Biz Markie and Big Daddy Kane on October 17; Eric B. and Rakim on November 21; and Public Enemy's debut show on December 26. The Run's House Tour featuring Run-DMC, EPMD, and Public Enemy came through town on August 23, 1988, notably, as the first packaged arena hip hop tour to hit the city. "What surprised me the most, I promoted it mostly to black people, however I would

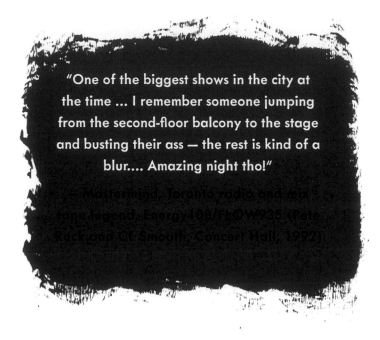

"One of the biggest shows in the city at the time ... I remember someone jumping from the second-floor balcony to the stage and busting their ass — the rest is kind of a blur.... Amazing night tho!"

— Mastermind, Toronto radio and mix tape legend, Energy108/FLOW935 (Pete Rock and CL Smooth, Concert Hall, 1992)

By the early 1990s, the Toronto hip hop concert market was thriving, and the city was becoming a required stop for major artists and groups. Hip hop was also going through a cycle of transformation, and the West Coast G-funk sound had taken over. Snoop would make his Toronto debut in 1997 as part of Lollapalooza. Dr. Dre's first appearance was as part of the Up In Smoke Tour in July 2000. Unfortunately, one of hip hop's biggest icons, Tupac Shakur, never played the city.

But while the West was enjoying its dominance, behind the scenes a New York rap renaissance was brewing.

By 1993, Ron Nelson had become disillusioned with hip hop, and transitioned to mainly promoting reggae shows. With his departure from the concert scene, many people tried to capitalize on hip hop. This created a Wild West environment in which promoters tried to make a quick buck by promoting rap shows. Many concerts would be oversold, or worse, the artists wouldn't show up. Several concerts ended in riots, like the Bring the Pain tour in 1994 (Redman, Keith Murray, and Method Man) and Rap Fest '95 (Common, Redman, and Craig Mack). It was during

have lost my shirt if it wasn't for the white people who showed up," recalls Nelson. Nelson brought Boogie Down Productions to the city on December 26, 1988; Ice-T on June 10, 1989; Queen Latifah on May 19, 1990; Cypress Hill and Pete Rock and CL Smooth on March 21, 1992; and Mobb Deep on July 10, 1993. With his groundbreaking radio program, concert production resume, and work as a producer, Ron Nelson's efforts contributed to the rise of a generation of talented artists from Toronto. It's no wonder he is widely considered the godfather of Canadian hip hop.

this tumultuous era that a young kid from Brampton came onto the scene.

Jonathan Ramos started promoting shows in 1993. "My brother and some friends DJed in high school, and at the time I was working for the Ontario government. Through my friend Errol Nazareth, I met Ron Nelson, who was a Toronto legend. Ron was transitioning out of hip hop into reggae, so I decided promoting could be something I could try out. Within two years, I quit my job and dove into it full-time," recalls Ramos.

Ramos founded R.E.M.G. and produced his first concert on June 21, 1993, presenting the Pharcyde, Bass Is Base, and a relatively unknown comic named Russell Peters. "I remember getting booed off stage. I wore a custom baseball jersey and tucked it in like an idiot. I was wearing red jeans and this fly baseball jersey. I was trying to keep it classy," recalled Peters on Power105's *The Breakfast Club*.

I asked Ramos what one of his proudest moments as a concert promoter was. "Working with the Roots was amazing. One of my favourite memories was promoting an outdoor Roots concert in the summer of

November 7, 1992, Bassline

March 5, 1994, Palladium

"Will remember this concert forever. It was the most diverse
crowd I have ever seen at a rap show ... I remember the
show opening with 'Brain Damage' ... Anyone remember the
giant mushrooms on stage?"

— Kasper Kennedy
(Eminem, Opera House, 1999)

1996 at the CNE Bandshell. It was a beautiful summer day, and it was a free show. Over 10,000 people showed up for a day of hip hop. We had Dream Warriors, Intrikit, Paul E. Lopes, Mastermind, Thrust, Choclair, and I just remember admiring the scene. Hip hop culture on full display in the park, just like the old days. It was hip hop 101. It was a community thing, and it was beautiful. Definitely one of my fondest memories as a promoter." R.E.M.G. would go on to have an impressive two-decade run as Toronto's pre-eminent urban concert promoter. They would go on to "break" a number of major artists in the city, including the Roots, Common, Goodie Mob, the Pharcyde, Outkast, Fugees, and Eminem. Jonathan's

commitment to high production values, reliability, and consistency ensured a first-rate experience for fans. Where Ron Nelson left off, R.E.M.G. picked up; a professional hip hop promoter that fans could count on.

Due to its proximity to New York, Toronto was uniquely positioned to host a spectacular run of concerts from the genre's most revered acts: Pete Rock and CL Smooth at the Bassline in November 1992; Mobb Deep at the Spectrum in July 1993; A Tribe Called Quest and De La Soul on March 5, 1994, at the Palladium; Wu-Tang Clan at the Warehouse in April 1994; and Nas at 488 Yonge in June 1994 (both promoted by Toronto hip hop legend Big Apple); Biggie Smalls in his one and only Toronto show

April 17, 1994,
Warehouse

on January 31, 1995, at an underground venue at Yonge and Gerrard (recently discovered footage of the event shows Smalls being swarmed by a mob of hard-core fans. He put on a 20-minute set before a mini-riot ensued and the show was shut down); Jay-Z, fresh off the release of his classic debut *Reasonable Doubt* performed at the Holiday Inn on King Street on July 31, 1996; the Hard Knock Life Tour featuring Jay-Z, DMX, Redman, and Method Man on March 10, 1999, at the Air Canada Centre (at the time, the largest arena hip hop tour in the city); and a controversial

THE "READY TO DIE" TOUR

the notorious B.I.G.

"JUICY"
"GIMME THE LOOT"
"THINGS DONE CHANGED"

"BIG POPPA"
"UNBELIEVABLE"
"THE WHAT"

FREESTYLE
RAP CONTEST

LIVE IN CONCERT
BIGGIE SMALLS

JANUARY 31st '95
AT THE APPOLLO
389 YONGE ST.
(corner of Gerrard)

MUSIC BY: DJX-C.K.L.N.-88.1 / CARL ALLEN / ELETE SQUAD

Ticketmaster   (416) 872-2222
Play De Record   (416) 586-0380   Traxx Music   (416) 977-4888
                                          Rock'n'Soul   (416) 298-8294

AND IF YOU DON'T KNOW, NOW YOU KNOW

January 31, 1995, Appollo

lyricist from Detroit named Eminem, who made his debut on April 10, 1999, at the Opera House in front of a modest crowd of 800 people.

By the end of the 1990s, hip hop had become mainstream and dominated popular music. In Toronto, promoters such as R.E.M.G., Kola Kube, Emerge, and Mass Appeal were bringing in a steady stream of the world's top hip hop artists. Even rave promoters were getting in on the act, bringing the likes of Run-DMC, Jungle Brothers, and EPMD to all-night dance parties. The tireless efforts of these risk-takers created the conditions for Toronto's current position as a global hub of hip hop talent.

(left) March 30, 1999, Guvernment
(centre) August 15, 1998, Molson Park
(right) April 10, 1999, Opera House

"A few things stick out. Meth and Red flying all over the place on the bungee cords ... incredible. DJ Clue handing us his business cards while he was spinning. The intro to Jay when they played the ROC family busting out of prison and Jay appears from the ground rocking a Charles Oakley Raptors jersey! At the end of Jay's set I clearly remember him saying 'for all my real fans let's go back to Reasonable Doubt.' And he performed cuts. Dope!!!!"

— Adam Morris (Hard Knock Life Tour, 1999)

(top) March 10, 1999, Air Canada Centre
(left) July 4, 2000, Molson Amphitheatre

April 13, 1995,
Club FX

16

CONTEMPORARY

R&B

The sound of modern R&B is often credited to Quincy Jones from his masterful production on Michael Jackson's debut album, *Off the Wall*. Incorporating synth-y bass lines, soul and funk, catchy vocals, and lots of sex appeal, contemporary R&B dominated popular music in the last two decades of the 20th century.

As was the case with most big tours, Toronto was a mandatory stop for many important artists of the genre. The Jacksons' 1984 Victory Tour could be considered the first modern R&B show to hit the city, when 30 trailers arrived at Exhibition Stadium for three sold-out concerts on October 5–7, 1984. Although it was billed as a Jacksons

TUESDAY JULY 22

New Edition

with special guest **112**

Energy 108 FM

July 22, 1997,
Molson Amphitheatre

show, it was essentially the Michael Jackson *Thriller* tour, with his four brothers acting as backup singers.

On August 19, 1985, lovers of R&B were treated to the Toronto debut of Boston quintet New Edition. The band was making waves with their hits "Candy Girl" and

"Mr. Telephone Man," and performed at the Kingswood Theatre at Canada's Wonderland. In the 1980s and early 1990s, you could spend a day at the amusement park, and for a few extra dollars, catch a show at night. The New Edition concert was five dollars! Although there was no review in the major publications, one irate fan wrote to the *Star* to complain about the unruly crowd, "Everyone stood on the arms of their chairs which are made of plastic and not even secured to the floor … if that wasn't bad enough some stupid person lights a sparkler. Don't people realize the danger in that?" Who knew Toronto crowds went crazy for New Edition! The band returned to Kingswood in the summer of 1986, and after a long hiatus, returned to Toronto in 1997 (sans Michael Bivins and Bobby Brown) to play the Molson Amphitheatre in support of their reunion album, *Home Again*.

Around the same time, a new band from the U.K., Sade, was transforming what modern soul could be. With their smooth and sophisticated sound, Sade planted the seeds for what would become the neo-soul movement of the 1990s. Their debut album, 1984's *Diamond Life*, was a critical success; however, lead singer Sade Adu and her band did not make it to Toronto until 1988, when, on August 24, Sade played in front of 9,500 fans at Exhibition Stadium in what the *Globe and Mail* called "a serene voice in a performance that seems as rich and ephemeral as the vapors that waft up from a snifter of cognac." The review also went on to call the visuals "one of the more intelligent light shows seen in recent years." Sade would return to Roy Thomson Hall in 1993 in support of her album *Love Deluxe*.

In 1986, Janet Jackson released her third album, *Control*. Produced by Jimmy Jam and Terry Lewis, it is widely considered to be one of the most innovative albums of the 1980s, profoundly influencing what would become new jack swing and contemporary R&B. The release of the album kicked off a hugely successful run of one of pop music's greatest stars. From 1986 to 1998, Janet consistently sold out Toronto's biggest venues, making her the number one R&B artist to play here in the '90s. On March 20, 1990, Janet brought her Rhythm Nation Tour to the SkyDome for her debut

September 29, 1998, SkyDome

Toronto show. The highly choreographed show thrilled the 24,000 fans in attendance, with the *Star* reviewer calling it "one of the crispest, most efficient bits of pop performance to hit a stage in recent memory," even going as far as to say, "the drops of sweat that ran down Jackson's forehead had their own choreographer." Jackson would continue to bring extravagant, critically acclaimed tours to Toronto, including the Janet World Tour with Tony! Toni! Toné! on November 26, 1993, and the Velvet Rope Tour with Usher (in his debut Toronto performance) on September 29, 1998, both also at the SkyDome.

Heavy D & the Boyz were one of the earliest acts to incorporate the new jack swing sound pioneered by Teddy Riley. The group made their concert debut at Rap Attack '87, an extravaganza promoted by Ron Nelson, which also featured Salt-N-Pepa and MC Shan and took place at the Concert Hall on August 22, 1987. The group returned to Toronto on December 4, 1989, performing at the CNE Coliseum with Kool Moe Dee and Rob Base and DJ E-Z Rock. However, it wouldn't be until Michael Jackson released his eighth studio album, *Dangerous*, that the sound of new jack swing would take over the world. Although the *Dangerous* world tour didn't stop in Toronto, one of the first shows featuring this sound was Bell Biv Devoe's concert at Kingswood on July 9, 1991. Billed as the MTV Club Tour, the bill also featured C+C Music Factory, Tony! Toni! Toné!, Gerardo, and Tara Kemp. The 14,000 fans in attendance paid a mere eight dollars for the show, with the *Star* saying BBD "had the crowd getting truly rowdy for the first time in the evening, right from the opening notes of 'Poison.'" New jack swing had arrived.

Contemporary R&B exploded in popularity in the 1990s. Fused with elements of hip hop, the sound was fresh, radio-friendly, and became a phenomenon with teens all over the globe. One of the biggest groups of the era was Philadelphia's Boyz II Men. The barbershop quartet made their Toronto concert debut opening for Hammer on August 1, 1992, along with TLC (in their debut appearance). And all that for nine dollars! It's worth noting that Kingswood was Toronto's only reserved seating, outdoor amphitheatre at the time, so it naturally hosted a plethora of incredible shows until the opening of the Molson Amphitheatre in May 1995. Boyz II Men was riding high off the strength of their monster hits "Motownphilly" and "End of the Road." The *Star* wrote, "This fast-rising quartet recalled the Temptations and the Four Tops, combined with a hip hop energy and collegiate banter that had every teenage girl in the house screaming." The *Star* would go on to say that Hammer was upstaged by both opening acts. Boyz II Men went on to be one of the biggest-selling acts of the 1990s, headlining the Molson Amphitheatre in 1995 with openers Montell Jordan and Mary J. Blige, and returning in 1998 to once again headline the same venue with opening acts Destiny's Child, Next, and Mya.

When you think of the biggest girl groups of the '90s R&B/hip hop era, TLC tops them all. The group had several chart-topping hits throughout the decade and three multi-platinum albums. As mentioned earlier, they debuted in Toronto opening for Hammer at Kingswood (fresh off their debut hit single "Ain't 2 Proud 2 Beg"). T-Boz, Chilli, and Left Eye returned to Toronto three years later to headline Kingswood on July 18, 1995, in support of their sophomore record, *CrazySexyCool*, which included huge hits such as "Creep"

July 4, 1995, Molson Amphitheatre

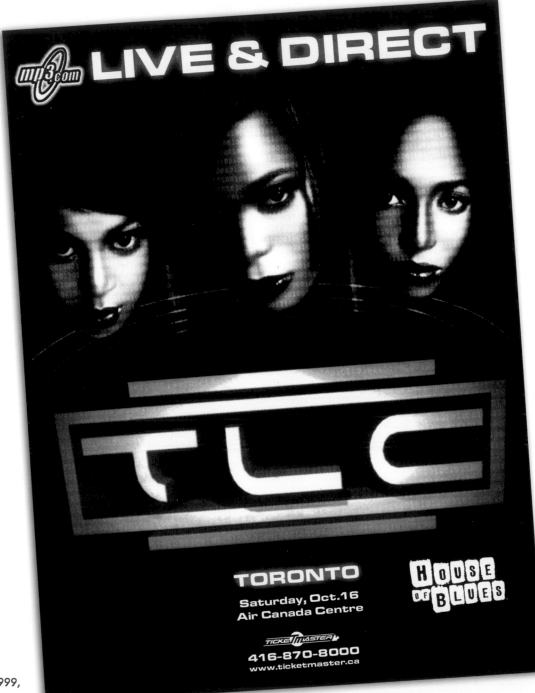

October 16, 1999,
Air Canada Centre

and "Waterfalls." Openers were Soul for Real ("Candy Rain") and Toronto R&B/funk outfit Bass Is Base. The *Star* gave the show high praise, calling it "shrewd, calculating, and on the mark." The 14,500 screaming fans in attendance surely agreed. The Atlanta trio would return for their final Toronto show (in their original incarnation) as part of the *FanMail* Tour on October 22, 1999, at the Air Canada Centre. Less than three years later, Lisa "Left Eye" Lopes would die tragically in a car accident.

With Sade planting the seeds in the 1980s, the mid-1990s saw the rise of a new organic R&B sound called neo-soul. With an emphasis on instrumentation, smooth soul, and elements of jazz and electronic music, neo-soul took popular music by storm with D'Angelo's 1995 release *Brown Sugar*. The album is considered one of the best R&B records of the 1990s. One could say the neo-soul movement first hit Toronto on October 20, 1995, when D'Angelo played for a sold-out crowd of 700 at the Opera House. NOW magazine said in their review that "the crowd was lifted for the entire evening, grooving along to the

October 20, 1995, Opera House

"I'd never seen a band so tight but so loose. They could turn on a dime ... Prince would call instruction to his band, and they'd nail it every time. He had charm, humour, sensitivity, spontaneity, and musicianship. Not to mention the show was over three hours long. And I couldn't look away for a second.... And somehow, he did it all again the next night, but with a completely different set list!"

— Ben Spivak, bassist and vocalist, MAGIC!
(Prince, Air Canada Centre, November 25–26, 2011)

caramelized harmonies he and his singers created. Of course, the key ingredient in this recipe was Brown Sugar." Another neo-soul stalwart of the era, Maxwell, wouldn't make his Toronto debut until 2001.

On February 11, 1997, Dallas-born singer-songwriter Erykah Badu released her debut album, *Baduizm*. The album was an instant classic, with much fanfare, and helped bring the neo-soul sound to the masses. She embarked on an exhaustive promo tour, remarkably making three appearances in Toronto in a span of six months. Her first gig was on March 1,

1997, at the BamBoo in a show that's still talked about today. She returned for the Apple Tree Café Tour on June 4, 1997, headlining the Guvernment (with opener Eric Benét), and finally closed out the summer by headlining the Smokin' Grooves Tour on August 23, 1997, at Kingswood, alongside George Clinton, Cypress Hill, the Roots, and Foxy Brown. The *Star* reporter was enthralled by her performance, stating, "Badu had no problem in creating a cozy environment … as she drew them into her quiet aura, with entrancing deliveries of numbers like 'On and On' and 'Next Lifetime'," continuing, "Far more tonal and textural … these songs were at once soothing and arresting."

After spending several years touring with her group, the Fugees, Lauryn Hill released her solo album, *The Miseducation of Lauryn Hill*, which became a global smash, and immediately propelled her to pop superstardom. The album was the best-selling record of 1998, and garnered her five Grammys. Ms. Hill made her debut Toronto headline appearance on August 10, 1999, at the Molson Amphitheatre. It was a triumphant and spectacular show,

May 6, 1997, Guvernment

August 10, 1999, Molson Amphitheatre

with the *Globe and Mail* stating, "The singer delivers her mini-homilies with a popular celebratory mix of humility and verve," calling the performance "a stirring seminar on black American music and spirituality."

The '90s R&B renaissance was a special time to listen to and experience live music. And Toronto crowds were better for it, as they were spoiled with a string of incredible shows from some of the genre's greatest and most enduring artists.

July 7, 1998,
Molson Amphitheatre

July 24, 1981,
Concert Hall

17
ELECTRONIC AND DANCE MUSIC

When it comes to electronic dance music, the city of Toronto has a storied yet often overlooked history. Today it's a hotbed of dance music, as witnessed by the rise of multi-day festivals such as Veld and Dreams, and the number of DJs and producers who call southern Ontario home. From Deadmau5 to John Acquaviva, Zeds Dead to Hatiras, Toronto is a global hub of electronic music.

Let's go back to 1968, when Dr. Robert Moog was developing the first generation of analogue, transistor-based synthesizers. Several scientists and musicians began learning about the potential of synthesizers, and one of the earliest adopters was a Toronto-based musician named John Mills-Cockell.

> "Amazing. Killer show. Aphex Twin [was] hiding behind the turntables. Bjork was wearing a bright-coloured garbage bag. Managed to get my hands on the live show audio years later."
>
> — Daniel Mekinda (Bjork, Warehouse, August 7, 1995)

On March 6, 1968, Mills-Cockell and his art collective Intersystems presented what's widely considered the world's first electronic music concert. Equipped with the 900-series that Mills-Cockell personally purchased from Dr. Moog (the fifth Moog synthesizer ever built), the night was billed as a presentation of "Light, Language, & Electronic Music." The *Globe and Mail* reported that the show "cast a spell over 200 people," and that "the sellout audience were drawn into an electrosonic world."

If electronic music was born in the lab of Dr. Robert Moog, it certainly had it's coming out party in Toronto. Soon thereafter, the Intersystems collective disbanded and Mills-Cockell established Syrinx, a group that further explored the potential of the synthesizer. Mills-Cockell is widely acknowledged as a pioneer of electronic music.

The synthesizer, along with other electronic instruments, would become a mainstay of popular music, featuring prominently in the recordings of Roxy Music, Vangelis, and Tangerine Dream, among others. The first week of June 1975 would mark a watershed moment in the rise of electronic music in the city. On June 2 a four-man band from Düsseldorf, Germany, called Kraftwerk made their Toronto debut at Massey Hall. A few months earlier they had released their critically-acclaimed fourth album, *Autobahn*. With its minimal and robotic riffs, the record redefined what electronic music could be and helped spearhead new genres, such as ambient, hip hop, synth-pop, and electro-funk. The review of the show in the *Globe* is a fascinating glimpse into how unprepared a music critic was for this new sound: "The results were an Andy Warhol dream come true: total reduction of humanity to being component parts in a vast machine.... Kraftwerk produced hypnotically repetitive rhythmic patterns that sounded like the thrum of generators in a power dam. Over that they laid intricate improvisational solos, slight, almost human irregularities in a mechanistic scheme," wrote Robert Martin. He continued: "Kraftwerk have pushed electronic music as far as it will go." Who knew that they had barely scratched the surface?

Around the same time, David Mancuso's parties at the Loft in New York were popularizing a new underground sound of syncopated bass lines and four-on-the-floor beats. These parties embraced a sexually diverse and racially mixed crowd, open-mindedness toward sex and drugs, and an emphasis on the music. The seeds of disco were laid here.

There's no definitive date where you could pinpoint when Toronto caught disco fever. We find clues in 1973 and 1974, when Barry White, the Ohio Players, and Isaac Hayes all played the city. These shows undoubtedly showcased the disco-soul and funk sounds that were becoming prevalent at the time. By 1975, disco had swept the majority of North American cities, and Toronto was no exception. A proliferation of swanky nightclubs with mirrors, fancy decor, and lit dance floors started cropping up in the city, including Pips, Cheeta, Heaven, Stages, and Club David's. These were all along the Yonge Street corridor, where Toronto nightlife lived. The first feature story on the disco phenomenon was a *Globe* article on November 15, 1975, entitled "A Fad Becomes a New Way of Life for Habitués of Downtown Discos." The article reads like Toronto's answer to the *New York Life* article "Tribal Rites of the New Saturday Night," which inspired the film *Saturday Night Fever*. It follows several young, hip disco fanatics as they navigate Toronto's burgeoning club scene.

There were two types of clubs: those that served alcohol (until 1:00 a.m.), and those that didn't and were open until 6:00 a.m. Needless to say, the after-hours clubs were where the real action was. It was also a time when disco dens with their in-house disc jockeys began to replace rock bars en masse. The disco clubs of the mid-1970s most certainly laid the foundation for the modern dance club.

Toronto was a tour stop for several major disco acts. The Bee Gees made their

October 20, 1978,
Maple Leaf Gardens

Toronto debut at the O'Keefe Centre on February 25, 1973. They graduated to Maple Leaf Gardens on September 29, 1975, after the release of their platinum-selling *Main Course* album, which introduced their new disco-infused sound to the world. Earlier Bee Gees shows had 20-piece orchestras, but this concert was slimmed down to just six pieces, including long-time collaborator Blue Weaver on the keyboard and synthesizer. Weaver is often credited as the "4th Bee Gee," and helped craft their new sound. According to the *Globe*, "the resulting sound was much funkier than the lush mush of the group's sixties hits … for the first time [the Bee Gees] are danceable … lots of churning rhythm with Weaver's synthesizer."

Disco reached a crescendo in popularity after the release of the film *Saturday Night Fever* in 1977. Consequently, the late 1970s saw a who's who of disco's biggest stars come to Toronto and turn the city's largest indoor venue, Maple Leaf Gardens, into a de facto discotheque. Donna Summer brought her road show to the Gardens on October 21, 1978. In their review, the *Globe* said, "Summer proceeded to demonstrate her gasping, moaning sentiments using the mike

as a stand-in lover. It was an astonishingly explicit performance, rotating pelvis and all, yet somehow it never felt lewd. There was, in fact, a sort of inspirational grandeur about Summer's movements here — as if she were a true priestess of the body." The first lady of the dance floor took Toronto's breath away.

Arguably the biggest novelty act of the disco era, the Village People played the Gardens on April 23, 1979, with Gloria Gaynor opening in front of a reported 16,000 people. "The band that started as a cult item for the gay disco crowd now sells albums in the multi-millions. While last night's crowd had its sprinkling of sailor suits, kinky leather and military uniform chic, the majority of the crowd were solidly middle-class white, many of them precocious teenyboppers with mom in tow," reported the *Globe and Mail*.

The Bee Gees returned to the Gardens on August 30, 1979, replete with a $1.5 million budget spent on "multicolored flashing stage, disco balls in two sizes, laser lighting, exploding charges, and instruments and speakers all in basic white and silver."

As the 1970s came to a close, musical tastes changed. As punk rock, hip hop, and

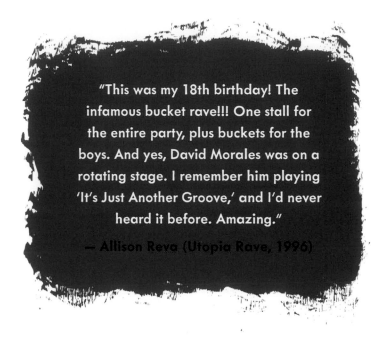

"This was my 18th birthday! The infamous bucket rave!!! One stall for the entire party, plus buckets for the boys. And yes, David Morales was on a rotating stage. I remember him playing 'It's Just Another Groove,' and I'd never heard it before. Amazing."

— Allison Reva (Utopia Rave, 1996)

the new wave artists started getting more mainstream acceptance, disco went into decline. However, the 1980s would see electronic music production become more sophisticated, ushering in a new era of dance music innovators.

Half a world away in Manchester, the band New Order (formed after the untimely death of Joy Division lead singer Ian Curtis, and the subsequent dissolution of the band) began experimenting with dance rhythms and incorporating drum machines into their music. New Order made their Toronto debut on November 15, 1981, playing to a sold-out audience at the Concert Hall. The band continued to experiment with electronic music and scored a massive hit with 1983's "Blue Monday." They would return to Toronto on August 4, 1985, with Factory Records label mates A Certain Ratio to play the cavernous International Centre in front of 3,600 fans.

Kraftwerk returned to Toronto to play their sophomore show on July 24, 1981, at the Concert Hall in support of their album *Computer World*. Rolling Stone hailed *Computer World* as one of the greatest electronic dance music albums of all time; however, the *Globe* was less than impressed, calling the show "mechanical, right-wing, and disturbing how the human element can be so easily replaced by the exchange of electronic impulses."

By the early to mid-1980s electronic dance music was percolating in cities such as Manchester, Berlin, and Düsseldorf, and was ready to explode in the warehouses of New York, Detroit, Chicago ... and Toronto.

As dance music evolved, one of the most important and influential Toronto nightclubs opened in 1980: The Twilight Zone. The Zone was the first nightclub to locate

"The closing party ... went until 8:00 in the morning. Deadmau5 headlined, which was very cool.... I remember walking through the crowd, with thousands of people shaking my hand and thanking me for the years they've spent there. There were thousands of people partying, cheering, clapping, stomping their feet. We had Mark's son Declan sing the opera song 'Con te Partiro,' which means 'Time to Say Goodbye,' and the room went silent. Thousands of partiers going all night long, [then at] 7:15 a.m., you could hear a pin drop. Incredible."

— Charles Khabouth, CEO, Ink Entertainment
(Guvernment nightclub, January 25, 2015)

in what was then a row of largely derelict garment warehouses along Richmond and Adelaide Streets in downtown Toronto. Owned and operated by the Assoon brothers, it was the first club in Toronto to focus on serving an eclectic variety of cutting-edge dance music, and welcomed a mixed crowd from every conceivable background. It was unlicensed, so partygoers could dance until the sun came up. "We were throwing parties around the city at places like Heaven and different rec rooms, but as our events grew in size, we realized we needed our own space. We started for a few months at 666 King Street West, but ran into some issues. So we started scouting locations and came upon 185 Richmond Street, which was an empty dance studio with a manufacturing plant on the upper floor. The landlord was a rabbi who was very supportive of us and our vision, and gave us a great deal on the space," recalls Albert Assoon.

The Twilight Zone catered to a sophisticated crowd who were serious about dancing. Friday nights were world beat and U.K. dance-floor hits spun by Toronto legend Don Cochrane. Saturdays catered to the "fashion" crowd, and featured electro-funk and post-disco tunes. "We had a great mix of people. Gay, straight, black, white, Asian, freaks, it was a total melting pot," recalls Albert. From 1980 to 1984 the club regularly played music by acts such as D-Train, the System, and Midnight Star, as well as new wave acts. "I remember being offered a new artist named Madonna who was making a name in the New York club scene with her song 'Everybody.' It was $1,500 to bring her up to the Zone in 1983. We declined the offer," says Michael Assoon, laughing.

What made the Twilight Zone truly unique was their state-of-the-art sound system. The Assoon brothers outfitted the space with a $100,000, 20,000-watt system. "It was important to us to ensure the sound was impeccable. So we asked Richard Long, who designed Studio 54 and Paradise Garage's systems, to come up and do the Twilight Zone," says Michael. Legend has it that people could hear the bass as far as Bay and Richmond. "Just follow the bass" was a common refrain when looking for the Twilight Zone in those halcyon days.

"At that time we were plugged in to the New York and Chicago scenes through Judy Weinstein, who ran the Def Mix label, and the New York record pool For the Record. We were getting incredible new dance records very early. Many were white labels and test pressings. This is how we were able to introduce house music to Toronto," recalls Albert. Records from the likes of Ron Hardy, Marshall Jefferson, and Jesse Saunders, with their synthesized bass lines and four-on-the-floor rhythms began entrancing Toronto dancers. In 1985, the Assoon brothers brought in one of the pioneers of this new sound, Chicago's Frankie Knuckles, to play a set at the Zone. Later that year they brought up Paradise Garage resident David Morales. "At the time nobody knew what this new music was. People called it 'Twilight Zone' music," recalls Michael Assoon.

Other DJs would come up to play, including Johnny Dynell, Dave Del Valle, and two young aspiring producers from

Detroit named Derrick May and Alton Miller. "They were too advanced. The crowds weren't quite ready for techno," remembers Michael. In 1989, Twilight Zone closed when the lease expired, and the property was sold; however, it left an indelible mark on the city, inspiring an entire generation of people, and influencing future Toronto clubbing institutions such as Club Z, Industry, and the Government. It was the place where Toronto first experienced house music, and it influenced a generation of local artists, including Dave Campbell, Nick Holder, Kenny Glasgow, and many others.

The mid-1980s also witnessed the rise of electro, Miami bass, and Latin freestyle music. Many popular artists made tour stops in Toronto, including Lisa Lisa and Cult Jam on July 6, 1985, at Heaven; Hashim at Club Z on October 5, 1985; Trinere on March 7, 1986, at the Concert Hall; Expose at 16 Phipps in April 1986; Force MDs at the Concert Hall in September 1987; and Stevie B. on May 4, 1989, at Spectrum. Early Toronto hip hop crowds gravitated to these acts, and the audiences were largely comprised of

Jamaican Canadians and West Indians. Hits like "Can You Feel the Beat," "Spring Love," and "Jam on It" were lighting up all-ages dance floors all over the suburbs of Mississauga, Brampton, Markham, and Scarborough.

As the '80s marched along, electronic instrumentation became more sophisticated, and the introduction of the Roland TR-808 and TR-909 drum machines transformed dance music. House music was becoming very popular in Toronto, and was routinely played in nightclubs, on radio, and sold in record shops such as Record Peddler and Starsound. Interestingly, Ron Nelson, who was the pre-eminent hip hop promoter at the time, was also one of the leading house music promoters. Two of his groundbreaking shows were House Craze '88 with Marshall Jefferson and Ten City at the Concert Hall (May 13, 1988), and Housebreak '89 with Tony Humphries and Phaze II at the Spectrum (March 24, 1989).

The Spectrum Club on Danforth Avenue was a popular concert venue for underground music until it closed in 1994. Royal House and Todd Terry played their Toronto debuts there on December 21, 1988.

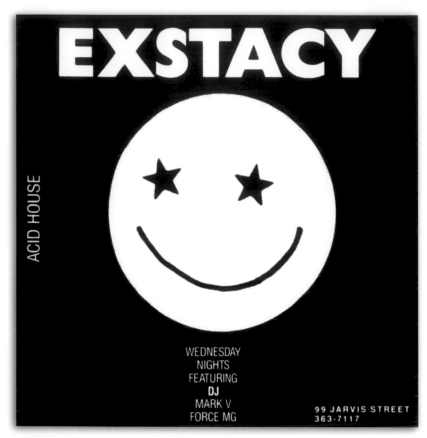

EXSTACY

ACID HOUSE

WEDNESDAY
NIGHTS
FEATURING
DJ
MARK V
FORCE MG

99 JARVIS STREET
363-7117

August 1988,
99 Jarvis
(Tazmanian
Ballroom)

the Copa, electronic dance music was gaining mainstream traction in Toronto.

In 1987 a new sub-genre based on four-on-the-floor beats and deep bass lines started gaining popularity. Powered by the Roland TB-303 drum machine, acid house may have started in Chicago, but it gained wide acceptance in Britain, where the second summer of love was underway. This book couldn't do justice to the history of acid house, but its impact is well-documented elsewhere. As Thatcherism took hold in the U.K., many British youths were no longer soccer hooligans and drinking in pubs. They were taking MDMA and dancing at clubs like Shoom, the Hacienda, and outdoor dance parties. Peace, love, unity, and respect would become the key tenets of rave culture, with the happy face as its unifying symbol.

Chicago's DJ Scrappy from the Medusa Club played the Copa in Yorkville on January 13, 1989.

With the support of Toronto radio personalities such as "Deadly" Hedley Jones and Chris Sheppard, who were playing dance music on CFNY (102.1) and at various clubs around town such as Klub Max and

As the U.K. rave scene exploded, Mark Oliver was getting his first taste of underground music. Born and raised in Scotland, Mark attended high school in Scarborough before returning to his native land to kick-start his DJ career. Mark is widely considered the pioneer of Toronto's rave scene. "Toronto was a rock city in the 1970s. I loved jazz, but commercial radio was playing heavier rock such as Zeppelin and AC/DC. However, in high school I started getting into Depeche Mode and industrial synth. My tastes were changing," recalls Mark. "And then I started going to Club Z and Twilight Zone. I remember hearing these new sounds coming from Detroit and Chicago. It blew me away." By 1988, the acid house scene in the U.K. was exploding. "Me and my friends were going over there, [then] coming back to Toronto, asking ourselves why this wasn't happening here."

Mark's first DJ gig was at a club called the Tazmanian Ballroom at Jarvis and Richmond. "Friday was called 'Rock n' Roll Fag Bar,' and Saturday we played acid house. We put the happy face on the flyer and played acid house all night. Tazmanian Ballroom was where the U.K. scene and the seeds of Toronto's rave scene were planted," recalls Mark.

As the 1980s wound down, electronic dance music began to splinter. "After the closure of Twilight Zone, that crowd, who were big into deep Chicago house looked for other places to dance. That's when after-hours parties started to pop up, including one called 'Kola,' which continued that warehouse vibe people were looking for. Dino and Terry played downstairs, and I was upstairs," remembers Mark. In the summer of 1990, Richmond Street was buzzing with clubs, and people were looking for places to dance after what was then last call at 1:00 a.m. To help fill that need, a new space at 318 Richmond Street, initially called 23 Hop, opened up. It would become the home of Toronto's early rave scene.

As Denise Benson writes in the excellent book *Then & Now*, "Toronto's embryonic rave scene can be traced to 23 Hop, as hybrid forms of techno, breakbeats, and bass began pouring out of the U.K. and caught ears here." Although there is an ad in NOW advertising a rave on December 31, 1989, we've been unable to find any corroborating information about it. Ask most ravers from Toronto's golden era, and they will say the first rave in Toronto was Exodus on August 31, 1991, at 318 Richmond. Exodus was a company founded by Scotland natives Mark Oliver, John Angus, and Anthony Donnelly. The DJs were Mark and fellow U.K. expats Dr. No, Sean L, and Malik X.

"Around this time I was playing techno, and early Plus 8 records. Malik X was doing the Pirate Radio thing on 88.1. At first the crowds were small, but week by week the crowds grew. Our parties had all the elements of a rave: the crowd, the hippie vibe, free love, and of course, the music," explains Mark. "I hate to say it, but the early days of raving were mainly a white crowd. Many came from Brampton. Perhaps it was the fairly large Scottish and British population that lived out there. We called that place 'Bramchester.'" Mark Oliver was known to drop Bob Marley's "Exodus" in the middle of the night to give the crowd a much needed breather from the thumping 130–150 beats per minute that clobbered them all night long.

With 23 Hop/318 Richmond as the home base, the city's rave scene exploded from 1992 onward. Several companies were founded to cater to Toronto's unending appetite for all-night dance parties. The first wave of companies, including Sykosis, Chemistry, Pleasureforce, and Nitrous, began throwing parties in nondescript warehouses all over the city, including carpet factories in Liberty Village,

> "The event that stands out for me was Vertigo at the CN Tower way back in the day…. I will never forget that night. I was dressed in mechanic's coveralls, four-inch platforms, and a fisherman's hat. Chris Sheppard dropped Prodigy's 'Out of Space,' and I exploded from the happiness!"
>
> — Natale Pizzonia, a.k.a. MC Flipside, DJ, producer, radio, and rave legend

airport hangars, and warehouses near the Cinespace studios on Eastern Avenue. Soon the scene blossomed into a full-blown cottage industry, with record shops, clothing stores, magazines, flyer designers, and radio shows supporting the scene. "I remember a party where we brought [U.K. group] 808 State, and Don Berns from CFNY came and fell in love with the music. He was very open-minded. The next day he went on-air telling everyone about the rave. He was hooked," recalls Oliver. Berns would eventually leave mainstream radio and start Nitrous, one of

August 29, 1992,
Concert Hall

August 27, 1994, Honey Pot Ski Lodge

the early rave companies in Toronto, and he started playing records under his alter ego, Dr. Trance.

Many argue that 1992 to 1996 were the glory days of Toronto's rave scene. There's no debate that during these years it was thriving and Toronto had one of the biggest scenes on the planet. Week in, week out, thousands of kids would meet at Union Station or Nathan Phillips Square to take a magic school bus to a mysterious venue in order to drop a pill and dance all night. Whether it was all-ages clubs such as RPM, where you could see Chris Sheppard or Terry Kelly spin, or all-night raves, a who's who of dance music's big names started playing Toronto: Crystal Waters, 2Unlimited, Orbital, Moby, Richie Hawtin, and Deee-Lite to name a few. Many artists from the Chicago school also came up to play parties, including Robert Owens, Farley "Jackmaster" Funk, and others. "One of my fondest memories is playing a sunrise set, and watching Lady Miss Kier (from Deee-Lite), this beautiful rave princess, dancing right in front of me. It was blissful," remembers Mark Oliver. It was a special time in our city.

As the music matured, Toronto's rave scene got even bigger, with companies specializing in certain styles of music; acid house evolved into many different sub-genres such as garage and hardcore — which spawned jungle and breaks. Destiny Productions came onto the scene in 1993 with an emphasis on progressive house and trance; meanwhile, Syrous Productions became the forebears of jungle and ragga, while Dose, with their focus on funky West Coast house and breaks appealed to the skater and alternative crowds. Even the venues got more and more creative, with raves being held at the CN Tower, Toronto Island airport, and several legendary parties were even held at the Ontario Science Centre.

The second wave of rave companies brought a non-stop series of parties to Toronto. Companies like Daybreaks, Better Days, Effective, Renegades, Out of Hand, Citrus, Delirium, Hullabaloo, Liquid Adrenaline, Transcendance, Subb, Alien, and many others were supplying Toronto ravers with an incredible offering of parties to choose from, each providing their own unique music and atmosphere. *Tribe Magazine*'s monthly rave calendar would inform everyone which parties were happening, and also allowed promoters to work with one another to choose dates so as to not conflict with each other. To say Toronto ravers were spoiled in the mid- to late 1990s would be an understatement!

"Before '96/'97, the dance music scene in Toronto was split into two camps. You had the ravers wearing baggy pants and holding glow sticks, dancing to techno, and you had the deep house purists who were doing their thing. They didn't really mix. That started to change when rave companies began booking some of the hot club DJs such as Nick Holder, Peter and Tyrone, and Kenny Glasgow. The scene got bigger, more unified, and the parties could accommodate each individual's preferred musical taste," recalls Steve Mealing, who co-owned Dose with his brother Wayne. "I remember we first brought DJ Sneak and Funky Tekno Tribe to an underground parking lot at 393 King Street West, and Peter and Tyrone was there too. It brought those worlds together. West Coast funky house and breaks with the sounds of Chicago deep house. It was called Two Nations, One Groove. It was an incredible party," remembers Mealing. "George

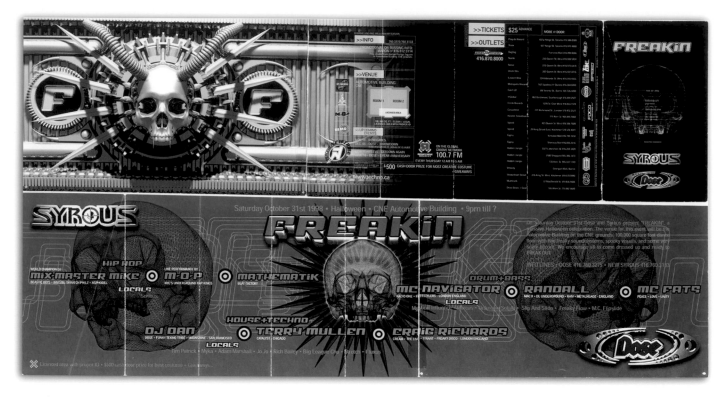

October 31, 1998,
Automotive Building

Hatiras and Liquid Adrenaline also did a great job bringing the sophisticated house sound to the rave masses."

Dose would also partner with Elliott Lefko at Universal Concerts to bring the Chemical Brothers and the Orb to the Warehouse on May 13, 1997, for their debut show. "Before they were known as the Dust Brothers, and I was dying to bring them to Toronto. But by that time, the traditional concert industry was jumping on the electronic bandwagon, and some acts were too difficult to book for raves. We partnered with Universal, and the show sold out in 11 minutes!" remembers Mealing. Dose would bring back the Chemical Brothers along with Death in Vegas and Derrick May for a party in November 1997. U.K. industrial-breakbeat band the Prodigy also made their Toronto debut on May 26, 1997, at Arrow Hall, promoting their record *The Fat of the Land*. By all accounts it was an incredible show for the sold-out audience of 6,000.

One of the most storied and beloved clubs to spring from this era was Industry Nightclub. The energy, atmosphere, and programming at Industry made it one of the most legendary clubs in Toronto history. Industry was a partnership between Matt Casselman, Mario Jukica, Daniel Bellavance, and Gavin Bryan. Gavin and Matt came from the FutureShock crew that included Jennstar, Ronnie Ferszt, Ben Ferguson, and DJ Gryphon. They broke ground at a dormant strip club space at College and Spadina and began throwing weekly parties for house music aficionados under the name BUZZ. The club would later be known as the Comfort Zone, a grungy yet beloved late-night venue for dance music fans. After a string of DJ equipment mysteriously disappeared, the group looked for another location to cater to their growing crowd.

Industry officially opened in July 1996 in an old country bar called the Saloon, on the ground floor of a commercial office building at 901 King Street West. The club was

May 13, 1997, Warehouse

outfitted with the old sound system that had previously occupied RPM (later known as Guvernment). "That first year was tough, as people weren't used to going to the same dance club every weekend," recalls Gavin Bryan. "What kept us afloat was doing Wreckshop Radio, which was live-to-air on WBLK 93.7 with regulars like Starting from Scratch, Baby Blue, Sean Sax, and promoted by Darryl Dark. It was hip hop and R&B,

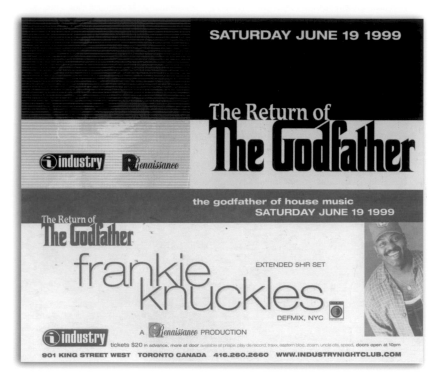

June 19, 1999,
Industry

create a model where every weekend was like a concert, where you could see the world's best DJs consistently. Subsequently, we gained a reputation within the DJ community about the vibe at Industry, so many of them would agree to take less money so they could play at the club," recalls Bryan.

Bryan's friendship with Chicago native DJ Sneak would help make Industry a favourite of DJs from the U.S. northeast and beyond, with artists like Derrick Carter, Carl Cox, Basement Jaxx, Daft Punk, Paul Oakenfold, Derrick May, Armand van Helden, David Morales, Victor Calderone, Mark Farina, Frankie Knuckles, Miss Honey Dijon, and Green Velvet all playing the club several times during its four-year run. Derrick Carter played Industry a record 16 times, holding down international resident honours with DJ Sneak. "Having the gay scene on board also certainly helped us. One of our owners was gay, and catering to that crowd was important to us. So we brought up Danny Tenaglia from NYC, and he instantly became a fan-favourite with both the gay, straight, and rave crowds. In fact, 'DT' was so special to us that he played Industry's closing party with a 15-hour set!" remembers Bryan.

and it was busy every Friday night, helping to cover costs running a 1,000-plus [occupancy] venue."

Toronto had never seen a club concept like Industry before. Each weekend would feature top-tier international DJs, just as the phenomenon of "superstar DJs" was becoming a thing. "The idea was to bring a special atmosphere and energy, in addition to world-class programming. We wanted to

"The snowstorm that night was so bad it took me over two hours to drive to Industry. Amazingly, Mills made it into town, and absolutely ripped the shit outta the place. I can still remember his first track off of Marco Carola's Question Series. SICK AF!! One of the best nights.... Dunno how long it took to get home, but I was smiling for a week after that jam :)))."

— Greg Gow, DJ, producer, techno titan
(Jeff Mills, Industry, January 2, 1999)

Industry was able to benefit from a committed ownership group who invested in decor production, weekly themed concepts, marketing, and stacked DJ bookings, and was boosted by Toronto's proximity to other booming dance music markets such as Montreal, NYC, Chicago, and Detroit. "It's no secret that Toronto was in this sweet spot geographically. Guys like Derrick May and Stacey Pullen would come from Detroit, Luc Raymond and Misstress Barbara brought the Montreal vibe, and, of course, being so close to Chicago and New York made an impact," recalls Bryan. This contributed to the growth of homegrown talent, as Toronto became a major producer of dance records, with imprints like Peter and Tyrone's 83 West Records and Mario J's Method 11:11.

"One of my craziest memories was a sold-out show in 1998 featuring techno legend Carl Cox. Carl had missed his flight from NYC, so we scrambled to charter a plane to get him, and inexplicably he missed that one, too. I get on the phone with DJ Sneak, and we managed to find another plane that would take him as far as Buffalo. Meanwhile,

SATURDAY APRIL 12 1997

"AN ALBUM WITH HUMOUR, FUNK, DANCEABILITY
AND FRENCHNESS, GOD BLESS 'EM"
      – ASHLEY BEEDLE

"10"   – MUZIK

"THE MOST INFLUENTIAL HOUSE ALBUM OF OUR
TIME"
      – UPROAR

"WORLD DOMINATION BECKONS!!!"
      – MIXMAG

Homework

daft punk

SLAM

industry

901 KING STREET WEST TORONTO CANADA
416.260.2660 www.isdustrynightclub.com

Virgin

LIVE FROM PARIS FRANCE

Daft Punk

THE WORLD CONQUERING FRENCH HOUSE MUSIC INNOVATORS IN
THEIR MUCH ANTICIPATED CANADIAN PREMIERE PERFORMANCE

ALONG WITH SPECIAL GUEST FROM CHICAGO

DJ Sneak

CREAM FUTURESHOCK SOLID SUNDAY RESIDENT

Mario J

A **SLAM** SATURDAY SPECIAL EVENT $15 COVER / $12 MEMBER   SATURDAY APRIL 12 1997   10PM – 8AM

UNCLE OTIS   SLAM   industry

April 12, 1997,
Industry

Matt C was on the mic at Industry giving hourly updates to the crowd. Ben Ferguson ended up driving to Buffalo to pick up Carl and his crew. We were all sweating bullets. Finally, by the grace of God, we got Carl on the decks at 8:30 a.m. and he killed it for three hours!" recalls Bryan.

Industry brought a special atmosphere and energy to Toronto's increasingly advanced club crowd. It was unlike any dance club the city had ever seen, where you could see the world's best DJs every weekend. They pushed the envelope, and set the template for subsequent

Toronto clubbing landmarks such as the Guvernment, System Soundbar, Turbo, and Roxy Blu. Sadly, due to pressure from other building tenants and rising rents, the club closed its doors in 2000. In the four years that Industry operated, it was a mecca of house and techno, leaving a profound and lasting legacy in the history of dance music in Toronto.

A watershed year for Toronto as a dance music market was 1997. The rave scene was huge, clubs like Industry, Limelight, and Guvernment were packed every weekend, and electronica moved into the mainstream. Clothing shops, magazines, and producers such as Hatiras, Troy Brown, Nick Holder, and the Stickmen were creating "Made in Toronto" dance floor bangers. On April 10, 1997, purveyors of fine French house Daft Punk rolled into Industry for their debut Toronto set. Riding high off the release of their smash debut record, *Homework*, Thomas Bangalter and Guy-Manuel de Homem-Christo played a DJ set for the house music faithful. The duo was interviewed by the *Toronto Star* the day before the show. "'We like the free-form base of electronic music,' says Bangalter. 'Rock

March 18, 1998,
Industry

music was becoming very boring in Paris. Even when it's good, like with Oasis, it's not new or original.' Time will tell whether the latest sound has significant longevity, or simply emerges as a kind of lambada with mechanical beats," said the *Star* reviewer.

"There was a lot of hype with Daft Punk, and DJ Sneak was good friends with Thomas [Bangalter]. So we packed 1,900 people into Industry, and they blew the roof off!" recalls Gavin Bryan. The band would return a few months later to the Guvernment on September 1, 1997, to perform live as part of their first official North American tour, Daftendirektour.

Drum 'n' bass was also getting in on the act, with Goldie making his debut at Industry on November 16, 1997. Pioneers such as Roni Size and Reprazent, and Grooverider would make their debuts also at Industry the following year promoted by Syrous, the company that single-handedly brought drum 'n' bass and jungle to Toronto.

In 1998, the Mealings partnered with Rob Lisi's Syrous Productions to form the largest rave company in Toronto, Lifeforce, and with that the era of the "mega-rave" had arrived. "Freakin' 98 at the Automotive Building [at the CNE grounds] was when things started to get really massive," recalls Mealing. "We went from 4,000 or 5,000 at one party to 12,000 at the next. We incorporated every best practice into Freakin'. Our street team was refined. We had Aaron Micks, and Neil Forester from Mass Appeal, we booked great hip hop acts through Jonathan Ramos, and the flyer was unreal. It was important to us that our flyers were pieces of art. And that's exactly

what our friends at Prototype Design in Vancouver did for us. We also harnessed this new thing called the internet by setting up a website and message board." The party featured an eclectic lineup including M.O.P., Mix Master Mike, DJ Randall, DJ Dan, and Terry Mullan. By this time, many traditionalists felt the scene was getting too big, and that the introduction of hip hop changed the dynamic of the parties. Steve, however, is unapologetic. "I made sure we only booked classic, respected hip hop acts: De La Soul, EPMD, Souls of Mischief, very musical, organic groups. They brought a great element to the party, and turned a lot of hip hop heads onto electronic music."

By 1999, the rave scene was hitting its apex, getting almost too big for its own good. After a couple of drug overdose deaths, the scene was under increasing scrutiny and media spotlight. Furthermore, due to political pressure, city-owned venues were no longer available for use. That didn't stop promoters from putting on some of the biggest and most talked about parties of the era. When Lifeforce brought Run-DMC to Toronto on May 15, 1999, it seemed as if every teenager in the city was there. "Jason Nevins's remix of 'It's Like That' was tearing up the charts, and I was a huge Run-DMC fan as a kid, so it made sense to us to bring them," remembers Mealing.

Later that year, Syrous brought back Daft Punk for their epic six-year anniversary party on September 4 alongside DJ Sneak, Josh Wink, and a huge jungle lineup featuring True Playaz DJ Hype, Pascal, MC GQ, and MC Fats. Personally, this was one of my favourite parties, and witnessing 10,000 people dancing in unison under the strobe lights while the world's best production duo rocked the house was truly spectacular.

Arguably, the final crescendo of Toronto's rave scene hit its stride on October 30, 1999, when Lifeforce presented its annual Halloween party, Freakin'. Headlined by EPMD, Rabbit in the Moon, Fabio, and Grooverider, the show almost didn't happen when the city-owned venue got pulled less than 72 hours beforehand. "We were scrambling to find a new venue. The city didn't want any raves at its properties. So we had to drop $50,000 to erect a tent on Polson Pier. I grew my first grey hairs that week," recalls Mealing. Freakin' 99 also saw a surprise performance by Public Enemy, who performed in Toronto for the first time in 10 years. Various estimates suggest 14,000 to 18,000 ravers were in attendance, easily making it the largest dance party in Toronto at the time.

In other circles, the mid- to late 1990s also featured an explosion of highly experimental, innovative, and influential artists who brought new perspectives to what electronic music could be. The advent of acid jazz in particular brought this new wave of talent to Toronto stages. Artists such as Galliano, Brand New Heavies, and Jamiroquai became fan favourites in Toronto. Jamiroquai's first show at the Opera House on November 7, 1993, is still talked about to this day. As the decade trudged on, new interpretations of jazz would be borne through experimentation with electronic music, most notably by artists on the Ninja Tune label. Artists such as the Herbaliser, Thievery Corporation, DJ Krush, Kruder & Dorfmeister, and Medeski Martin & Wood would become Toronto favourites with the efforts of local promoters such as Carlos and Pedro Mondesir (Hot Stepper) and Izzy, Felix, and Gani, who threw the beloved Milk parties. The JVC Acid Jazz Festival was a high watermark running from

November 7, 1993, Opera House

1996 to 1998, featuring an ensemble cast of the world's most innovative electronic jazz artists of the time, including Roy Ayers, Nightmares on Wax, DJ Greyboy, Groove Collective, and Gilles Peterson.

Clubs like the Guvernment, Factory, Buzz, Industry, RPM, and Limelight made Toronto a truly exciting place to experience dance music. Promoters like Syrous, Empire, Next Junction, and Vinyl Syndicate made our city a globally recognized drum 'n' bass mecca. And festivals like Destiny's World Electronic Music Festival created the template for all dance music festivals thereafter.

It goes without saying that one chapter can't do justice to the incredible history of Toronto rave and club culture. There's simply too much to tell, and hopefully one day someone will write a definitive account of that era.

(left) August 31, 1991, 23 Hop
(right) June 12, 1999, Industry

ACKNOWLEDGEMENTS

We would like to give a shout-out to the relatively recent activity by a number of writers who have documented Toronto's incredible musical life. Of late there have been a spate of books on Toronto punk and hardcore, including Liz Worth's *Treat Me Like Dirt: An Oral History of Toronto Punk and Beyond 1977–1981*, Dan Pyle's *Trouble in the Camera Club: A Photographic Narrative of Toronto's Punk History 1976–1980*, Nick Smash's *Alone and Gone: The Story of Toronto's Post Punk Underground*, and, most recently, Derek Emerson and Shawn Chirrey's *Tomorrow Is Too Late: Toronto Hardcore Punk in the 1980s*. Denise Benson did a wonderful job chronicling dance club culture in Toronto in *Then & Now: Toronto Nightlife History*. Benson has also written some superb online articles on various venues that can be found on the internet by searching "Then and Now: Toronto Nightlife History."

Mark Miller has written a number of books on Canadian jazz that include a wealth of information on activities in Toronto. Two of his books, *Cool Blues: Charlie Parker in Canada 1953* and *Way Down that Lonesome Road: Lonnie Johnson in Toronto, 1965–1970*, focus nearly exclusively on Toronto. Nicholas Jennings chronicled the Yorkville scene of the 1960s in *Before the Goldrush: Flashbacks to the Dawn of the Canadian Sound*. The Ugly Ducklings lead singer Dave Bingham's *Noise from the North End: The Amazing Story of the Ugly Ducklings* also has much useful information on the Yorkville scene. Mark Campbell has published a pictorial history of Toronto hip hop in *Everything Remains Raw*.

David McPherson's recent book *The Legendry Horseshoe Tavern* is the first to cover the history of a Toronto music bar, while Michael Hill's *The Mariposa Folk Festival: A History* is an eminently readable account of the changes Toronto's legendary folk festival has gone through over the years.

It should also be noted that Doug Taylor's fascinating *Toronto Theatres and the Golden Age of the Silver Screen* was an invaluable reference tool for many of the long-lost theatres mentioned in this book.

There are also a number of dissertations and theses written at York University and the University of Toronto on vaudeville, minstrelsy, the Mariposa Folk Festival, and early Canadian black religious ensembles. We have drawn on all of these in addition to our interviews and newspaper research.

Finally, we would like to thank the following people who helped one or both of us obtain high-resolution copies of various flyers, provided memories about shows they promoted or attended, or dug into their files for otherwise unavailable information so that we could be as accurate as possible. We are grateful to all: Ralph Alfonso, Cleave Anderson, Sarah Anderson, Derek Andrews, Albert Assoon, David Assoon, Michael Assoon, Sonny Banerjee, Marlene Bauer, Dave Booth, Jeff Brandman, Jon Bronski, Colin Brunton, Gavin Bryan, Karen and Oswald Burke, Morgan Cameron-Ross, John Catto, Ed Conroy, Stephen Cribar, David Dacks, Mike Daley, Andrea D'Andrea, Mark Dantas, Derek Emerson, DJ Filthy Rich, DJ Greedo, Jesse Feyen, Richard Flohil,

Neil Forester, Mark Gane, Adam Gill, Peter Goddard, Gustavo Gonzales, Hamish Grant, Evan Gray, Arthur Fogel, Greg Cow, Hailey Graham, Jonathan Gross, Sunil Gupta, Patti Habib, Ian Harrison, Jill Heath, Piers Hemmingsen, Al Hooper, Howard Hughes, i2i Art (Brittany Lobo, Angela Dunning, and Isabelle Zelonka), Paul James, Paul Jarvis, Martha Johnson, Denise Jones, Ian Kamau, Aaron Keele, Gary Kendall, Adrien King (DJ X), David Kingston, Rohan Koomar, Grit Laskin, Geddy Lee, Elliott Lefko, Mark Lewkowicz, Todd Linton, Paul E. Lopes, Rick Lourenco, Gordon MacBain, Johnny MacLeod, Jian and Page Magen, Richard Martin, Mastermind, Stephen McInally, Mike McKenna, David McPherson, Steve Mealing, Wayne Mealing, Max Mertens, Howie Moore, Mark Moore, Tricky Moreira, Gareth Morgan, Vivienne Muhling, Dave Murray, Ron Nelson, Liam Nickerson, Jennifer O'Brien, Mark Oliver, Trevor Payne, Jonathan Ramos, Kevin Richards, Volkmar Richter, Kevin Ritchie, Harris Rosen, William Russell, Mark Oliver, Margaret Saadi Kramer, Lorraine Segato, Kevin Shea, Brock Silversides, Mike Smith, Cyrus Songad, Ken Stowar, Andy Strote, Adam Swinbourne, Gary Tate, Doug Taylor, TO Live Archives/ Meridian Hall, Dave Tollington, Gary Topp, Richard Trapunski, Lorne Van Sinclair, Kaitlin Wainwright, Bob Wegner, Colin Watts, Bobby Wham, Brad Wheeler, Darby Wheeler, Bob Wiseman, as well as Laura Boyle, Saba Eitazaz, Scott Fraser, Allison Hirst, Kathryn Lane, Elena Radic, and Dundurn Press.

If you have interesting memories of shows or flyers and posters that you would like to share, please let us know. I can be reached by email at rbowman@yorku.ca. Daniel can be reached at dantate@gmail.com. Check out The Flyer Vault at www.theflyervault.com.

IMAGE CREDITS